From Darkness to Light

by
Andy Bates

**Kingdom
Publishers**

From Darkness to Light

Copyright© Andy Bates

A catalogue record for this book is available from the
British Library.

All Scripture Quotations have been taken from the New King James.

ISBN: 978-1-911697-53-4

1st Edition by Kingdom Publishers

Kingdom Publishers, London, UK.

You can purchase copies of this book from any leading bookstore or email contact@king-
dompublishers.co.uk

Dedicated to Joan and Bertha Williams beloved Mum and Grandma

Contents

INTRODUCTION

I know the thoughts that I think towards you, says the Lord, Thoughts of peace and not of evil, to give you a future and a hope. (Jeremiah 29:11)

The future that Nigel Williams was facing was one seemingly without hope. Taken into care from a young age and stuck in a cycle of crime and prison, plagued with such serious issues as mental health problems, depression and self harm, the future looked so bleak that the only way out appeared to be suicide. But something, or rather someone, happened to Nigel that changed his whole life and gave him a future and a hope.

This is his story. One he wanted to be told because not only has he have a passion to help people but he also wants anyone who is in the midst of the darkest trials to know that there is hope and redemption. Indeed, he believes that same redemption can be experienced by everyone and not just those whose lives are in chaos and disarray.

This is the amazing story of how he came from darkness to light.

Andy Bates

2022

But rise and stand upon your feet, for I have appeared to you for this purpose, to appoint you as a servant and witness to the things in which you have seen me and to those in which I will appear to you, delivering you from your people and from the Gentiles—to whom I am sending you to open their eyes, so that they may turn from darkness to light and from the power of Satan to God, that they may receive forgiveness of sins and a place among those who are sanctified by faith in me. (Acts 26:16-18)

PROLOGUE

They were coming in...

The sound of the metal door beginning to creak and crumple under the iron pincers of the door-jack made that obvious.

I looked around at the wreckage of the small cell, which I had smashed to smithereens. Desperately surveying the carnage, I reached down and picked up a chair leg, my fingers curling tightly around my makeshift weapon. I planted my feet, and gritted my teeth, ready to batter and bludgeon whatever came through the barricaded door that was about to implode.

A moment later, the door gave up its futile fight and the first guard rushed in. Each officer dressed in full riot gear; because of the narrow doorway, they had to come one by one. This would give me a chance to do some damage. I swung back the chair leg ready to bring it crashing down on the assailants that were about to engulf me...

Chapter 1

Early Years

I was born in Kings Mill Hospital in Mansfield on the eleventh of December 1970. The Met Office records the day was cloudy and overcast. It seems strange I can find out that the sky was grey and dull over Nottinghamshire on that fateful day but I have never known the name of my Father. I was, apparently, the product of a one-night stand. Growing up I asked my mum why I didn't have a Dad. All the other kids in my village had one and it seemed strange I didn't. Mum wouldn't tell me anything about him; I just knew he wasn't around. Maybe it was painful for her to talk about him. It left me with a simmering resentment and anger towards whoever and wherever he was. He'd left me and my mum to cope alone. He obviously wanted nothing to do with us, so why should I spend any time worrying about him?

My mum suffered from paranoid schizophrenia, which meant the home life I knew, was very different from the average household. Mum's illness would cause her to repeat phrases over and over again. It also affected her body, her limbs would involuntary jerk around, and her legs constantly shake uncontrollably from side to side. Smoking was her comfort; she constantly had a cigarette dangling from between her lips. She would chain smoke her way through eighty a day. Our walls were stained yellow with nicotine and a cloud of smoke always hung in the air.

She loved me as any other mother loved her son but her mental health problems would confound and confuse her mind. She would sometimes throw plates at me because she was convinced I'd stolen something trivial like a bottle of brown sauce from her kitchen. I would grow up to steal many things but Mum's brown sauce was never one of them. Thankfully, we had Grandma who lived with us to help care for Mum and me. But Grandma had problems too and also suffered from depression and anxiety. It can't have been easy caring for us and coping with her illness. She would self medicate by drinking two bottles of Sherry a week. It was hardly a nurturing environment for a child to grow up in but you don't get to choose the circumstances into which you're born. But I know Mum and Grandma did their best and I loved them.

These days there is most likely more help and support available but this was the early 1970's and mental illness was seen as an embarrassment and something to fear. So this was my family, my mum, Joan, Grandma Bertha and me, Nigel Owen James Williams.

Chapter 2

Life on Lowmore Road

We lived in Kirby in Ashfield, a small town about five miles from Mansfield. 120 Lowmore Road where we lived was a two-bedroom terrace on the outskirts of town. Although it had two bedrooms, we not only all slept in the same room but in the same bed. Maybe this was due to the fact the house had no central heating system and in the cold bleak Nottinghamshire winters we would keep each other warm with our body heat. We didn't have a bathroom. I was washed in our big Belfast sink for my first few years.

When I outgrew the kitchen sink, bath nights would be in a big tin bath in front of a roaring fire. After I'd finished Mum and Grandma would have a strip wash in the water that had cleansed me from the grit and grime. My first ever memory, I must have been about two, was sitting looking out of the window and feeling a sense of wonder and awe at the outside world. Dreaming of adventures and yearning to get out and explore. In my childlike mind, the world seemed full of possibilities. I would have the same feelings many years later looking out of another window; feeling joy in my heart despite the fact that I was behind the bars of a secure mental hospital.

But, I have many fond memories of the old terrace house on Lowmore Road. I remember thinking it a good idea to practice forward rolls down the steep staircase. Need less to say, my fledgling gymnastic career ended with a literal bump and I finished up at the bottom of the stairs with a sore head. The house was basic and the décor was tired and old. New furniture and fittings were luxuries we could not afford. My mum and Grandma weren't able to work so relied on benefits. Money was always tight.

The one and only time I can remember us getting a new carpet it ended up ruined due to a practical joke I played on Mum. Shoving my slipper under the new carpet, I shouted to my mum that we had a rat in the house. She screamed and ran out of the door in horror at the rodent shaped bulge I was showing her lurking under the new carpet in the living room. I burst out laughing, a highly delighted four year old. I wasn't laughing long though as the door burst open again to reveal our next-door neighbour brandishing an axe followed by my distraught mother who pointed to the bulge in the carpet. Terry ran over and wielded two or three mighty blows at the suspected intruder.

My slipper stayed obligingly still for him as the axe cut through and shredded the brand new carpet. It was in a right state due to the rat exterminating skills of our next-door neighbour. But, it was soon plain for everyone to see who was really to blame as Terry held up my sorry looking slipper shaking his head in disbelief at my mum. She spun round and glared at me, appalled at the damage I had caused.

Sometimes Mum would give me some pocket money; it didn't stay in my pocket for long but was soon behind the counter of the local corner shop in exchange for sweets and especially chewing gum, which I loved. We could never afford holidays and my Christmas presents were donations from the local working men's club. In the run up to Christmas, any families struggling to buy their kids gifts were allowed to take three small bags of presents each. These were mainly filled with chocolates and small toys. I remember Mum and me picking up the bags and carrying them home; the sense of excitement outweighing any embarrassment that we needed the charity of the local community.

My first ever ride in a car turned out to be in a police car, sadly it was a taste of things to come. One day when I was four years old, I'd gone out to play alone. A couple of streets away was a waste ground that had massive concrete tubes strewn around awaiting some building project or other. I had a whale of a time scrabbling through them and climbing up and jumping off these; pretending I was a super hero. I must have lost track of time because Mum had become worried when I hadn't returned home. She had looked all over and couldn't find me anywhere so had rung the police and reported me missing.

The first thing I knew about it was when a police car drove down the lane towards me. I thought I was in big trouble when two Bobbies got out of the car and told me they had been looking for me. They duly escorted me home, chauffeur driven in a Panda car and much to Mum's relief. She threw her arms around me giving me a big hug. This mode of transport grew to be a familiar one a decade or so later. But for now, I was excited to be returned to my family home in the company of two uniformed officers. Sadly they never sounded their blues and twos for me but it would be a sound I would come to know all too well in later years.

At five, I started school like any other kid. On my very first day I was involved in a fight, I punched a kid in self-defence knocking him to the floor. I hadn't wanted the fight and felt unsafe in these new surroundings. I decided I didn't like school and when I got home, I told Mum I wasn't going again. I was determined not to return after this harsh first taste of education. I imagined violence would be part of everyday school life, which horrified me. It was some considerable time before I would pick up my education.

Around this time, I started hanging around with the older kids at the local fields or we'd meet on the back garden of my friend Lee's house. His garden had old disused cars strewn all over it and stacked on top of one another. His dad used to strip down old cars and sell the parts. Sometimes we'd sit in the cars pretending to be getaway drivers screeching away from the police. Little did I know that my make-believe efforts of trying to escape capture would soon become a grim reality. Often I'd wait for Mum and Grandma to go to bed then slip out of the house into the night and away to see what mischief I could get up to.

We'd meet up and then go into people's gardens looking for apples and rhubarb. On one occasion, we had a lucky escape. We were up in the branches of an apple tree relieving it of its juicy bounty when the owner came bounding down the garden towards us. He threatened to let his dog out on us. This wasn't a prospect we would have relished as his dog was a big nasty German Shepherd. It's safe to say we jumped down, running as fast as we could before scrambling back over the wall.

We didn't let our near miss halt our fledgling thieving activities. We were just more careful to avoid the snarling fangs of any dogs that lived in the gardens where we were fruit picking. I knew from an early age that stealing was wrong but it was fun and it never seemed a big deal. All the older kids did it and I took to it like a duck to water. Mum even used to leave a bowl of sugar out to dip our stolen rhubarb in. She never asked me where I got it from and didn't seem to mind, as she had no hesitation in using the fruit to bake tasty apple and rhubarb pies.

It was also when I was five that our house was engulfed in a nasty fire. Mum and Grandma were already in bed when I came home from playing out. I headed straight upstairs and wriggled my way eel like between Mum and Grandma. It felt safe there cocooned between my family and I soon drifted off to sleep. I'm not sure how long I'd been asleep but it didn't seem long when I awoke with a dry throat and desperately needed a drink. I sneaked out of bed to quench my thirst with the fizzy orange pop Mum kept on the dresser to take her many tablets. Gulping down the sweet sugary liquid I spotted something that made me turn my head. Smoke was seeping under the door curling its fingers towards us.

"Mum. Mum. Fire. Fire." I bellowed, running over to Mum and shaking her awake. My mum roused Grandma and then threw open the bedroom door and disappeared into the smoke.

I later found out she'd gone to phone the fire brigade. This would involve her dashing down the road to the phone box, as we didn't possess a telephone in our humble abode. Grandma too ran from the room to get a bucket and water in an effort to douse the rising flames. I was all alone and didn't know what to do or where to run. Terrified, I vainly sought sanctuary under the ageing creaking wooden bed.

The smoke began to fill the room stinging my eyes and filling my lungs.

The bare floorboards underneath me got hotter and hotter. The palms of my hands and my knees were beginning to burn with the intense heat so I had to curl up into a ball, my hands tucked into my body to stop them blistering. Where were Mum and Grandma? I could see the fire on the stairs. Suddenly the strong arms of a fireman reached under the bed and pulled me out. Picking me up in his arms, he threw me over his shoulder and carried me downstairs. I still remember clearly the smoke and flames I viewed during my rescue. I'm grateful for his bravery risking his life to save mine, and for his colleagues too, busy putting out the fire while he took me safely outside into the fresh night air.

I was taken to hospital and had to spend the night there. After that, we had to live with one of the neighbours who kindly put us up while our house was made habitable again. Surveying the charred wreckage that had once been our living room brought home to us the gravity of the situation we had been in and the fierceness of the flames that had engulfed our house. A six-foot black pit was all that was left of our floorboards.

I look back now and shudder at what would have happened had I not woken up when I did. We would have probably been burned to a crisp and this book would never have been written. At the time, I would have just put it down to coincidence but now I firmly believe it was the mercy and grace of God. It didn't feel like mercy having to share someone else's home but the important thing was we were all alive. When we were able to move back to our house I expected life to continue as it had always done but I was in for a shock. A big shock. One that would rip me from the bosom of a loving family and put me amongst strangers.

Chapter 3

Foster Care

The simple sound of a knock at the door didn't fill me with foreboding at what was about to happen. I had no idea that on our doorstep stood a social worker accompanied by a number of policemen. Like the fireman, they'd come to take me from my house. But this time I wasn't being rescued but forcibly removed. It may have been the fire or the fact I wasn't attending school that had alerted the authorities of my plight. It subsequently came to light that the fire had started because Mum had left a smouldering cigarette in the ashtray, which somehow must have dropped onto the settee setting it ablaze. But, whatever the reason, I didn't want to go anywhere away from the love and care of Mum and Grandma.

I know now they were trying to act in my best interest, but to a frightened six-year-old nothing could seem further from this; being dragged away from my distraught and heartbroken mum. The police had to physically restrain her and hoisted her unceremoniously above their heads, carrying her out like a rolled up carpet and into the waiting police van. I was literally snatched from her grasp and bundled into the car of the social worker. I can still recall her distressed cries all these years later.

As I sat there being driven off to the house of a stranger I felt a wave of anger wash over me. For all the faults and shortcomings of my family life, it felt wrong to be taken away. I knew I was loved at home. They had torn us apart and I didn't care about their reasons. I was powerless. Deep in my heart, a seed of hatred and distrust had been sown against the police and authorities. Each turn of the wheels took me further away from my own family and towards an unknown life in a new home with a foster family.

I didn't like living in foster care. I had to move to a village called Huthwaite, which was three miles away from Kirby, which had been my home for the first six years of my life. My foster mum was called Anne. Her husband had died of cancer some years previously. They had a son who was five years older than I was who didn't take too kindly to me coming into his home. He hated me and the feeling was mutual.

I am not sure if his dislike came from a sense of frustration and resentment at having to share his house and the affections of his mother, but we just didn't get on. It was as plain as the nose on his face; he didn't like me and he wasn't shy in letting me know it. I didn't let my size and age disadvantage stop me from sharing what I thought of him and his name-calling. I would repay any taunting he gave me by attacking him and things usually ended with him sitting on me to restrain me. My foster mum would then have to try to restore peace and calm. Thankfully we both slept in separate rooms, mine had bunk beds in.

My foster mum was an emergency foster carer. However, I stayed there for ten years and shared the bunkroom with a variety of foster children. Sometimes they would turn up in the middle of the night and I would be woken with a sleepy introduction to the latest kid to be housed by the authorities for their own well-being. After a brief introduction, Anne would leave the room and the poor kid would be left alone in the darkness of a stranger's bedroom having to come to terms with being taken away from everything they had ever known.

I knew first hand of the pain and bewilderment they were experiencing. Many of them had been victims of the vilest abuse and would tell me of the horrors that had happened to them. Others suffered stoically in silence, while some broke down sobbing and I knew I was in for a sleepless night. I would try to comfort and reassure them. Explaining I was their friend and they were safe here and things would seem better in the morning. While I tried to calm them down, sometimes sadly, my kindness was curtailed by my desire to sleep and I had to tell them to shut up and be quiet. In the morning, I would feel bad and try to help the newcomers feel at home in their new and strange surroundings.

On my first night alone in that room away from Mum and Grandma, it was me that had to bear the crushing weight of grief, fear and loneliness; traumatised at being ripped from my childhood home and the safety and security of all I had known. While I hadn't grown up in a normal nuclear family, I felt sharply the pain of being separated from the two female figures I loved and knew loved me.

Anne was a nice lady, but she wasn't and never could be my real Mum and I was unhappy. I was used to my mum's lack of rules and being able to come and go as I liked, to prowl around with the alley cats late into the night. Now there was no chance of anything like that, I had a six o'clock curfew. From my new bedroom window, I sat miserably gazing into the night sky, looking at the stars. On clear nights, they were out visible for the world to see, unlike me who felt like a caged tiger.

I was sent to a playgroup with a view to easing me back into school life. I hated it, and what happened on the very first school day was to become a pattern. Whereas I wasn't totally to blame that day, I couldn't say the same about the many fights I was now getting into.

I hadn't been back at school long when I landed in serious trouble, which would lead to a sense of shame I still carry with me today. A lad called Lee and I decided it would be good fun to flood the school. One break time we sneaked back into school and slipped into the girls toilets. Taking the paper towels, we stuffed them into the sinks and turned on the taps as fast as they would go. We waited until the sinks started running over and then bolted outside into the schoolyard.

Unbeknown to us, someone had seen us, as we found out when were summoned to the front of the class after break. Our teacher had two potties placed on tables at the front of the class. Then to our horror, Lee and I were ordered to stand on the tables and to pull our pants down and sit on them. The reason given was we weren't responsible enough to use the lavatories in a proper way so would be treated like babies. When we refused to comply, the teacher came behind us and pulled our trousers and pants down for all the class to see. Thirty pairs of eyes could hardly believe what they were seeing and their delight was matched by our humiliation. This teacher's mode of discipline thankfully would find no place in today's society.

Our behaviour certainly warranted discipline but the teacher's inappropriate response was cruel and callous. I have many scars visible on my body today from all the physical trauma I've faced. The scars caused from violence soon begin to fade but that's not always the case with the wounding of our feelings. If this was a shock tactic to get me to conform and behave, it didn't work, and only served to deepen any alienation I was feeling.

I was still missing Mum and Grandma terribly. I was able to see them but it just wasn't the same. the visit always came to an end and I would have to leave my real family, my real home, and go back to a house where I didn't want to be. It didn't feel right being away from Mum and Grandma. But there was not a thing I could do about it. I had to accept it and get on with life. The weeks turned into months, which drifted into years.

Chapter 4

Growing Up, Sinking Down

I was ten years old when I had my first experience with drugs and it was a very unpleasant one. I wish it had put me off drugs for life but unfortunately, that didn't happen. I was visiting Mum and she had run out of cigarettes so she gave me a few pennies and sent me next door telling me to ask the neighbour for some. A woman answered the door and invited me in. I followed her into the kitchen and my eyes were drawn to a strange looking object. She picked it up and asked me if I wanted a go.

I didn't know it was a bong, an instrument used to inhale cannabis. I didn't know how it worked or what to expect. But even so, I said yes. Not knowing what I was saying yes to or what I was letting myself in for, she passed me the bong, watching me closely. I couldn't change my mind now. I sucked the drugs quickly into my lungs and immediately I felt sick and dizzy. I had a coughing fit and couldn't catch my breath, much to the amusement of the woman. I snatched the four cigarettes from her hand and fled. I didn't say a word to Mum who was oblivious that her son had just had his first taste of drugs. Needless to say, I never went back to that house.

Not long after this incident, I felt I'd had enough of being in care and decided to run away. I enlisted another kid staying at my foster house as my wingman. Our ill-conceived plan was to wait for the cover of night, then walk to a motorway, and hitchhike to London. We threw some food and clothes into a bag and when the house was noiseless and with everyone asleep, we sneaked through a window and into the cold night air.

We were two ten year old boys walking through the quiet late night streets of Huthwaite; hoping to reach the bright lights of the big smoke. We imagined the streets of London were paved with gold and somehow we'd be able to thieve enough to live off. We'd been walking about half an hour and had nearly reached Sutton when a Land Rover pulled in beside us and stopped. It was a friend of my foster mum whom we knew as Uncle Keith. He naturally wanted to know what we were doing walking away from home at a time when we should have both been tucked up safely in bed.

"Running away" was the blunt and honest answer to his concerned question.

He escorted us back to our foster home making sure we were safely deposited back in to the care of my foster mum. I expected a right telling off. But she didn't raise her voice she just sent us to our rooms. The next day instead of punishing us, she took us out and bought clothes and food. She really spoilt us. She must have been worried we were going to run away again.

I didn't try drugs again for the next two years after my unpleasant introduction to them but by the time I was twelve I was already drinking. That all changed one winter's night. I'd gone with two friends to a party and we were all drunk on vodka. Walking home one of them offered to show me how to sniff glue. Why not I thought, I'll get grounded anyway for being late back. Besides, if he did it, why not me? It sounded like a good idea. He said he kept some glue hidden under a gravestone in a cemetery on our route home. We made our way through the cemetery past the gravestones covered in snow until we reached the one where my friend kept his hidden stash of glue.

He showed me how to hold the bag to my mouth and squeeze while breathing in deeply. I didn't hesitate but took a big gulp of fumes. I immediately collapsed, slumping against the icy gravestone. The other two laughed and kicked the snow from the ground onto my prostrate body, but I didn't care. As the particles of snow flew towards me, they changed hues, an ethereal kaleidoscope of beauty. The flakes became a riot of rainbow colours dancing before my eyes. I was tripping; my body lay in the snow and ice but I was unaware as my mind soared skyward in a drug-induced trance.

Lost in my own private ecstasy I remember thinking this is the feeling I want to have for the rest of my life. Little did I know the pain and damage drugs would cause. They have been a wrecking ball to my life. They damaged my mind and while other factors would contribute to my future torments, I have no doubt they have caused paranoia, anxiety and have made me mentally unwell. The consequences with which I'm still living all these years later. But to a twelve-year-old boy in foster care laid prone in a cemetery in the dark of the night they offered a chance to forget my pain and separation from my family. I took that chance with both hands and started sniffing glue whenever I could. And not just glue but pretty much any solvent I could get my hands on, gas, aerosols and petrol, even Tippex.

Walking home from school, I would fish out the Tippex from my school bag and stick it under my nose. I guess I had something in common with all those that used the white fluid. They used it to erase what they'd done. The only difference was, while they carefully painted over their mistakes I inhaled it as deeply as I could to forget mine. Later I would graduate on to magic mushrooms found growing in the local fields. I would often eat them without washing first, careful so as not to arouse any suspicion by taking them home and eager to experience the psychedelic escape I hoped would follow. I greedily gobbled the shrooms seeking to be shot to the stars but this wasn' t always the case as they could sometimes cause bad trips. Nothing dimmed my desire to get stoned and I wasn't fussy what substance I used.

Back then, before I discovered the mind-bending effects of fungi I even tried petrol. Around this time, my foster brother bought a motorbike. I would take a rag to the fuel tank, soak it in petrol and then inhale it to give me a high. But my staple diet of solvent abuse came from gas canisters. I would purchase these from the local shop at fifty pence a time. There was no chance of nicking them as the man who ran the shop kept them locked up behind the counter. I would buy enough to keep a team of drillers constantly busy producing it.

The shopkeeper must have known I wasn't using the gas to power my homebuilt space rocket but he never once asked me what I was using it for. The reality was he would have known. I would stick the nuzzle against my teeth and use my lips to form a seal around the canister and breath in the fumes. I did this so often I will now never be able to advertise toothpaste. The gas rotted away my teeth and made me a dentist's worst nightmare.

To fund my glue and gas highs I started stealing. My foster mum kept a big glass bottle for any loose change. I made it a bit looser by liberating the coins into my pocket. I'd also go into the school cloakroom when no one was around. My mate Michael would act as lookout as I rifled through bags and coat pockets. I'd take money and new pencil cases to sell. Often I'd find dinner tokens, which cost 50 pence and would sell them for 20 pence. We were always careful never to take all the tokens we found. If one bag had five tokens, we'd take one or two so as not to arouse suspicion. It worked and we were never caught for our cloakroom skulduggery. I made money this way and would spend it on sweets and food as well as the solvents I was abusing.

Sometimes I would buy chip butties from a cafe in nearby Sutton we called the rat cafe. If there were any lads from school, who hadn't any cash I would buy them chips. It felt good to be able to buy stuff for people. I was totally oblivious that sometimes the same people I was robbing at school in the day, I'd be buying for later. I was certainly no Robin Hood who had plied his trade just down the road from where I lived. He robbed from the rich to give to the poor. I robbed because it was fun and I was able to get the things I wanted and needed. The times when I had no money, I would resort to stealing. I remember once going into the hardware store with a big bag, using my arm to sweep glue containers into the bag and then walk as nonchalantly as possible out of the shop and around the corner. Once out of sight, I legged it as fast I could away down the street.

Sometimes I would play truant. I would visit my mum or go to my favourite secret bolthole. A nearby private school had a shed on their ground that was locked. But I found I could prise the door wide enough to wriggle through, taking whatever solvents I could with me. Other times I'd find somewhere quiet to lose myself and take away the pain for a short while. That was the trouble and is always the trouble with drugs. Reality returns and leaves you feeling cold, empty and unfulfilled. You're left desiring bigger and bigger highs and all the time addiction gets its grubby little fingers in an ever tightening strangle hold.

At twelve years old, I was beginning a descent into a pit of crime and drugs, a slippery slope that would lead me to the jaws of death and hell. It would be many more years before my life would turn around and I'd finally find a life that was truly rewarding and fulfilling.

Two other things happened when I was twelve. The first makes me feel angry and sick and I have deliberated over whether to include the sordid details. But it affected me deeply so I'm reluctantly including it. My foster mum dropped me at an elderly man's home who she knew needed help with some DIY. I was going to put bubble wrap on his windows to stop the draft blowing through the house. Standing on a chair to reach the window, he came up behind me and started to touch me in a place I certainly didn't want him to touch. Thankfully, I was no shy wallflower and shouted at him to stop.

Going home in the car that night, Anne asked me how I'd got on. I never said a word thinking she wouldn't believe me. I felt revulsion and shame at what had just happened. I felt dirty even though I played no part in it. Let's move on quickly to the second thing because it had a positive influence on me. It was something, which gave my life structure and discipline that also happened around this time.

Chapter 5

Army Cadet

My foster mum became increasingly concerned with my behaviour. Knowing I had an interest in anything associated with the military, she contacted the army cadets. Unfortunately, I wasn't allowed to join until I was thirteen. Anne pleaded with them explaining my situation and told them she didn't know what to do with me. Eventually, the army took pity on her and allowed a delinquent twelve year old to join their ranks and become a cadet.

I loved it and excelled at all the exercises and physical activities. We spent time with the Grenadier Guards and were shown how to fire assault rifles, Browning pistols, Bren machine guns and even a bazooka. We got to ride in a Challenger tank and went on training trips all over the country. We were taught to forage and live off the land long before Bear Grylls had been heard of. You may have thought for someone who struggled with rules and discipline I'd hate it. You couldn't have been more wrong. As usual for me, I still managed to get into trouble.

Our army trainer was the typical Sergeant Major: short, squat and muscled, with a voice that could curdle cream from fifty yards. He would catch me doing something wrong and command me to get down and give him fifty press-ups. I would do them as quick as I could and spring back up and smile at him. This always annoyed him and he'd make me do another fifty. He seemed to single me out by throwing fire crackers next to me as I squirmed my body under the barbed wire of the assault course. You had to be careful not to panic otherwise you end up with barbs embedded in the back of your head. The crackers were designed to mimic the sound of explosions and let off quite a racket that made your ears ring like a church bell. I'd seen these things thrown into a lake and they would cause an instant geyser with water spraying up to twenty feet into the air.

On one particular manoeuvre I wasn't careful and ended up injured and in agony. We had gone away for the weekend and been divided into teams for a military exercise. Most of my team had been captured and I decided I was going to try and free them from the outbuilding in which they were being held. Trying to creep up stealthily, I was spotted by the enemy. I ran as fast as I could seeking to evade capture but in my haste I didn't see the little wire fence in my path. I went flying and landed squarely on my shoulder.

Although I jumped straight up and legged it, the pain was excruciating. I never said anything to anyone hoping it would wear off after a good night's sleep. The trouble was I couldn't sleep; the pain was so bad. In the morning, I stood on the parade ground lined up with the others. While my company stood straight and proud I had to support my shoulder with my other arm. This soon came to the attention of the Sergeant Major who wanted to know why I was making the place look untidy. He didn't seem too impressed when I told him I thought I'd broken my shoulder.

"There's nothing wrong with you Williams," he barked, jabbing his cane into my painful shoulder.

My cry of agony attested to the fact I wasn't exaggerating and there was certainly something wrong. I was sent to hospital. It turned out I had dislocated my shoulder and it had to be popped back into place by a doctor. This was not a pleasant experience but it was worth it to stop the agony. In spite of this, I still loved the cadets, the adventure and exercise. I soon found out I had a natural talent for the physical training and excelled at it. This was a new experience for me.

At school, I was struggling to read and write and was always behind the other kids. This was not the case on the assault course though. Despite being the youngest, I was also the quickest. It felt good to be the best at something for once. One time all the cadets were entered into a sit up competition which I won by managing sixty-two in a minute. It appeared that annoying the Sergeant Major had its positive side. I knew then I wanted to join the army. There was so much of my life I couldn't control but I loved training my body, building it up. I loved having a purpose and being part of a team. I felt useful and that I belonged. I was stepping up and making progress and life seemed to be offering me something. I was going somewhere. But then everything came crashing down, my Grandma died.

Chapter 6

Grief and Gaffes

I guess it shouldn't have come as a surprise that Grandma died. She was eighty-four, had been a heavy smoker for over sixty years and quaffed at least two bottles of sherry a week. But it was a shock; in fact, it hit me like a sledgehammer. Only a couple of days before, I'd been due to visit her in the hospital but was unable to go, as she had been too unwell. I knew she'd been poorly but no one had warned me how seriously ill she was. As far as I was concerned, she had always been around and I never contemplated that one day she wouldn't be there with her love and support for me and Mum.

She'd been a rock to us. Now that rock wasn't there, who would be there for Mum? I knew she would be distraught at losing her mother. I wasn't wrong. At the funeral, Mum was overcome with grief and had to be physically held up. She nearly fell into the grave that my Grandma's coffin had just been lowered into. I'd seen her in some pretty bad states down the years but I'd never seen her this bad. On top of dealing with the grief and loss of my Grandma, I had the worry of what would become of Mum living all alone.

My cousin and uncle came to the funeral too. Their friendliness and my uncle's gift of a few coins felt like a small ray of sunshine on an otherwise bleak day. That night when I was in my room all alone, I broke down. I didn't usually cry, in my mind it was a sign of weakness and after all, I was now fourteen. The river of tears wouldn't stop flowing for the next week as I mourned the loss of Bertha Williams and all she had meant to me. What would we do without her?

It wasn't long after that Mum told me my dad had died. I don't know how she found out and didn't care. It may seem cold and callous to say this but I really wasn't affected by it. After all, I had never known or even seen him. It wasn't until many years later, I wondered if he had ever given me a thought or if he had even known about me. I was fourteen and really all alone in the world except for my mum who was falling apart. Yes, I had my foster mum who I had been with for eight years but I found it hard to cope with my loss and the worry over what would become of Mum. The thunderbolt of death and the dark clouds of anxiety caused me to rebel and my behaviour worsened.

At school, I was becoming a real problem for the teachers. Stealing, swearing and fighting became daily habits. My backside was well acquainted with the chair outside the headmaster's office. Afterwards it usually stung from the whack of the ruler used as punishment for the most unruly of which I was certainly one. I was still abusing solvents and continually needed money to fund my addiction. I recruited friends from school, foster care and my neighbourhood to aid and abet my one-man crime spree. We would get drunk when we could get our hands on booze and we came up with a scheme to make sure that happened on a regular basis.

The local pub had a garage attached to the side that was used to keep its supplies. We knew if we could get inside, we would find a treasure trove of intoxicating liquor. While the door was fitted with secure padlocks, the roof was old and ramshackle. We were able to lift part of the roof off and climb in. Once inside we would get to work on the beer bottles. When we'd had our fill we would carefully replace the roof as we left, being sure to take with us all the empty bottles. We were onto a good thing and got away with it for quite a while. Until one fateful night, returning home after our boozy bonanza, I realised I'd left my hat and a beer bottle top in the garage.

I hoped against hope that nothing would come of it and we could continue our illicit drinking sessions. It seemed like a long shot though because unless giant mice had taken to wearing beanie caps and opening bottles with their penknives, the game would be up. Sure enough, the next time I passed the pub the garage roof was covered with razor sharp barbed wire. No more free beer and I'd lost my favourite hat into the bargain. As we could no longer steal booze, we resorted to waiting outside the corner shop with money we'd scraped together and asked any adult passing by if they would buy it for us.

Skol lager was our usual poison because it was cheap and our taste buds weren't refined. Dom Perignon it wasn't but it was good enough to get us high. We would eventually move on to Diamond White cider, which was much stronger. Back then, we'd urge those old enough to be served alcohol to get us as many cans as our coin-kitty could buy. The more responsible citizens of Huthwaite politely declined to facilitate our underage drinking sprees but normally we wouldn't have to wait long before we could convince someone to buy lager on our behalf. Off we'd go to the park to drink it, laughing and larking about.

It was on this same park we got into an argument with some travellers that had invaded the local fields. Our turf. Some of the younger ones had been tearing around the fields on a motorbike. One day a few of them were stood round the motorbike, which was parked up. After exchanging heated words with them, I decided to jump onto their precious bike and rev it up just to annoy them. Before I knew it, the motorbike and I were wedged in a hedge ten yards away. I prised myself from the branches and we all legged it away from the angry crowd and startled dog walkers.

It was also the same area that saw a violent attack of which I was the perpetrator. I can't say it happened by chance because I'd gone looking for a certain local lad known as Tucker. But it wasn't just me looking for a fight as I had a good reason to confront him. I was sharing a room at my foster mum's with a lad called Jason who had also been taken into care. Jason had been complaining of being picked on and came home one day in tears. After calming him down, I was able to establish that Tucker had been his tormentor-in-chief.

This made me angry as Jason was three years younger than I was while Tucker was in my year at school. I decided to do something about it and went looking to warn this bully to behave himself. I knew the park

34

was his usual haunt and, sure enough, I found him in the ginnel at the park entrance. I can honestly say I was only going to warn him and hadn't planned on anything else.

Tucker was bigger than me in both height and weight, especially the latter if you get my drift. I marched straight up to him, told him to leave Jason alone, and if he touched him again there would be trouble. He looked at me scornfully, I can't remember what his actual words to me were but they probably ended with 'off'. I punched him as hard as I could and he fell backwards. I walked away when he didn't get up and my intervention seemed to do the trick. Jason never had any trouble from his tormentor again. Years later, I would once again provide protection for Jason but on that occasion, it wasn't in a foster home but prison. Back then, I would never have imagined this was in our future as we were just two teenage lads thrown together in care.

If losing Grandma had exacerbated my bad behaviour, it had devastated Mum. Without the care and companionship of her mother, she was overwhelmed with loneliness. She was struggling to cope alone and would invite anyone into her house to break her bleak and barren existence. Dozens of times I would go and visit my mum to find the house full of older teenage boys. They would be running amok in her house, stealing her money and bullying her. She was an easy target with her mental illness. They would even bring their motorbikes into the kitchen and use the place where Mum was supposed to prepare food as a garage. Oily, greasy bike parts were often strewn on the floor and kitchen work surfaces.

When I turned up to find these youths over-running the house, I would throw them out. It didn't bother me they were bigger and older. They were in my mum's house and I was indignant that they had descended like locusts on my poor vulnerable mum. They didn't argue with me. They must have sensed the fury and wildness I felt at their behaviour. I needed to be with my mum all the time instead of living miles away in foster care. I wasn't able to protect her and they would return as soon as I left.

I found out later that they had urinated in the corner of the living room next to the television and eventually it blew up due to this disgusting act. Words fail me at their behaviour but it added to my feeling of anger and revulsion towards the police and authorities. I vented my spleen to my social worker, telling her what was happening and confiding my concern for Mum. I'm thankful she not only listened but reported what was going on. A one -bedroom flat was found for Mum in Sutton. While I missed her like crazy, at least it gave me peace of mind knowing she wasn't being preyed upon by a marauding mob.

When I was fifteen, I made my first sortie into the world of nightclubs. I looked older than I was and never had a problem passing for eighteen and getting past the bouncers. The loud throbbing music and girls made this a heady cocktail for a young adolescent lad.

Chapter 7

Broken Dreams

At sixteen, I enrolled in a two-year youth training scheme. The first six months was spent studying construction at Mansfield College, followed by a further six-month work placement. I was assigned to work with a small building firm in nearby South Normanton. This would then be repeated for the second year, after which it was hoped the experience I'd gained would lead to a permanent position.

But I knew what I really wanted to do. I'd known since the moment I had joined the cadets. I wanted to be in the army. This was my hope and dream. As soon as I was old enough, I applied and waited to hear from them whilst I continued with the YTS. For my application to be successful, I would have to pass three tests: a written test, a medical and a physical test. While the latter two held no fears for me, I couldn't say the same for the first. The written test filled me with apprehension.

I've already mentioned I struggled at school academically so I sought the help of the officers in charge of the cadets. They were able to give me the previous year's written test papers. While I hated every aspect of school and had never completed a single piece of homework, I worked hard revising the old test papers to prepare me. Thankfully, there weren't any spelling tests and most of the questions were multiple choice. I was still very nervous because I knew this test stood between me and my dream of joining the army. This desire had only been strengthened by attending a cadet training camp in Belgium.

We were sent to a working army base training with real soldiers. We were split into teams, set many challenges, and encouraged to work together to solve them. One such challenge saw two teams of five tasked with getting a big heavy log up a massive steep hill without it touching the floor. And by log, I mean something resembling the trunk of an oak tree. Halfway to the top, it felt like our legs would buckle and our shoulders explode. Each step seemed to take an age as we slowly climbed upwards. First, one of our team dropped out saying he couldn't go on and then another gave in, beaten.

Three of us refused to give up and inched our way painfully to the finish. Whilst we didn't win the race, it felt like a victory as we lay panting, as proud as if we had conquered Everest. We also went on night marches and manoeuvres. I had the time of my life. On the final night, we were invited to join the real soldiers in the NAAFI, or the army clubhouse. They bought us our beer and were all well impressed by my drinking abilities.

As usual, I overdid things and a burly solider came to my rescue by picking me up and depositing me outside via the window. It was just in the nick of time, as I was swaying like a reed in the wind, and about to vomit. I puked my guts up and then returned to the clubhouse ready to start again much to the amusement of the soldiers. I loved the adventure and camaraderie, the sense of brotherhood and belonging. This was the life I wanted and I would have gladly stayed if I could. But it was back to reality and my job as a builders mate.

I was paid twenty-five pounds while on the Youth training scheme. Normally this would have been a small fortune to a young lad like me from my background. But I never saw that money. Twenty pounds went to my foster mum for my board and lodging. The remaining five pounds didn't last long and soon found its way into the tills of pubs and nightclubs. All my mates I was knocking about with always had much more cash from their jobs and made sure a pint of lager was in my hand even when my pockets were empty.

The day finally dawned for me to take my army entrance exam. I found myself sitting in a room with a group of ten other lads at an army-training centre in Mansfield. If only they gave places for passion and desire then I wouldn't have been sat there sweating like a turkey in late November. The papers were passed out and it was all over in a blur. I thought I'd done okay but still faced a nervous quarter of an hour while our exams were marked. It was a tense time but I was finally told I'd passed. Relief and joy burst out in equal measure.

My foster mum was waiting in the car and could tell from my broad smile and shining eyes I'd passed. She presented me with a new watch to congratulate me. She knew how much it meant to me and it was a fulfilment of an ambition I'd had since being a boy. Or so I thought. The army doctor who took my medical had other ideas.

He told me that whilst I was obviously in good shape physically, both my eyesight and hearing didn't meet the required standards and I wouldn't be able to join the army. I was devastated, my boyhood hopes destroyed. I had been a cadet for a long time now and was sure the army would be my ideal career. I knew the training would be no problem and was ready for the tough physicality of army life, in fact I was longing for it.

Okay, I wouldn't be able to become a sniper able to take out the enemy a quarter of a mile away but I knew how to handle weapons and how tanks worked. I could run through mud with a twenty-pound backpack on and crawl silently through undergrowth without being seen or making a noise. I was a perfect fit. It was what I was supposed to do. It was what I was good at. It was my passion and now they were taking it away from me forever. My dreams were left in tatters and I felt angry, hurt and upset. What made it worse; I got sacked by the building firm where I was doing my training.

The first incident that put me in the bad books was when Dave (one of the two guys who ran the firm) asked me to tie some long pieces of wood to the roof of the van. This I did, or at least I thought I had. Half a mile down the road, a loud clatter told us otherwise. Dave was furious; the wood had come loose and flown into the road. I guess we'd been lucky, as it could have easily shot through a car window if anyone was behind us. It's fair to say he wasn't best pleased. We retied the timber, this time he showed me how to do it properly and we restarted our journey but I knew he was upset with me.

Once we got to a quiet road, he pulled the van in and offered to fight me. It was a fight I knew I had no chance of winning. I was sixteen and he was a fully-grown man, his body built up by years of manual labour. I wasn't stupid and told him I wouldn't fight and if he wanted to punch me that was up to him. He eventually calmed down but I knew my job prospects would be limited if I made another cock up. Sure enough, it wasn't long before I did.

The youth training schemes were a mixed blessing. They were created by the government at a time of high unemployment. If someone was on a YTS, they didn't register as being 'on the dole' and weren't included in the unemployment figures. It was brilliant for some because it lead to an apprenticeship and a trade. But these were probably the minority and for many small firms, especially if they were struggling, it was a chance to exploit cheap labour. Whilst I know most people start at the bottom and work their way up I can't help thinking I was used as a workhorse.

It was my job to mix the cement for the builders. I was given the task of keeping three bricklayers supplied. If they were kept waiting then I would get into trouble. I knew the correct ratio to make cement, two parts sand and two parts water. But under pressure and with the builders hassling me, I would get it wrong when trying to rush. The mixer just wouldn't go fast enough to keep a trio of bricklayers going. So I filled it fuller to get more cement and the consequence of my ingenuity was to break the brand new mixer and transponder.

Needless to say, I was fired on the spot. No army, now no job, and no trade for me to learn to provide a living. Fuelled by rejection and teenage hormones, I felt the rage inside me building. My life was at a crossroads and I was about to take the wrong turn.

Chapter 8

Partner in Crime

At first, things began to look up, as I wasn't unemployed for very long. My foster brother mentioned that a local shoe factory was looking for workers. I applied and after assuring them at interview I was a good worker and wouldn't let them down, I was given the job. But my words were just hot air and not only did I go on to let them down but I would go on to damage and defraud the company and my new workmates. I was given the job of working on a lathe and it was my job to remove the glue from the shoes after the sole had been stuck to the main body of the shoe. I hated it and found it monotonous and boring. Excuse the pun but it was truly soulless.

There are many hard working people all over the country that are employed in factories that faithfully graft for a living but the prospect of me stuck in this job for the rest of my life, wasn't one I relished. I should have been serving my country and seeing the world instead of the grey four walls of a factory, doing the same thing over and over again.

It was a chance meeting around this time that would send my life spinning out of control and down the dark road of crime. I didn't know it that day as I hung around the park and just started chatting casually to a guy my own age. His name was Bill Stacey. Bill had had a rough childhood and attended a special school for kids with behavioural problems. He had grown up angry, violent and unstable, which mirrored the way I was feeling about life at that time. I had met a kindred spirit. But, whereas I had stolen from shops and blazer pockets to feed and pay for my desire to get high, Bill was already robbing houses.

That day on the park, we both talked about where our lives were heading. With the benefit of hindsight, I now look back and realise we made the wrong choice. The anger and rejection in both of our lives made us unable to see through the black clouds of pessimism. We concluded the only life worth living was one of crime. In Bill I knew I had found someone I could team up with and to watch my back. I now had a very literal partner in crime.

In the foster care system, when you reach the age of seventeen you're expected to go out into the world and make your own path. I decided I was too old to move back in with my mum and anyway her place only had one bedroom. A small flat was found for me. Living alone, I lacked the motivation and discipline I needed to keep working at the shoe factory. I quit the job because I hated the Groundhog Day existence.

Now I had my own place I could do as I pleased and what pleased me wasn't a nine-hour shift de gluing shoes over and over again. I didn't have a clue about paying bills, cooking or taking responsibility for my life. I began to neglect myself, eating meagrely for days and then binging on fast food. I was more interested in getting high on gas and glue. It was a cure for the boredom and disappointment at the fact Her Majesty had declined to let me join her royal forces. But to fund my slacker lifestyle I needed money I didn't have. I turned to crime.

I was already well acquainted with stealing from shops and cloakrooms and was about to progress to the much darker art of burgling homes. I teamed up with Bill to break into houses and steal money, jewellery and anything valuable we could lay our grubby hands on. Our method was to hit the back of the house so we couldn't be seen from the road. Often we would choose houses with hedges big enough to shield us from any prying eyes.

I'd carry a crowbar down my trousers and use it to jimmy open windows. My childhood habit of climbing through small gaps and onto roofs and buildings stood me in good stead for my illegal activities. My nickname as a kid was monkey as I was so agile. I was well known for being able to shin up lampposts. You could say I was a human baboon. I'm ashamed to say I wasn't swinging through trees but through windows to break into properties.

If there wasn't a small window through which to squeeze, I would put tape around the edges of the pane of a larger one. This would serve the dual purpose of dampening down the noise of breaking glass and protect me from cutting myself when I broke in. Once inside the property, I would look for the back door key or release the Yale lock so Bill could join me. An open back door made a very handy escape route if the homeowners arrived home unexpectedly. We always kept the front door locked; this would give us extra time to make our escape out the back. We'd use gloves to avoid leaving fingerprints. If we didn't have any, we would wear our socks on our hands instead. We were careful not to leave any evidence behind that would incriminate us.

We didn't restrict our breaking and entering to residential properties. We would also target factories. I suggested robbing the shoe factory that had been my place of employment only two weeks previously. I was about to bite the hand that once fed me and it turned out to be more than just a nibble. We hit the place from round the back with me smashing a window and reaching through to release the handle. Once inside, I led Bill to the office that contained the safe.

I knew it was housed in the room where I had collected my wages. Of course, the skill set of a couple of scallies like us didn't include being international safe breakers. We were hoping we would be able to find the keys to the safe. We rifled through the office drawers and desks. In the bottom of one drawer, Bill came across a key that gave us the golden ticket to access the safe. Contained within were all the staff wages in their pay packets. We had hit the jackpot.

We hastily made our exit and decamped to my flat to divide the spoils of our thievery. There was just over two thousand pounds in cash but we didn't divide it equally. As we were going through the wage packets, I came across one with my name on it. I told Bill I was keeping that one for myself as I had earned it. I had no such qualms about anyone else's hard-earned wages. Instead of it paying people's mortgages and putting food on the table, we used it for drugs, new clothes and alcohol -fuelled nights out.

We would also steal from shops. Morrisons in Mansfield was one of our favourite haunts. This was until one day when we had a close shave in every respect. Bill and I separated so if the store detective got wise to one of us, the other would be left free to fill his boots or in my case, the large empty plastic carrier bag I'd placed in my trolley.

I'd just about shoved the entire stock of Gillette razors into my bag. I was reaching for the last pack and about to call it a day when the security guard walked round the corner and clocked me with 197 quid's worth of shaving tackle tucked away in my bag. I quickly pushed my trolley away and left it marooned in the next aisle and made my way towards the exit. I thought I was safe waiting for Bill outside, as I did not have any stolen goods on me. The security guard had other ideas though and proceeded to follow me out and grab hold of me.

Pleading my innocence, I brazenly challenged him to search me if he liked. He declined and instead marched me back into the shop informing me the police had been called. As we returned to the store, who should walk out past us but Bill. I hoped he'd been more successful as he nonchalantly sauntered past ignoring me.

When the police arrived, there was nothing they could really do. In fact, they cracked a few jokes asking me if I was planning on growing a long beard. They wanted to know what a kid with a bit of bum fluff on his top lip would want with a shed load of razors. They couldn't arrest me, as I hadn't committed a crime. They sent me away with a warning, which I chose to ignore and carry on regardless.

We went on to rob countless houses in our hometown but eventually we targeted a new area, Derby. It was here Bill made a mistake that would cost us dear.

Chapter 9

Pain in the Neck

Bill came to me with a sure-fire way to triple our ill-gotten gains. He knew of a poker game played amongst the taxi drivers. It wasn't quite like taking candy from a baby but he assured me we could make big money. It made sense to me. It seemed easier and less risky than what we'd being doing. Fleecing gullible taxi drivers out of their money seemed better than breaking and entering. I didn't know a royal flush from a toilet flush but as long as Bill knew what he doing, everything was fine.

As it turned out, our main problem was Bill didn't know what he was doing either and these cabbies were no mugs. We lost and we lost big, all our savings down the drain. Five hundred pounds of which nearly half was mine. Watching the winning taxi driver scoop up his winnings, most of which had been our money, brought a lump to my throat.

"Let's rob him", I whispered to a shell-shocked Bill. "Come on let's get our money back". "Just leave it", he replied aggressively as the driver drove away taking with him our precious cash. We needed to make money back and fast. But how? By the only means a pair of degenerates like us knew. We were back on the rob. But whereas we'd always got away with our crimes, things were about to change.

At first, it seemed the county capital would prove fertile soil for our illicit trade. Knocking on a door to check no one was home before attempting to break in brought the next-door neighbour out, she obligingly informed us the occupants were away on holiday. After thanking her, we disappeared, only to return and proceed to practically empty the house over the next couple of days.

We found a local shop that sold furniture just around the corner and handed over the poor holidaying homeowners prized possessions in exchange for cash. Imagining the reaction on their return from a sunshine break, I can now only grimace. Back then, I didn't care. We were about to get the comeuppance our cold callousness deserved in our next attempted burglary. We deployed our usual modus operandi. Bill stood on guard at the front while I forced a window round the back and slithered through into the house.

I'd been in the house only a minute or so and had grabbed what valuables had been on offer when I heard voices outside. I froze and listened in with horror. It was Bill arguing loudly with the owner of the property who had returned. It was Bill's way of warning me and trying to buy me some time. I legged it and forced the bigger back window open so I could slide through with my swag. Before I was out of the property, I heard the man come charging through the house in hot pursuit.

I made it outside and jumped through the hedgerow in the back garden, running for my life. Bill had done the same and we bumped into each other a few streets away. Breathless, sweating and laughing at our close shave. We weren't laughing long as a police car pulled up and two officers grabbed hold of us. We had all the stolen goods on us and there was no use denying it. We were arrested and taken down to the police station.

We were charged with burgling three houses but because it was our first offence and we were only seventeen, we were released on bail. We walked out of the court relieved and unrepentant. On the way out, as we were going down the steps of the courthouse, we passed by the couple whose house we'd robbed. The man who'd argued with Bill then chased me challenged us.

"Why did you do that to our house?" he wanted to know. Bill just stared at him and coldly spat back a mouth full of obscenities. We were free and it should have been a wakeup call. We should have realised how lucky we were not to be behind bars but we didn't care. We would carry on, oblivious of the obvious outcome our continued career in crime would bring about.

Although we were free, the court had ruled we both be sent to different children's homes. They wanted to spilt us up in the hope of reforming us. I hadn't been there very long when I cut my thumb opening a tin. It was a fairly deep cut and I had trouble stemming the bleeding so I took off my shirt and wrapped it round my hand. When the staff saw me half- naked and soaked in blood they wrongly assumed I'd tried to slit my wrists and commit suicide.

They called the police who came up to find me sitting in my room. They just barged straight in and refused to believe what I was telling them. I asked them to go in no uncertain words. They refused, and then things went from bad to worse. I shouted at them to clear off. When they tried to get me I threw a soda bottle, it whistled over their heads and smashed into the wall showering them with broken shards. There was no way I was willingly going with them. I'd seen what they did with my mum and I was determined to stay. A fight ensued and they had to restrain me. The two of them couldn't get me out and into a police car so they called for reinforcements.

I was eventually bundled into the back of a police car but not before I'd put up an almighty struggle. If you have ever seen a child refuse to be put in their pram by making their little bodies rigid than you will get the idea. I managed to get one leg on the roof while they were trying to wrestle me into the vehicle. One frustrated officer took out his truncheon and began pounding my shins. I did my best to make myself the square peg going in to a round hole but eventually their numbers prevailed. What others thought at the sight of a shirtless bloodied youth being folded into the back of a police car by several burly police officers, I can only guess.

Once at the local nick, I continued in my non -compliance refusing to remove my belt and shoelaces. For those unaccustomed to police station protocol, these seemingly innocent items must be removed before being banged up in a cell so the prisoner is unable to use them to attempt to take their own life. My motive for refusing this simple request wasn't born out of a death wish. That unfortunately would become a tidal wave waiting to engulf me in the coming years. But at that moment, I just wished to seriously annoy the police. I was forced to comply by one policeman who picked me up by the throat and rammed me against a wall.

I was never charged with any offense and was eventually returned to the children's home with my pride and rebellious spirit intact, but also a neck injury, which I sustained in my tussling with the long arm of the law. It would cause me pain for many years. I would go on to reciprocate the injury the police gave me by becoming a constant pain in the neck for the constabulary.

Once I even ended up stealing from them, much to my glee. Fleecing the force. One night I came across a small rural police station whose front doors were locked up. The door at the back, however, wasn't locked. Opening it, I shouted out expecting an officer to answer. When silence met my tentative probing, I slithered stealthily inside. I can't say I was like a kid in a sweet shop because there wasn't that much on offer. But what was on offer was a coat and wallet inside an unlocked locker. Of course, I took it, pleased to be giving the proverbial two fingers to the boys in blue who I despised and disdained.

But I'm getting ahead of myself. I only mention it here because it highlights the hatred I held in my heart for the police. A hatred so deep rooted it would take a heavenly hand to pull it out and replace it with love. But, like I said, I'm getting ahead of myself.

Chapter 10

Alfreton

I wasn't enjoying life in my new home. Feeling isolated and alone, I decided to track down Bill Stacey to see what fun we could get up to together. I knew the name of the children's home where he was staying, so I sneaked out and went to look for it. I couldn't just knock at the door and ask if he was coming out to play, after all we'd been separated for a reason. I decided to climb onto the roof and have a look around, to check if I could see him come out or where his room was.

While I was perched on the roof, I heard the unmistakable voice of Bill. I clambered back down and could see him arguing with one of the staff through the kitchen window. When he was alone, I caught his attention; he didn't need any further encouragement and was soon out of the door. Then we were off. We resumed our life of skulduggery. Falling back into it, like we'd never been away. The old saying is crime doesn't pay and we were about to find out the hard way just how true that was. We were soon caught by the police again.

Our demise came about when we attempted to burgle a house in Alfreton. I knocked on the door of our chosen property. When no one answered, I knocked again loudly just in case a shift worker was in bed or someone was in the shower. If there had been an answer, I would have made up some pretence like trying to find someone living in the area or ask directions to a nearby street. There was still no answer, so I slipped round the back to check out the property while Bill watched the road.

I soon returned to my partner in crime telling him we needed to give this one a miss. The back of the property was in plain view of a host of neighbouring kitchen windows, and in my opinion, it was just too dangerous. Bill didn't share my apprehension and told me we just needed to get it done carefully and quickly. I told him I wasn't comfortable and it didn't feel right but I let myself be swayed, against my better judgement. I knew I could easily get into the property but the prospect of prying eyes troubled me. Once round the back, I scanned the windows opposite and, when I couldn't see any nosy neighbours, I quickly crowbarred the kitchen window open.

Once inside, I moved quickly and Bill came to help me. We'd only been in a couple of minutes when I heard sirens in the distance. The sirens suddenly stopped. This was standard police procedure to cut the noise as they got nearer so they wouldn't alert the perpetrators. We needed to get out. I knew my worst fears had been realised and we climbed out of the window and sneaked into a neighbouring garden. It was in the nick of time because as we did we heard the slam of a car door. The police had arrived.

We sought sanctuary in a neighbour's garage. Bill wanted to sit it out and wait until the police had gone. I was in favour of using the two bikes that were stored in there to make good our escape. It was listening to Bill that had got me into this situation in the first place. I wasn't prepared just to sit here while the police had time to search all the nooks and crannies for us. I wheeled the first bike out and quickly mounted my steed with Bill close behind me.

Before we got halfway up the drive, a door opened and a woman ran out and made a grab for Bill. He lashed out and managed to escape her grip. Once out of the drive, I turned left and Bill went right. After I'd gone round the corner, I turned left again and down the hill, as I did so I passed a policeman with a dog. Seeing me, he released his canine partner who gave chase. I was thankful for gravity as the gradient I was speeding down was quite steep. I felt confident of outrunning the German Sheppard. What I wasn't so sure of was winning the race against the police car I saw turn the corner as I looked back. Sure enough, the car was right on my back wheel in no time.

My only chance of escape was now a ginnel or field. Before I had chance to find any of these, I was knocked from my perch by the police car colliding with me. There was nothing accidental about it though as the over-zealous copper had deliberately driven into me. The way he drove was better suited to policing the mean streets of the big apple and not a small sleepy Derbyshire town. Yes, he got his arrest but he could have killed me in the process. I guess I would only have had myself to blame if that had been the outcome.

Derbyshire's answer to Starsky and Hutch would later tell the court I fell off my bike trying to escape. This was actually true but only because his car had rammed me from the road. The bike shot straight into the air and me with it. I landed on the back of my head and shoulder on the hard concrete, along with the pain, I now had two policemen for company. Then the police dog arrived and joined the party. I'd been caught good and proper.

It turned out Bill had suffered the same fate. He had ridden his stolen bike a couple of streets away and dumped it in another ginnel, then hid behind a shed. Someone must have seen him as plod was soon on the scene to feel Bill's collar. The police wanted to take me to the hospital to get my head injury checked out. I refused and was reunited with Bill at Alfreton police station. We'd been nicked, and this time there would be no slap on the wrist. It was March 1989 and I would be seeing in the 90's behind bars. We were sent to prison on remand. I was full of fear and foreboding at what lay behind the prison gates. I was about to find out.

Chapter 11

Personal Joey

If you ever get the chance to visit the fair city of Lincoln, I would recommend it. Parts of its city centre streets are quaintly cobbled and it has a cathedral and castle well worth seeing. If you get the chance to visit the jail, I really wouldn't bother. Whilst the old brick building may be aesthetically pleasing from the outside, the hospitality inside certainly leaves a lot to be desired. That was my conclusion as I stood in a line of naked men in a cold bare room. We were all sprayed with a white antibacterial powder. Fumigated like a bunch of unclean animals.

I suppose in some people's eyes we were animals. Most of us in there had behaved worse than any animal would. Yet we were still human and able to feel shame at being debased. The humiliation of it all was added to by the taunts and jeers of the prison guards of whom one was female. She pointed at us laughing at the sight of grown naked men doused in what looked like baking powder.

I surveyed my neatly folded clothes carefully stowed into a box with my few belongings, ruefully thinking it would be some time before I saw them again. In their place, I was handed a blue striped shirt and a pair of brown trousers, which seemed apt given the anxiety I was feeling. These were an indication I was on remand and therefore easily differentiated from the convicted prisoners in their blue trousers. The officers escorted us to our cells.

There are four levels at Lincoln. Level One was for young prisoners, Level Two for sex offenders and Levels Three and Four for ordinary adult prisoners. Despite the fact I was three years away from being counted as a regular adult prisoner, I was taken to a cell on Level Four. I was shown into my cell and the door clanged shut. I gazed around my new home. There were three beds, all of which, to my relief, were unoccupied. I was given a toiletry bag with a comb, soap, shampoo and shaving products but no razor. These were to be handed to us tomorrow.

I sank down onto the bed and was suddenly engulfed with a feeling of loneliness. The night crawled along as I tossed and turned, wondering what the new day would bring and what prison life would turn out to be like. A couple of months ago, I was still harbouring hopes of serving in her majesty's army and now, just a short time later, I was being detained at her majesty's pleasure. Daylight crept into the cells and time passed but the door to my cell remained shut.

I was beginning to regret being alone, my boredom and loneliness outweighing the fear and uncertainty of who I could be stuck with in a small cell. In the dark recesses of my imagination I had envisioned being alone in a cell with a six foot six serial killer who had made himself a weapon of torture from the bed springs. I wanted someone to tell me about prison life, what and what not to do. How long were they going to leave me in here? There was a bell on the wall and my finger hovered over it.

I knew it was a bell for emergencies and I didn't think the guards would consider that my loneliness met those criteria. But I was going stir crazy and couldn't stand it any longer. I rang the bell, my boredom finally overcoming my fear. Apparently, what you never did was ring the bell. The prison officer warned me if I ever touched it again, unless I was dying, he would take me down the block and beat me. His complaint that he'd had to come all the way up to my cell to answer it, was peppered with swearwords. He made it clear he didn't like my question as to what time was breakfast and, "how long will you leave me alone in here?"

The next day, I was thankfully transferred onto A1, the place where all the young offenders were put. I was pleased and remember well the sense of relief I experienced as I made my way out of the adult section. At least I would be with others my own age and would have someone to share a cell with that I could talk to. Maybe prison life wouldn't be too bad. I couldn't have been more wrong. I was put into a cell with two others.

I found out later they were both awaiting transfer to another prison. They knew each other well because they had committed their crime together and been placed in the same cell. As soon as the door locked behind me, I introduced myself to them. Their greeting to me was to push me into a corner, strip me naked and beat me. They never touched my face, as this would arouse the suspicions of the prison guards. One thing they did was to make what's called a rat's tail with a twisted towel. It was only a towel but used as a weapon it could do great damage.

These two clowns were malicious, in fact, they often soaked the end of the towel in water to make it heavier and increase its effectiveness in doing maximum damage. They would then hold me down and whip my back with it. This homemade instrument of torture is able to slice its way through thick cardboard so you can imagine the damage it did to the tender flesh on my back. Unfortunately, for me, I didn't have to imagine.

It took the skin off my back, flaying me and it hurt like hell. This happened day after day. Sometimes they'd make me stand naked in the corner of the room and took turns in belting me as hard as they could with their self -made scourge. They also made a list of things for me to buy from the prison shop: cigarettes, soap, Rizlas, matches, tobacco, toiletries, toothpaste, chocolate, bottles of pop and even toilet paper. All this was purchased with the money my mum would send and I would be forced to hand it over to my two tormentors.

I later found out this is what is known in prison as taxing. Often fear, violence and intimidation would be used not just to exhort goods from the weaker prisoners but also to do anything their oppressors wanted. Jail had its own dialect and being able to command and rule someone was known as having your own Personal Joey or PJ for short. It was modern day slavery with the poor Joeys jumping to command. While I didn't experience the worst level of abuse possible, the fact was that these two bullies were inflicting mental and physical torment. That was the trouble, there were two of them and both were older than me.

They made my life a living hell and because I shared the cell with them, there was no escape. They even took my canteen away so I had no water to drink. This went on for over two weeks. Then one day I came out of my prison cell to take my breakfast tray out, forgetting I had no shirt on. One of my cellmates shouted at me to get a shirt on but I was on the landing by then. I turned around to go back and get my shirt but a watchful officer had seen me and heard the shout from my cellmate.

"Who's done that to you?" the guard wanted to know, surveying the whip marks that crised crossed my back and must have looked like an aerial map of spaghetti junction.

"I've just fallen over," was my unimaginative and false reply.

I certainly had no love for my two cellmates who were making my life an abject misery but I knew grassing on people wasn't right. Despite a clear lack of morals, ratting, or telling on people just wasn't done. It was a point of honour you didn't break. It was ingrained into the criminal psyche. But, the guard was no mug and immediately sussed the situation.

"No you haven't, they've done it to you, haven't they? Them in there" said the officer gesturing towards my cell, which contained my two tormentors.

I said nothing, refusing to answer. I was taken to the first aid centre to be patched up. I had over fifty wounds on my back that had to be cleaned with cotton wool soaked in antiseptic lotion. I was returned to the level and thankfully allocated a new cell. The ordeal I endured at the hands of my two former cellmates was thankfully over. My new cellmate, although only a couple of years my senior was well versed in the harsh realities of prison life.

"If you don't stand up for yourself in here," he warned, "you're not going to make it."

I listened to his words and vowed if it ever happened again, I would stand up for myself, come what may. I hoped it wouldn't come to that. But this was prison, where life was often brutal and the likelihood of living in jail without intimidation and violence was a very long shot. And so it would prove to be. But for the moment, I'd found in my new cellmate someone to help, guide and protect me. After what I'd been through, it was certainly the calm after the storm.

I settled down to prison life, which was extremely regimented. We had a shower only once a week along with a clean set of bedclothes. Every day, we had to take our blankets off the bed and fold them neatly into a bed pack. The blankets and sheets had to be neatly placed in a certain order and had to be without a crease. These blankets were supposed to keep us warm but after using them, I felt a little too warm around my private parts. The blankets can't have been washed on a high enough temperature because I caught pubic lice or crabs.

I had to endure a male prison guard putting what looked like wallpaper paste from my feet to my neck from behind. Thankfully, I could do the front myself. I had to keep it on for two days until the itchy little pests died off and I was then allowed an extra shower. It was one of the few times I used the prison soap they provided us with, as you smelt worse after showering with that soap than before.

The toothpaste for smokers was foul too, bright green in colour and tasting of rotting sprouts. Well what did I expect? After all this wasn't the Ritz was it? I know you may be thinking that it served me right for the life I was living, committing crimes and I'd have to agree. Every Sunday morning, we would have the Governor's inspection. He would come into our cells, casting his eagle eyed gaze over them.

If the Governor could find any dust on the doorframe or under the bed there would be a consequence for our slovenliness. If the cell was unclean in any way or if he deemed our bed-packs not neat and tidy enough, we would face a punishment that hurt. We would not be allowed to go to the cinema, which was located in the church. Every week, we'd get to watch a new film but only if our cells met the approval of the Governors critical eye. It was a treat I didn't want to miss so I always endeavoured to keep my living quarters shipshape.

Not that I liked cleaning you understand, I resented my daily task of scrubbing the wing floors, which were the length of a football pitch. We'd have to get down on our hands and knees. We were given a bucket, soap, cloth and scrubbing brush and had to work from the back wall up to the kitchen like a scullery maid.

Thankfully, we had some free time, which I spent participating in sport. I would enjoy playing football and used to push my body doing circuit training. I found it kept me fit and wore me out so I would be tired enough to get a good night's sleep. To enrol on any educational courses, you had to submit an application form but this was difficult for me. At the time, I didn't know what dyslexia was or that I had it. I certainly wouldn't have been able to spell it because I could barely write. And if I couldn't write then I couldn't get help with my writing or further my education. I was hampered by my disabilities from getting help.

If you needed a phone card or wanted to see the doctor or dentist, an application had to be submitted in advance. This meant I wasn't able to access these services when I needed to, as I couldn't spell any words longer than four letters. The few occasions I did submit applications, was when I swallowed my pride and asked for help with writing and spelling. Sometimes when things were at their worst, I would ask Mr Green, a prison guard, how to spell certain words. He would furnish me with the correct order for the vowels and consonants I required. Little did I know he would be instrumental years later in saving my life. Prison life ticked along slowly, minutes dragging into hours and the hours trudging into days which crawled into weeks and months.

Chapter 12

Not so Great Escape

Summoned to Derby crown court to face trial, I was given a sentence of eighteen months and duly shipped out to an open prison near Nottingham. Inmates here had much more freedom. We could come and go anywhere within the prison. But open prison was still prison and convicts were still convicts. Their surroundings may have become a little less oppressive but their natures were the same. Intimidation and violence wasn't peculiar to Category A establishments, as I was to be reminded one breakfast time.

Four of us used to sit together at meal times. Unbeknown to me, one of these guys was being picked on by another prisoner. The first I found out about it was when he picked up his metal tray and walked over to where his tormentor was. He never said a word to the rest of us, just sauntered casually over to this chap. He had obviously had enough of his bullying and after a brief exchange of words, and much to our shock; he hit him as hard as he could square in the face with the metal tray.

He knocked him clean off his chair, sending him flying over the next table and rearranging his facial features for a good few weeks. I never saw either of them again. They were moved to separate prisons. I too craved a move but not to another place behind bars, I wanted to taste freedom again.

If I'd kept my nose clean, I could have been out in under a year. Instead of getting my head down, behaving myself and doing my time, I began to look out for opportunities to escape. It wasn't long before I began to formulate a plan that would give me a flight to freedom. At the open prison, we had to check into every department we went to.

Everything worked on a timing system and the authorities would be alerted if you were missing for any length of time.

Every day, on my way to and from work detail, I would pass by a skip. It was full of old plasterboard and cardboard. It was also used by the kitchen to dispose of any rubbish. Being nearly full to the top, I knew it would offer me a good place to hide whilst the heat wore off. If I waited until it began to go dark and they still hadn't found me, I reckoned I would have a good chance of making it out. Of course my genius plan really only went as far as breaking out.

Once out, I had a vague plan of heading back to Huthwaite and kipping on some mate's floor, not really considering it would be the first place the police would look. I was just desperate for a way out of the prison life I hated, instead of thinking things through and doing my time. I listened to my inner impulses. I checked out of work detail with the guard and told him I was off back to my cell, as I was feeling unwell. Instead, checking carefully nobody was watching, I hopped into the skip burying myself under its dirty contents and settled down to wait.

It must have been a couple of hours later when I heard guards walking past. One of them was talking into his radio asking if there had been any sign of him. I knew him meant me and my heart hammered in my chest. Would they search the skip? The sound of their voices faded as they walked straight past my hiding place. I lay safe and undetected in my yellow refuse refuge.

I may have even fallen asleep if it wasn't for the slop bucket being emptied in to the skip. Prison food is never good at the best of times. It certainly wasn't good dripping down between cardboard and plasterboard onto my head. But there wasn't much I could do about it except lay still, hidden from the guards. I was banking on them assuming I'd already made it outside in my bid for freedom. I was right and no one bothered me in the sanctuary of the skip.

Hours passed slowly until I thought it safe to get out as twilight was falling. Jumping out and looking around, I made a dash across the prison fields and over a fence, out into an industrial estate without meeting anyone. Climbing over another fence, I broke into a power station and stole a coat. I'd only been out five minutes and I was again on the rob. I was tired and night was fast approaching. I came across an old caravan that seemed to be empty. I decided this would make a good base for me to get my head down in for the night. I broke in and was pleased to see a full whisky bottle smiling at me from a small table inside.

I took solace as the harsh liquid warmed my throat and eased the voice of my conscience, telling me I shouldn't have escaped. I asked myself what I was going to do now I was alone out on the streets and a wanted man. I passed out into a deep drunken sleep. I woke before it was light and it took me a few seconds to realise where I was, that I wasn't in my cell.

I set off straight away and headed for the nearest road. It was too far to walk home so I decided to hitch a lift. One hour and one lift later a considerate but unsuspecting motorist was dropping me off on the motorway slip road on the outskirts of Huthwaite. From here, it was only a twenty-five minute walk into town and the sanctuary of my mate's house.

Before I had the chance to call on any of them to ask them to stow me away, a familiar car drove towards me. It was my foster mum and it was too late to hide, she had seen me. What luck. I'd spent hours evading the guards only to run into my foster mum as soon as I set foot on home turf again. Pulling in and winding down the window, a look of shock registering on her face, she was clearly upset to see me and wanted to know what was I doing out of prison.

I told her I'd been released early but she instinctively knew I had escaped. I tried to deny it but she was having none of it and urged me to hand myself in. She told me she was off to the funeral home to pay her respects to her mum who had recently passed away.

There was no wonder she looked distressed. On top of the shock of seeing her foster son, an escaped prisoner sauntering down the street, larger than life, she had to deal with the bereavement of her beloved mum. I don't really know what kind of reception I was expecting when she saw me. I guess I couldn't really have imagined she'd throw her arms around me but her reaction gave me a reality check. It made me feel awful and poured cold water on my hopes and plans of enjoying a life of freedom.

I should never have done a runner. I decided to turn myself in. Instead of a mate opening the door for me and letting me have a soak in the bath, raiding his fridge and watching television with a cold beer, I made my way back down the road and towards Sutton Police station to hand myself in. I never reached the cop shop though. I was saved the journey as two unmarked cars came skidding to a halt and four plain clothes CID officers jumped out and pinned me to the car.

I was arrested and taken back to prison. For my Cool Hand Luke impression, I had fifty days added to my sentence. My career as an escape artist was far from over though. Due to my stupid antics, I forfeited the right to serve my sentence at an open prison and was moved on somewhere more secure.

Chapter 13

Hokey Cokey Reprobate

Onley prison near Rugby was next on the list. As seems to be usual for me, I was yet again placed on the wrong wing. This time I was housed on the Black and Asian wing. Even though it was the early nineties, non-white prisoners were somehow still considered to be more dangerous than white offenders. While we all know now, it's not the colour of skin or the country a man comes from that determines how dangerous he is. The fact is it felt incredibly intimidating to be in such close quarters with convicts I had been conditioned to fear more than others I had encountered, and not only to live with them but to do so as someone different to them.

I felt like I had a big target drawn on my back. I don't mind admitting it I was scared. I needed protection and sought it the first chance I got. One night, at dinner I made a beeline for a prisoner I recognised, he was housed in the cell opposite mine. He was sitting eating with his mate. I took a chair across the table from these two well-built cons. My presence was greeted by silence and stares so I didn't beat about the bush. I offered them half an ounce of tobacco a week for protection. The mate was interested and was up for it but my cell neighbour just eyeballed me.

"I want your radio from you when I come upstairs." He informed me coldly.

Needless to say that was one mealtime I didn't enjoy. I made my way back upstairs with fear in the pit of my stomach. I didn't want to lose my radio but more importantly, I knew if I gave it away, it wouldn't stop there. The words of my former cellmate came back to me warning me I had to stand up for myself. But the guy was older and bigger than I was. Maybe he wouldn't come, maybe it was just threats designed to scare me. The sound of his footsteps in the corridor told me that wasn't to be the case.

"Give me your radio", he demanded, barging into my cell and blocking the doorway with his considerable bulk.

"No" I heard myself tell him.

I saw the punch coming but wasn't quick enough to get out of the way and it caught the side of my ear. My head was ringing like an alarm bell but he was now off balance. Before I had time to think, I hit him as hard as I could. I landed three or four blows and he fell back onto my bed. I quickly followed up, punching his face three or four times until I realised he wasn't moving and was covered in blood.

Still in shock, I ran out of my cell, across the hall, and into his cell. What had I done and what was I supposed to do now? My mind racing with equal amounts of fear and adrenalin. Should I go back and see how he was? I never got the chance as an officer poked his head around the door.

"Is this your cell?" He asked.

"Yes" I lied instinctively.

He looked at me and locked the cell door. I looked down to see what he'd been gazing at to see my shirt covered in the blood of my attacker.

It turned out it wasn't just my shirt that had been splattered with human claret from the unconscious prisoner. The walls and sparse furniture of my cell had been sprayed vivid red from the impact of my fist on his face. Thoughts crowded in on me as I sat waiting in that cell, not least, the irony that all this violence had come about through me asking for protection.

I knew the news would spread fast about what had happened and people would probably see me in a new light. I hoped any newfound respect would keep me from being seen as a target. The officer returned with reinforcements and opened the cell door demanding to know what had happened and why I looked like an extra from a Vincent Price film. I didn't say a word and I didn't have to, it all became clear as the dishevelled bloodied figure emerged from my cell opposite.

The guards quickly put two and two together and he was led away to the hospital and I was locked back inside my own cell. When I saw the guy the next day, he never even looked at me. Even if he had, he would have struggled to see me because his eyes looked liked cracks in the pavement and his face was bloated and bruised. I'd made a right mess of him. Maybe I wouldn't need protection after all.

But the truth was if I had stayed on that wing, I would have needed a team of bodyguards, as the convicts housed there weren't too impressed with the fact I'd hospitalised one of their comrades. Thankfully, I was moved for my own safety. Life turned out to be a lot less dramatic on the new wing. I started to learn to play chess and draughts. I entered the Christmas competition for both games and won. I was pleased and proud to be the winner of chocolate bars, some tobacco and phone cards.

It felt nice to find something I was good at other than stealing. When my sentence was up, I was released from prison. I couldn't get a job though. No one wanted an ex con who couldn't read or write very well. I would get sent to appointments for which the Probation Service was supposed to help me prepare, but no one there really took an interest.

It felt as if people just regarded me as a no-hoper, a man whose path was already carved out in life, someone who would never change, a Hokey Cokey reprobate, someone who was destined to be in and out of prison all his life. But I really did want to change. I hated prison and didn't want to end up being banged up again but I had no support network nor was I offered any help or training.

I was given ninety-four pounds as a discharge grant to last me two weeks. Two days later, it had gone on food, drink and drugs. Before I knew it, the debts were piling up. I stopped going to the meetings as I felt there was no point. I should have returned home but I didn't want to be a burden on my mum or foster mum. What was I to do?

I returned to the only thing I knew, stealing. I fell back into burgling houses. But now I had form with the police and was known to them as a convicted thief. Any crimes committed in the area and guess whose door they would come knocking on? Sure enough, it wasn't long before I was arrested again and sent back to Lincoln prison on remand. I found myself on the very same wing where I'd been housed on my previous stay. I was locked up once again after only twenty-eight days of freedom.

Chapter 14

Falling Apart

Back inside, I began to suffer from depression. It would prove to be the beginning of a variety of mental illnesses that still plague me to this very day. Back then, the spectre of being locked up again began to cast a dark shadow over my innermost thoughts. I was seemingly stuck in an endless cycle of long term imprisonment then release into a society that didn't want me and in which I could find no place.

Was this all there was to life? In and out of prison, never to find happiness whether I was caged or free. If, in the eyes of the world, I was scum, it only echoed the feelings I had for myself. I was on remand awaiting trial but the prospect of remaining in jail for some considerable time seemed certain. I was in all probability facing the next two years behind a cell door.

The thoughts of the endless monotony of prison life loomed like dark rain clouds, ready to wash away any hope I had left. The desolation I felt engulfed me in a tidal wave of depression. I couldn't see the point in living any more. Lying in bed one night, I broke open my disposable razor, placed it on my arm and started to cut. I sliced deeply into my flesh and the pain seared through my body. I didn't know how long it would take to bleed to death or how I would feel as the light of life slowly faded into blackness.

Looking down at my arm, I experienced the strange sensation of seeing the exposed intricate labyrinth of veins in my arm, like pictures in a biology textbook. The blood pouring out was a painful reminder this was only too real and the cord that kept me tied to life was about to be severed. The blood flowed freely and ran down from my top bunk onto my cellmate in his bed below. He jumped up, alarmed at the sight of my blood splattering his blankets. He shouted and screamed for the guards, banging on the cell door. It's strange to think my life was to be spared because I slept on a top bunk. This wouldn't be the last time that providence prevailed in thwarting my attempts at ending my life.

Whilst some may chalk it up to fickle fate or blind chance, I'm convinced, even back then, that the guiding hand of God had intervened. I was rushed to the hospital wing where the doctor took one look at my wounds and called an ambulance. He was asking me my name and prison number and I was unable to answer him. My body was shaking; I had gone in to shock. He asked me about the pain in my arm and I wanted to tell him it was nothing compared to the agonies in my head. I needed to share my inner turmoil with him but I couldn't even tell him my name.

I was taken to Lincoln hospital. My one good arm safely handcuffed to the prison guard that accompanied me. The doctor there refused to attend to my wounds until they freed me from my restraints. Reluctantly the guard unshackled me and the doctor began his examination. He warned me he needed to close the wound and it would be extremely painful. I told him to get on with it because the quicker I got back to prison the quicker I could get on with undoing all his handiwork. I fully intended to finish the job I'd started.

He repaired my wounds but the real problem was in my head and that was left untreated. They stitched me back together but in reality, I was falling apart. I had fifty-two stitches in just one of the cuts in my arm. It measured eight inches long and half an inch wide and stretched nearly all the way from wrist to elbow. It's still visible today, a living reminder of my former agonies. A map of my previous madness that people's eyes are drawn to when I'm wearing a t-shirt in warm weather.

They treated my wounds and I was sent back to Lincoln and thrown into a strip cell for my own safety. These cells are sparse and barren containing only a bucket for our toilet needs, a mattress and a strip blanket. Once inside, you stayed there 24/7. The door would open three times a day to bring meals and empty the bucket. There was no human interaction and I was left to myself all day and night with just the cockroaches for company. I hated these cells and it only further added to my torment and mental troubles.

Through the years, I would go on to spend a lot of time in these six by eight torture chambers. Because of what I'd done, I had to be checked on every hour by the prison guards. They saw I had been as good as my word to the hospital doctor. I had ripped off the bandages and was trying to pull out the stitches. I was warned they would put me in a straight jacket if I carried on. It was bad enough in the strip cell without being trussed up like an oven ready chicken. I was fearful at this prospect and decided to bide my time until I had the chance to finish the job properly.

The following day, I was visited by the prison doctor. He prescribed two drugs he thought would help to bring stability to my troubled mind. The first was Stelazine. They were little blue and white ball-shaped pills that looked like they could have been sweets. I would discover that they were anything but. After all, no one to my knowledge has ever become dependent on Tic Tacs. The other was called Largactil, a brown liquid that quite a number of prisoners took. You could tell at a glance which ones took this not so happy juice. The way they walked gave it away. Their ambling was known as the Largactil shuffle as it not only dulled the mind but slowed our movements. It would prove to be just the start of my long years of dependency on prescription medication.

The doctor informed me that because I had tried to commit suicide, he thought it would be good for me to move to a dormitory housing other prisoners. So, I was moved. Although I was thankful to be out of the strip cell, I doubted if living in the dorm would make any difference to my depression. I was wrong; I made a good friend in Paul who was serving life. The camaraderie of the other men and especially my friendship with Paul, served to lift my spirits and while prison life was still hard, it became bearable. Life in Lincoln limped along until the day of reckoning in court finally came around.

Chapter 15

Probation

The day of my court case dawned and I had grim expectations of being banged-up for a lengthy spell. I'd just served nine months and had once again re-offended almost as soon as the prison gates clanged shut behind me. I stood in the dock lamenting that my taste of freedom had been all too brief and I'd be heading back to some hellhole cell. To my surprise, the judge issued me with a two-year probation order.

I was to serve the first year at a probation hostel and then be released into the community on a twelve-month probation. This was so I could be monitored and to prepare me for life as a fully integrated member of society. The judge had been lenient; perhaps he imagined after my second stretch of prison, I was ready to be reformed. He was sadly mistaken.

It was the start of the summer of 1991 and I was shipped off to Colchester to the probation hostel that was intended to be my home for the next year. I tried to settle down to life but if truth be told, I didn't try that hard. There was nothing particularly wrong with the place and the people, what was wrong was me. I was bored, miles from home, and with no one I knew. I got on okay with the lads in the hostel who were a mixture of youths, all seemingly gone off the rails and sent to Colchester for rehabilitation.

My efforts to reform entailed me breaking into the safe kept in the office one night when no one was around and stealing a wad of cash. Stuffing the few hundred pounds into my trouser pockets, I set out to leave and escape. Once again, I was no master planner; I just walked out and kept walking. I hadn't planned where I was going or indeed how I was going to get anywhere at all. I was bored, and once again felt like a caged lion. Before I'd walked more than a mile or two, I saw a group of men heading towards me. It turned out it was the guys from the hostel returning from a rave. They wanted to know where I was going and tried to persuade me not to do a runner.

Eventually I agreed to return with them. They had no idea I'd robbed the safe and I knew there would be trouble the next day when the staff found the safe empty and the money gone. Sure enough, we were all interviewed by the staff and the police trying to find out who the culprit was. Of course, I told them I'd no idea who would commit such a low down dirty act. Lying and thieving are natural bedfellows and I was as proficient at both.

My patience didn't last long and two weeks later, I broke probation and was on the run. Picked up by the police, I soon found myself back behind bars on remand. This time Glen Pava, Leicester Prison, was my new home. Thankfully, I was only there a short time before yet again, I stood before a judge and, once again, I was given a two-year probation order. This time I found myself travelling North instead of South.

Fir Tree Grange hostel in Durham was my new abode. The place was set in its own grounds and we were tasked with cultivating the land to grow our own vegetables. Most of the lads in there had only committed minor offences and I found myself being looked up to by the others. Once again, I hadn't been there long when I told them I was leaving and walked out. I was found by Yvonne and Ian, two of the staff, who'd driven round the streets looking for me.

Once again, I was persuaded to return. I then repaid this patience and care by going on the rob. I stole keys to all the other rooms and hid them in my room underneath the carpet under my bed. I got on well with the other inmates but not that well that I wasn't prepared to nick from them. It only highlights the man I was that I suffered no moral qualms for the thievery committed against my new associates with whom I would play football and generally lark around.

Although I was nicking from the residents, I enjoyed the camaraderie and the mischief we got up to. There was one occasion when my horseplay went a bit too far and it literally ended in tears. The weeping wasn't a product of emotional distress but one of physical pain. It probably won't surprise you to learn I was the perpetrator and not the victim. I was larking about play fighting with another resident when I picked up the fire extinguisher, pointed it straight at him and pressed the release valve.

I wasn't expecting anything to happen. What did happen was the foam sprayed directly into his face. The stuff got into his eyes causing him severe discomfort. He wasn't best pleased and tried to wipe the foam from his eyes. The more he tried to rub the chemical - filled foam away the worse it got. I had to lead him to the toilets and spent the next twenty minutes continually rinsing his eyes with cold water.

Eventually the pain and discomfort began to subside but the irritation at my behaviour took a little bit longer to dissipate. I was lucky my stupid prank hadn't done any permanent damage to his sight. Although my actions had caused my mate pain, I can honestly say it was down to naiveté not nastiness on my part. I hadn't planned on hurting him but my recklessness could have ruined his retinas.

It wasn't all messing around at Fir Tree Grange. We were given jobs picking the vegetables we'd grown. Sometimes, I would ask to be excused from work duty telling them I wasn't feeling well. I would then sneak into the other rooms using the keys to gain access and take cash or clothes. Once again, I was careful not to take too much from one room, as I didn't want to give myself away. I had to find a place to hide my stash in case my room was searched.

Fir Tree had an old stairwell and I removed the cladding so I had a place to secrete my ill- gotten gains. I would place my contraband in a plastic bag and store it in my dark dank hideaway; stuffing it behind a pile of old bricks just to be extra safe. Once again, I robbed the safe using a set of stolen keys to clear it out. I'd gotten friendly with a lad called Gordon and gave him some of the cash. He took the cash and duly grassed me up, telling them where I'd stashed the loot. My old friends, the police, and I were soon reacquainted and I found myself in the back of a Panda Car under arrest then taken before the Magistrate.

I was bailed to a hostel in Newcastle. I really enjoyed life here. The food was great and we played in the local five-a-side football league. I'm sure some people reading this may feel upset at me being housed in a bail hostel at the taxpayers' expense, living the high life. But I didn't care. In fact, we lived it up a bit too much. The lads from the hostel and I would go out drinking and doing any drugs we could get our hands on. The problem was we needed money for these two intoxicants.

Again, I naturally turned to stealing. The other lads didn't take any convincing to join me in my illicit trade. We would shoplift and then go into pubs to try and sell the gear we'd ripped off, using the money for drugs and beer, a corrupt merry-go-round of feeding and fuelling my desires to get high. As much as I enjoyed life in Newcastle, I began to get itchy feet and wandering eyes. I knew the pending court case would in all probability serve to sever my freedom and see me back behind prison walls. Frankly, although it's what I deserved, I didn't much fancy that option. Once again, I started to think about moving on with no thought or care about the trouble I would get in.

Chapter 16

On the Run

One day, I stole a pushbike and set off back to Mansfield. My timing could have been better as autumn was dying and the first icy touch of winter was beginning to leave its frosty fingerprints. Choosing to bike my way the hundred and fifty miles, as the cold kicked in wasn't the smartest of moves. I faced the biting northeast wind that could chill you to the bone. I would have to peddle through the rain and the raw conditions to reach the sanctuary of my mum's. Even then, I knew I couldn't stay for long, as the police would be looking for me. Still I wanted to see her, no matter how brief it was.

So I began my journey and it turned out to be a very eventful one. There was no way I could sleep rough as the temperatures plummeted like an Olympic diver once darkness fell. Not having the money to book myself a penthouse at the Savoy, I had to be resourceful in acquiring accommodation. I adopted a policy of looking for farms or outbuildings that wouldn't be used in the evenings, that could afford me shelter, privacy and little chance of being disturbed, or so I thought.

It worked like a dream in the beginning. I broke into a church the first night and helped myself to the hot drinks on offer. More tea vicar is a phrase I've heard, but seeing as the guy with the dog collar wasn't there to ask, I helped myself. I put my feet up with a nice cuppa and settled down to watch the telly I found in the back room. It took me a while to get a picture and had to stick a fork in the back of the telly to act as a makeshift aerial but I had a very comfortable night's bed and board.

The next few nights weren't to prove as serene. I forced a window on a school and wriggled inside. The inside door was locked so I had to break it open to gain access to the main building. Replacing the lock as carefully as I could, I began to explore. I found the school had a swimming pool. I had begun to look round further when I heard a noise, the unmistakable sound of voices, one male and the other female. I took cover behind the large tarpaulin they used to cover the pool. A short time later, a man and a woman entered the poolroom. While he walked straight through, to my amazement the woman started to undress and then dived into the pool. The only costume she had was the one she was born with, she was totally naked.

I guessed the man was a caretaker and the starkers swimmer his wife or girlfriend. After a few minutes, the man retuned and, much to my relief, he didn't join her in her aquatic adventures but urged her to hurry up, telling her he could get in trouble. The woman told him to relax, as no one would find out as no one could see them. She never knew that less than twenty feet from her, peering out from under cover, was a pair of eyes belonging to someone on the run from the police.

Finally, they left and I could relax and explore the rest of the place. To my delight, I found a large stash of canned lager in a shower. Hopefully it was for the teachers upcoming Christmas party as I couldn't see boozing being part of the curriculum. I started the party early for them, quaffing the cans and passing the time by ringing everyone I knew on the school phone. I set off early next morning probably weaving from side to side, due to the excesses of the previous evening. My head was pounding like a sea at high tide beating against the rocks.

I was thankful I'd awoken early before some science teacher caught me snoring in their classroom but that wasn't to be the case a couple of nights later. I had found a stable, which contained horses on one side and hay and straw on the other. Not wanting to disturb the livestock, I crept into the hay pile, tired from my day's effort on the bike. I must have been exhausted because the next thing I knew I was awakened by a young lady, asking if I was alright. Trying to think fast through the fog of early morning grogginess, I told her I was homeless and had just kipped here for the night. She told me to wait where I was and left.

I was then faced with a choice to remount my chariot and peddle away quickly or to do as she asked and stay put. Had she gone to get someone in charge, or even ring the police? I decided to wait, as she had seemed genuinely concerned for my welfare. I reasoned that the people that keep horses usually weren't short of a bob or two and perhaps she might come back with a note with a picture of the queen on it. Although that didn't happen, something equally as good did. She returned bearing gifts, a carrier bag full of food and a piping hot drink that made for a nice early morning breakfast. After thanking her, I resumed my journey.

Next on my list of abodes, I chose to spend the night in was a sports pavilion. Once inside, I secured the door, wrapping some string I'd found around the handle and the nails embedded in the door. After my two previous close calls, I didn't want an unexpected visitor disturbing my sweet dreams. But to dream, you need to sleep and I was freezing. The place was no more than an old wooden shack and as such, offered little protection from the cold. I looked around and found some old paint pots. I filled these with pieces of wood and paper and set light to them. They stopped the chattering of my teeth and I dozed off to sleep.

I awoke with a shock, coughing due to the smoke. I think it must have been the remnants of paint in the pots and splashes on the outside of the tins that had proved combustible or perhaps some burning paper had dropped onto the floor. I had nothing to put the fire out with and it was already too well established to stamp out. My eyes were stinging from the smoke and noxious fumes. I decided to get out of there fast, only that wasn't possible because some idiot had tied the door securely shut, namely me. I'd done such a good job that no matter how hard I pulled, the door wouldn't budge.

I knew I had to get out as the flames had begun to take hold and if I didn't escape, I would be burnt to a crisp. I kicked the door with all my force to no avail. I kicked again with the strength of a desperate man and the door came off one of its hinges but not enough for me to make good my escape, the smoke was quickly filling the room stinging my eyes and invading my lungs. Thankfully, the door folded outwards on my third try and I made my way out into the cold night air, thankful still to be alive.

I didn't hang around, as I knew it wouldn't be long before someone saw the pavilion going up in flames and called the fire brigade. I pedalled to a nearby hill and watched. Five minutes later, the building collapsed, the yellow tentacles of fire pulling it to the ground. It was a sobering thought to know I would have been consumed by the flames if I hadn't woken when I did. A couple of days later I reached my mum's house, alive and in one piece.

Chapter 17

London

I knew this time I couldn't stay home because I'd soon be picked up. After seeing my mum and gathering a few belongings in a backpack, I set off once again. I had quite enough of travelling by bike and was ready for something much more easy on my legs. Sitting on a train, or at least sitting until the ticket guard approached and I felt the sudden desire to use the toilet. I decided to head to our national capital. Reviving my boyhood plan of moving to the bright lights of London.

Now, I was old, cynical and experienced enough to know its streets weren't paved with gold and I wasn't going to be some modern day Dick Whittington. I was heading south alone and uncertain about what life in London would be like. I had a few belongings and a small amount of money in my pocket. I had nowhere to sleep and no idea of how I was going to support myself. Exiting the train, I headed to the tourist information, explaining my plight of being homeless and all alone. They told me about a hostel that had been built whose patron was Princess Diana that provided a bed and two meals a day for the homeless.

It was away across the city so I was directed to catch a bus. I got off the bus in the general area but I was unable to find the hostel. I called into a shop where three or four people were gathered and asked directions, telling them I was homeless and trying to sound as dramatic as possible. They didn't offer much assistance so I resumed my seemingly aimless wanderings. Then one of the women, who I had asked directions of, pulled up in her car and told me to get in and she would take me. Never one to look a gift horse in the mouth, I duly obliged. I was pinning all my hopes on getting in at this hostel. Five minutes later, she dropped me outside a big building informing me this was the place I was seeking. She said goodbye, thrusting a tenner into my hand and wished me good luck.

It turned out I would need it as the place was all locked up, it wasn't the hostel I was searching for. I'd had enough of traipsing the streets for one day and when I came across a hospital nearby I made my way inside and tried to get my head down for the night. I drifted off to sleep, laid out on waiting room benches only to be awakened by staff asking me what I was doing there. Fobbing them off with some tale, I then sneaked into another department and once again slipped into a restful sleep.

I can't have been asleep long when, once again, I was disturbed from my slumbers by hospital staff. This time, it was security who informed me I couldn't sleep on the premises. I was severely naffed off at being woken up and forced to vacate the warm refuge of the hospital. I left the guard in no doubt what I thought of the hospital's hospitality and made my way outside into the cold night. Homeless and without a place to bunk down, I began to question my decision to leave Newcastle and a place that had supplied me with a warm bed and good food.

I managed to stumble across some cardboard and bubble wrap underneath the hospital concourse that had probably been used as a make shift den by a homeless person. Using the cardboard as a mattress and the wrap as a quilt, cocooning it tightly round me, I settled down and spent my first night in London, shivering on the streets.

The following day, I finally managed to locate the hostel. I painted a sad picture to the staff using the maudlin brush strokes of self-pity. They swallowed my story and offered me a room. I had to give them a false name, as the police were no doubt by now looking for me.

I kept my first name, thinking I would be less inclined to make a mistake and changed my surname. So I now had somewhere to stay, at least for the short term.

I have to say life in London didn't live up to expectations and was a disappointment to me. I'd secretly hoped to get work with a crime syndicate or fall upon some scam that would line my pockets and give me a carefree lifestyle. Of course, I can look back now and see my aspirations were pure pie-in-the-sky and the reality was always going to be a lot less glamorous. I don't want to upset anyone that lives in our fair capital but in the midst of the iconic sights that everyone associates with London, there is a seedy underworld of grime, squalor and shame that exists below the surface.

I took to begging, asking people for spare change. I'd always been good at blagging cigarettes off prison cons and now turned my skills to try and relieve the public of their hard-earned cash. I used this to keep me fed during the day and to fund my other dubious pleasures. Once again, to supplement my income I took to robbing the rooms of my fellow boarders. Heartlessly, I would steal anything valuable I could find.

Another scam I pulled at this time fills me with shame even to this day. I can offer no excuse because there is none. I've done some truly awful things in my life but this was the worst. You will read, years later, of me trying to atone for what can only be described as the lowest of the low. I understand people reading this book will be sickened by my actions because it sickens me.

I was in a pub in central London, just finishing a pint before going on the rob when I saw a man selling poppies. Every year people buy these poppies to commemorate and honour those brave men and women who gave their lives fighting in wars for our country. They gave the ultimate sacrifice to preserve our liberty and freedom. These thoughts never entered my head as I introduced myself to this fella. Turned out he was ex-army and every year he'd give up his time to sell these famous paper flowers to help and support our troops and their families.

I explained I too also served in the forces and regaled him with tales from my army cadet days in Belgium and Germany. I told him I'd like to volunteer to be a poppy seller and he gave me his address, saying he would be glad of the help and promising me a box of poppies to sell. Of course, the only thing I really wanted was a pocket full of cash for my next high. This seemed like a much easier way of getting it than robbing shops or houses. So I made my way over to the address he gave me at the appointed time and again spun my tangled web of deceit.

I walked out with a tray of poppies and a collection box and off I went. I stood outside some shops for a while and sold a few. Being eager to make money quicker, I decided to visit a busy London park. Instead of waiting for folks to come up and purchase the poppies, I began to approach people, asking them to give generously to such a good cause. Little did they know that the cause their hard-earned cash would be squandered on was squalid and selfish.

I had no intention of the British Legion getting a single penny. Instead, I would use the cash to buy drugs and alcohol to get high. I should have had a red face but all I was interested in was getting off mine. My hard sell brought me to the attention of a park ranger who told me I wasn't allowed to approach people to sell to in the park.

As I had no ID and probably proverbially sniffing a rodent, he began to question me. I lied to him about my good intentions and desire to help support the heroes that fought for us. I told him he could phone the man I was selling them for if he didn't believe me. The perceptive ranger confirmed he did want to speak to someone who could verify my story. I was soon explaining to my poppy supplier that I was being prevented from selling my wares in the park by a policeman. I thought that promoting him to a copper for the sake of my story would butter him up a bit. I then passed the phone to the park ranger to speak to the man himself. the man confirmed I was supposed to be selling the poppies and the ranger sent me on my way with a semi-apology and instructions to relocate to the shopping mall.

I made my way out of the park. Instead of standing outside a bunch of shops, I decided to visit people's houses. I went door to door with my dishonesty. After finally selling the last one, I dumped the empty tray, took the money out of the box and headed off to get high. The fact it was an appalling, low and disrespectful thing to do didn't bother me then. It was just another trick I pulled whilst living in the capital. The thought of it now makes me feel sick and ashamed.

I never really enjoyed London; I didn't like the frantic constant pace of life. If Sinatra sings that New York is the city that never sleeps, then London is an insomniac's dream, life constantly on the go, with thousands of people buzzing about like wasps round a jam jar. One day, at the hostel, I began to suffer with a violent migraine. My head felt like it was going to explode as lights danced before my eyes.

I made my way to the local GP's surgery, desperate for some relief to the vice like pain squeezing my temple. They wouldn't let me see a doctor because I wasn't registered there. Explaining my situation and begging to see someone for just one minute made no difference, as did my shouting and swearing. I left and groped my way slowly down the road, slipping into a church, I sank into the back row of a pew.

I knew what pain was like, I'd endured beating and stabbings from myself and others but the pain in my head that day was horrendous. I found myself praying for relief and asking God to heal me. Sitting quietly, I found after a short time, the pain was beginning to ease and fade. It wasn't long before it disappeared completely. I was relieved and thankful. I soon forgot about the pain and all about the gracious God who had answered my prayers.

I fell back into living only for myself, a life of stealing and lying, of blagging and scamming.

I was always playing some angle or scheme. The capital offered me plenty of opportunities to eke out a dishonest living. After a couple of months, I tired of London and desired somewhere more relaxed, with a slower pace of life. I decided it was time to go and live by the seaside. I chose Blackpool as my next port of call. I never saw the Tower or illuminations because I never made it there. This would be a decision that would once again see me back behind bars.

Chapter 18

Beside the Seaside

I bid a not so fond farewell to London and made my way to the nearest motorway slip road. I stuck my thumb in the air, seeking to hitch a ride to Lancashire's premium seaside resort. It wasn't long before I was offered a lift from a guy going to Southport. That was close enough to start with.

Unfortunately, when I arrived, I could not find a hostel. Although the coldest winter weather had passed, it was still Baltic and the wind whistled in from the Irish Sea, chilling me to the bone. A shop doorway became my shelter for the next two shivering nights. I needed to find somewhere warmer and soon.

I ambled around the town to check out what was on offer, looking for easy pickings to steal. I searched quiet back streets to see if anyone had left anything tasty enough in their cars to interest me. Unbeknown to me, Southport had been experiencing a string of car thefts and I was walking into a police sting. They had set up a clandestine watch on the motor vehicles parked on the very road I'd come sauntering down, peering into cars. It was obvious to them I was up to no good.

The only reason I didn't smash a car window was that there was nothing on offer I fancied. I'd caught the attention of the police regardless, acting as suspiciously as a wolf at a sheepdog trial. I was hungry so I decided to abandon my recce of the parked cars and try my luck at the shops, where I knew there would be more on offer to my liking. My actions had put the plod onto my case and I was oblivious I was being followed.

I got busy filling a bag in Woolworths, planning to hide it underneath my coat and slip outside when the coast was clear. Being an experienced thief, I always kept my wits about me, checked and double-checked if anyone was watching. It had reached a point I could almost sense the eyes of anyone taking an unhealthy interest in me. I'd only been down a couple of aisles when the alarm bells of suspicion began to ring in my head. Out of the corner of my eye, I clocked a man following me. Taking my time, I pretended to examine the packaging of a box as he rounded the corner. I knew for sure from his demeanour that he was watching me. Taking my goods to the till, I explained to the cashier I'd lost my wallet so wouldn't be buying anything. I dumped the goods on the counter and exited the shop straight into the waiting hands of six policemen.

They wanted to know who I was and what I was up to. I explained I was homeless and gave them a false name and date of birth, borrowing both from a friend. I acted more like a fiend than a friend to him by giving his details to various authorities around the country. Pleading my innocence, I urged the police to check the story of losing my wallet with the cashier. As I hadn't actually committed a crime, they had to let me go. I was free to continue my meanderings around the cold streets of Southport, alone and without a place to stay.

I returned to the shop doorway but was beginning to yearn for somewhere warm. My thoughts turned to home but I knew I couldn't return there, as I'd be picked up. The idea of a nice warm jail cell with bed and breakfast provided was beginning to sound like heaven. So I found a local solicitors, went in and plonked myself on their couch. After explaining my situation, I asked if they would represent me and they agreed. The next day, lawyered up, I marched into the police station and told them I was a wanted man on the run.

I was duly locked up and brought before a judge a couple of days later. The judge instructed that I be taken back to Durham to face the music. The next day, some officers were despatched from there to pick me up. I spent the journey joking with them as we travelled back to the northeast. Once again, I was heading towards prison life.

I was sent to Lower Newton jail in the north of England on remand. I found myself being singled out by the other prisoners because of my accent. My Nottinghamshire twang made me a target for abuse and violence. I was hardly a southerner but the 130-mile difference set me apart as if I was from another planet. Prisons are often tribal places with cliques and groups bonding together because of geographical or ethnic ties.

Sometimes, just the place a prisoner was born and the way he talks, can earn him a beating and isolate him from other inmates. That was the case for me in Lower Newton. Thankfully, I found myself sharing a cell with a guy who was top dog in the prison. No one messed with him as he'd fought his way right to the top of the prison tree. But, for all his fearsome reputation, I got on with him very well. He seemed to like me and it didn't bother him where I was from.

He took me under his wing. It was a safe place to be, the other inmates soon realised if they gave me any trouble, it would be repaid with interest by my cellmate. It wasn't long before my case came up and I stood before the judge, fully expecting to be given a custodial sentence for habitually breaking probation orders. Once again, leniency was shown, I was sentenced to 160 hours of community service and placed back on my probation order.

Due to my previous bad record of flying the nest from hostels, and having no home of my own, I was sent back to my mum's in Sutton. It was from here I was to perform my community service. Spending life again with my real mum presented many challenges. Her mental health hadn't improved and I found it hard to cope with her anxieties. She would constantly complain people were stealing her things and thought they had broken in to take her food.

I'm afraid I wasn't the most patient and understanding of sons at her perpetual paranoia. My mum had seemingly lost all concept of time and would often start vacuuming at three in the morning when I was trying to sleep. I would get mad and shout at her to get a grip on reality. I was also struggling mentally.

I remember calling in to see my foster mum and taking the dog out for a walk to clear my head. Whilst in the local park, I rashly decided my medications were doing me more harm than good and disposed of the lot in a rubbish bin. That night, back at my mum's, I felt like my head was about to explode with pain. The hours crept slowly by in sleepless suffering.

In the night, I was beside myself and needed the pounding in my brain to stop. I went to the local doctor only to be refused treatment, as I wasn't registered there. Desperate, I begged them to phone me an ambulance. Again they refused and I took to punching the seats in frustration, shouting and swearing. I guess I was lucky they didn't ring the police or get me sectioned. Eventually, in an effort to bring peace back to the surgery, they gave in and rang an ambulance.

They gave me an injection that immediately made me feel better and silenced the hammering in my head. The doctor informed me they were keeping me in for a couple of days because I needed to have some tests. I told him I was going home. He advised me against this and, of course, I paid no attention at all and proceeded to get dressed. An hour later, I was back home at Mum's. That night, the pain in my head returned and I had to take to the comfort of my bed.

I was unable to find any solace as sleep just wouldn't come. I was shaking and sweating, curled up in a tight ball trying unsuccessfully to find a position to stop the pain. The night dragged on endlessly with no relief. Eventually, exhausted, I fell into a fitful sleep as the light began to bleed its early morning colours through the curtains.

When I woke, I felt better but the rot had begun to set in. The illness that plagued my mum was not only knocking on the door to my mind but breaking it down. Very soon, I would understand the mental anguish she was experiencing and would myself, descend into a deep pit of mental torture.

Meanwhile, my mum would be on the end of my vociferous complaints at her strange fears and bizarre behaviour. The following day, I brought her a bunch of flowers to apologise for losing my temper. I hadn't been back long before I was due to start my community service. From what you've read about me up to now, I'm sure it will come as no surprise I had no intention of doing a minute of it.

I had no respect for authority and was only interested in doing what I wanted to do. And what I wanted to do more than anything was to get high on drugs and alcohol. Of course, the authorities weren't best pleased with my lax attitude, insisting I make amends for my misdemeanours by serving the community. Soon the letterbox was rattling and the phone ringing off the hook with people wanting to know where I was.

Chapter 19

Birmingham

I was lazy and selfish but I wasn't stupid. I knew before long the police would come knocking. Explaining to my mum that I had to leave because I would be arrested, I gave her a hug and hit the road, homeless and on the run once again. This time, it was the second biggest city in England to which I was heading: Birmingham.

Sally Anne hostel was located on a big roundabout on the outskirts of the city. It was a hostel for the homeless and it afforded me the comfort of being off the streets, with somewhere warm and reasonably safe at night. I would only go there to sleep. During the day, I'd head to The Bullring, a city centre shopping complex. It presented lots of opportunities to a light-fingered thief like me. I needed the money to feed my drink and drug addictions. One of my favourite tricks was to brazenly walk into hospitals and find the workers lockers. The good doctors and nurses would often return from a shift to find their lockers prized open and belongings gone.

I would also knock on the doors of houses I'd been watching. If the curtains were open and no sign of activity then I would investigate. Once assured there was no one home, I would break-in and rob the place. The things I've done fill me with shame and I'm well aware of the pain, misery and distress I must have caused. I would, one day, endure a battle with guilt and shame at my behaviour but at this time, the reality was I just didn't care. I would rob a blind man of his white stick if I could flog it for a wrap or a bottle of booze.

My lifestyle didn't endear me to the staff at Sally Anne and I ended up leaving after failing to obey what I then considered draconian rules. If the truth be told, I just didn't like being told what to do. I found a different hostel on the backstreets. While staying there, I met a fellow ex-con who was also homeless. We shared stories of our thievery and he told me about a job he was about to pull and asked me if I was interested. This was like asking a horse if it wanted a sugar cube. Of course, I was interested.

He told me that nearby there was a car rental firm. People returning the cars they'd hired would park up and post the keys through the letterbox when the office was closed. We thought if we could nick a car on a Friday after closing, it wouldn't be reported as missing until Monday morning. My new found friend, Ron, showed me his secret weapon of a piece of string with a magnet tied to it and a couple of days later, we went fishing through a letterbox although we were seeking to catch Subaru not Salmon. We were soon driving away in a fancy new hire car. I can't recall what make and model it was but I remember thinking it was dead flash. That would do very nicely thank you.

I couldn't drive but Ron could and we travelled for miles and miles. The consequence of which meant we needed fuel. Stopping at a petrol station, Ron got out to fill up and I kept an eye on the staff. No one was taking any notice of us but I'm sure that changed that a minute later when Ron replaced the petrol nozzle on the pump, got back behind the wheel and floored it. A couple of hours later it was my turn to take the lead when we stopped at a small supermarket.

We parked up a couple of miles away and enjoyed a car picnic of stolen sandwiches washed down with looted lager. I say enjoy but in reality Ron was starting to get on my nerves. He was the type of bloke who'd done everything, been everywhere and knew it all.

If you'd caught a carp then he'd harpooned a whale. We moved the car off the road for the night. Trying to bed down in a motor wasn't a great idea. Though it was a nice car, it was a rotten bed. I only managed a couple of hours fitful dozing and my lack of sleep only heightened my growing dislike of the man in the driving seat.

I told Ron to drop me off, I'd had enough and he could do what he wanted with the car. In fact, I'd had enough of Birmingham altogether and decided to look up a mate who I'd met at Onley prison. His name was Steve and he lived in Wolverhampton, trouble was I didn't have his address or phone number. I planned to ask around in the city centre pubs hoping someone knew him. Like most of my plans, it was a spur of the moment decision and I set off walking along the canal.

I had spent a lot of time walking the canals in Birmingham, as I loved the waterways, the scenery and wildlife. I would open the locks for people if they needed help. I guess it was one of the few times opening locks was a good thing. It took me a fair few hours to reach the Black Country. Once there the search for my former jail mate proved fruitless.

Asking around if anyone knew an ex-con called Steve only raised eyebrows instead of any credible leads. Turned out, I would be reunited with Steve soon enough when we became fellow cons once again, in the grim surroundings of Stafford prison. Going back to my wandering about in Wolverhampton, I came across a traveller's camp. I marched boldly in explaining I was homeless and asking for a job. I told them I was fit and strong and I could tarmac driveways. They offered me a small caravan and the promise of cash if I agreed to wash all their vans down. I agreed and was thankful to have a place to sleep.

My gratitude didn't last long. That night I found out, I wasn't alone in the dirty caravan, I was sharing with thousands of bloodsucking fleas. I only lasted a week with the travellers, as they didn't pay me properly for my hard work, scrubbing the vans clean of tarmac, day in day out. The travellers were okay but I wasn't one of them. Also, I had to flee the fleas and the servitude. Once again, on the move, I headed north. My days of freedom were about to come to a shuddering halt.

I said vaguely that I moved north, the only reason I know this is because my criminal record tells me I stood trial in Nottingham Crown Court. I've spent weeks racking my brain trying to recall exactly where I went and what I did, all to no avail. The events of thirty years ago remain shrouded in mystery. Well, as far as my exact location goes that is. It's no mystery what I was up to because it stares back at me in black and white. My long list of misdemeanours numbered five counts of burglary and theft.

I'm not sure why my mind draws a blank when trying to piece this particular part of life's jigsaw together. I can recall events before and after this time period with no problem. Actually, it's a miracle I can remember anything at all with the amount of intoxicants I consumed. You'll probably begin to understand why my mind sometimes feels like mush as you read of the breakdown and bedlam that lay in store for me.

Two years and fifty-six days was the just desserts handed down to me that day at Nottingham Crown Court. Two years was the sentence for the burgling exploits and the extra fifty-six days was because, again, I had broken probation and community service. It was December 1991. My Merry Christmas and Happy Birthday would once more be spent in a cell. In just six days, I would turn twenty-one, this milestone birthday, key to the door. How ironic. I would long for a key that would unlock the gates of Hatfield prison. Of course, the guard wasn't so obliging so I decided to escape. But first, I would be sent to another jail, where trouble once again awaited me.

Chapter 20

Escape from Hatfield

Ashton Opcn was thc prison I was sent to this time. It wasn't a bad nick but I hated being inside again. I hadn't been there long when I began to watch the activities of the guards. I made a mental note of everything and began looking for any weak points I could use to my advantage for an escape. I noticed the bin lorry would come every week on the same day and around the same time, to collect the refuse. The place they parked when emptying the bins would leave a small gap on the side out of sight of the guards. A gap I knew I could squeeze through and maybe cling to the underside of the lorry without being noticed. It was risky though. I knew if I fell off, I could end up under the wheels and suffer the same fate as the rubbish crushed in the back. I never got the chance to put my plan into action at Ashton but my career as an escape artist was far from over.

Meanwhile, to ease the boredom and humdrum existence of everyday life, I started to play chess again. I found a guy who was a good player and we had some epic tussles trying to trap each other's king in checkmate. I also got on with him very well and we formed a good friendship. The problem was many other inmates didn't share my taste in friends. My mate was black, and shocking as it sounds, racism was prevalent in Ashton.

He wasn't a big bloke and didn't really know how to handle himself. This was a green light to the bullies who picked on him and made his life hell. The way he was treated made me angry and began to get me into situations. I would stand up for him and this would lead to scraps and confrontations. It also put me on the radar of the guards who began to mark me out as a troublemaker. It felt unfair, but then again, who was I to complain about unfairness?

I guess the guards were there to keep the peace and weren't too bothered about the rights and wrongs of convict disagreements. This feeling of injustice at getting in bother whilst trying to defend my mate, further fuelled my disillusionment with the guards. It wasn't long before I ended up in an isolation cell.

These cells did what it said on the tin. You were left alone and without human contact. The bare cell was furnished with a bucket and a table made from cardboard. This was so it couldn't be smashed up and used as a weapon or an implement of self -harm. The bucket served as the toilet. It was only emptied once a day, so sometimes you would have to put up with the smell of your own excrement all day long. I would not only have it assault my nostrils but my eyes too when I had to urinate in the same bucket.

I hated the barren and lonely existence of the strip cell. They habitually became my temporary home in many prisons due to my self-harming and breaking various rules. Once out of isolation at Ashton, I was moved on to another nick. I was transferred because the defence of my mate had marked me as a troublemaker. I never saw my friend again and I can't even remember his name. I don't know how things turned out for him but my life was definitely about to get much worse. I was moved to a prison near Doncaster called Hatfield. I hated this nick so much that I was desperate to escape.

Here the prison was run like a training camp for the military. We had to perform exercise drills. We were given blue suits to wear and forced to march on the spot and run. If anyone misbehaved, they would be given penalties of press-ups and sit-ups. It won't surprise you to hear I was often given these punishment exercises. I guess the idea behind it was to teach us some discipline. I didn't mind doing these exercises to keep fit but resented being made to do them. It wasn't the army and never would be and I quickly grew sick of life at Hatfield.

On top of being treated like a kid, the food was awful. I began to look for a way to escape. The fences weren't really a problem, but if you went missing for any length of time, the police were notified. They would be told the exact time you were last registered and based on this information they would know how far you could have gone. A cordon of police would then circle in to pick you up. Wearing our blue suits made us easy targets to spot.

I figured the only way to have enough time to get myself clear of the police was to escape at night. The only problem with this plan was we were locked in, twenty -five feet up, with regular checks throughout the night to make sure everyone was accounted for. Still, I wasn't going to let these little inconveniences deter me from leaving this glorified boot camp.

I waited until lights out, rolled up my spare clothes as a makeshift body under the bed cover and finished off by sticking a pair of boots at the end to mimic my feet. All that was missing for any inquisitive guards was the sound of me snoring. That didn't sort the problem of gravity and me being a long way above the ground. I squeezed through the window and lowered myself down swinging off the window ledge still twenty feet above ground. I hung midair, bracing myself for a landing I hoped wouldn't result in a broken leg or twisted ankle.

Thankfully, I was young and fit enough to survive intact from the impact and now all that was left between me and freedom was the fence. I'd already chosen a spot in the corner with bushes behind it. I made my way over as speedily and stealthily as possible and clambered over the fence and through the shrubbery. I soon came upon a railway line and I followed this for hours. The plan was to get as much distance between me and the prison before they realised I'd disappeared. Hopefully, not before the morning roll call.

When I was satisfied that I'd gone far enough, I found a nearby road and hitched a ride. I'd walked all night long but now I was tired. I needed a faster mode of transport to take me as many miles as possible from the prison. I knew my exit was about to be discovered. Soon my name would be echoing over every policeman's radio in the vicinity.

Thankfully, a van driver stopped and gave me a lift.

He dropped me at junction 28 on the motorway slip road. This was a couple of miles from Sutton, and the sanctuary of my mum's house. I knew it wouldn't be safe to stay there for too long, as Old Bill was liable to come knocking. All I needed was a change of clothes, some supplies and something to eat as I was starving. After completing the last few miles on foot, I reached my mum's. She opened the door and I gave her a big hug. I asked her to get me something to eat and went to pack a bag, explaining I couldn't stay long.

My mum asked me where I was going; she didn't really understand the trouble I was in due to her mental illness. I told her I had to go away for a few months but would be back. I hurried to change and pack a few things while mum retired to the kitchen to make me a cheese sandwich. A minute or so later, I had just come into the kitchen ready to devour my sandwich when there was a loud knock on the door. I just knew from the sound it was a copper's knock. I told my mum to stay exactly where she was and I hid behind a cabinet.

The knock came again and again. I figured they must have seen my mum and decided I'd better come to her aid. I opened the door as big and brashly as I could, sure enough a policeman stood on the doorstep. I asked him a question in the best tone of righteous indignation I could muster.

"This is about my brother isn't it? What's he done now?" "You don't have a brother, Nigel" came the reply.

For once, I was lost for words. After a few seconds racking my brain and coming up with nothing, I asked him if I could finish my cheese sandwich before being nicked.

"No Nigel, you can't, you've got to come with me", said the stern faced bobby.

It probably says a lot about me that I was gutted in equal measure both at the prospect of being returned to prison life and the fact I never got to eat the cheese sandwich lovingly made for me by my mum. She was in tears, distraught; our brief reunion was ending with the arrest of her son.

Chapter 21

Lindholme

I was shipped back to Hatfield. They took great delight in giving me lots of physical exercise as a punishment. They also wanted to know how I'd escaped but I wouldn't tell them. They said I'd be moved and I'd never escape from a prison again, they were only half-right. I was moved to Lindholme from which I would perform my most daring and dramatic escape. In my long and industrious career in crime, I would frequent some prisons more than once and Lindholme proved to be one of these. It wouldn't be from this particular stretch I was serving that I would launch my successful bid for freedom.

Although in the first week or so, I would wish for it with all my heart due to the bullying and intimidation, I would receive at the hands of the other inmates. I was put in a dormitory with eleven other men with my bed being in the corner. These men were all older than I, as I was no longer classed as a young prisoner. My fellow boarders at her majesty's pleasure saw me joining them as a chance to have what they saw as a bit of fun. But to me it brought misery instead of mirth.

The first night, I lay down on my bed and was beginning to drift off until a boot bouncing off my head, startled sleep away. It was then followed by an arsenal of objects that either hit me or crashed against the wall. This would carry on till my tormentors had run out of things to throw. Then the only thing left they had to throw in my direction was the poison of profanities and threats. I remember sobbing silently into my pillow, imagining how unbearable life would be living at Lindholme amongst such brutal bedfellows, I wasn't wrong.

At night, when the lights were turned out, I was made to run up and down the passage in the middle of the dormitory while the rest of the prisoners stood at the end of their beds. They would pummel me with pillowcases filled with boots and other heavy objects that they swung at me as I ran past. One night, they made me and another lad from York, wrap towels around our hands and have a boxing match. They probably expected me to cop a hammering but I held my own as we bludgeoned each over with blows. It went on for quite some time without one of us going down, much to the delight of the others who shouted their encouragements.

Despite the noise from the baying mob surrounding us, no guards came to see what was happening. It ended in an exhausted draw and we retired to our beds, bruised and battered. But that night, no missiles were fired in my direction. It seemed I'd earned a newfound respect. The next day, Yorkie came to see me and told me we wouldn't let them get away with making us fight again.

Another incident that raised my respect levels, followed shortly. The hardest bloke in the dorm was bragging about the power of his punch, so I challenged him to hit me as hard as he could in my midriff. He thought this was a good idea, as did everyone else. I stood there waiting for him to level his best swing at my stomach. I tensed my muscles, nervously hoping that the many years of sit-ups would stand up to the challenge.

That didn't prove to be exactly the case as he hit me as hard as he could. I stepped back from the force of the blow but managed to disguise my discomfort with a smile. He couldn't believe it. The toughness of my torso raised my profile and the other men now accepted me as one of them. Life at Lindholme became bearable. In fact, we teamed up to create a few added facilities to our shared dormitory.

The dorms slept twelve and the toilet block was connected to them. The guards were able to look into the dorms through the viewing panel on the door but couldn't see into the toilets. Having a sauna and being able to cook ourselves a full English weren't included in the luxuries prisoners enjoyed and yet, due our opportunistic thievery and a fair amount of ingenuity, these were exactly what we fashioned for ourselves.

We stole a big vat of cooking oil from the larder and rolled the barrel into our dormitory. We cut the top off the barrel, emptied it and filled it with water. We then nicked a metal food tray that we used to eat off. I bent it in the middle until it folded in two. We then bored holes in either end and fastened two pieces of wood to it. Passing a wire through the holes, we connected it to the electric light switch with razor blades and dropped our device into the barrel. In a short time, the water was steaming and we had our homemade sauna.

I remember one time jumping from chair to chair in the toilet block, one wise prisoner told me to stop as I was larking about too near the barrel. If you knock it over we will all be fried he said. Safe to say, I heeded his advice. We also used the same system to cook the bacon, eggs, sausages and beans we'd nick from the kitchen. We had to be careful though we didn't set off the smoke alarm and alert the guards to the fact we were having our own mini barbecue. Often, there was a group of prisoners furiously wafting away the smoke before it drew attention to our sizzling exploits.

Some were excluded from the companionship and camaraderie among the cons. Although I was now accepted, it wasn't the case for everyone. One day, we had a new prisoner allocated to our dormitory, a quiet man with thick-rimmed glasses. When asked what he was in for he refused to answer. His failure to disclose his illegal activities with us other cons only served to arouse the suspicion that he was a sex offender.

I doubt now that this was actually the case as those sorts of prisoners were always housed together for their own protection. But his secrecy damned him in the eyes of the other prisoners in our dorm. They began to plan retribution and I was nominated to execute the sentence the kangaroo court inevitably reached for all such crimes. There was a strict hierarchy among the heinous. In the food chain of prison life sex offenders dwelt at the very bottom. Hated and reviled, causing disgust even in the eyes of violent, dishonest convicts.

The plan was to set his bed on fire while he was asleep so his feet would be burned. I should have recalled my initial bedtime torment and refused. But, me being me, I took a rag and slipped stealthily out of bed and over to where he lay. Using a lighter, I set the bottom of his blanket alight. I retreated to my bed and waited to see what would happen. I didn't have long to wait as the smoke, heat and flames soon awoke the poor man. He jumped up in panic and ran to the door, banging on it shouting for help.

Help came in the shape of the guards whose subsequent investigation drew a blank in trying to find out who was the arsonist amongst us. Thankfully, my reckless actions did no lasting harm apart from a nasty shock, the man was thankfully, unharmed and was transferred for his own safety. I was soon to follow, with Nottingham nick being my new home and a place where, once again, my fragile mental health would begin to crack and splinter.

Chapter 22

Nottingham

There were 192 lifers in Nottingham. Now you don't get a life sentence for being a boy scout. These were serious criminals that had committed the worst crimes. Apparently, I missed out on meeting one of the infamous Kray twins by one week. He'd left just a few days before I was transferred. It wasn't my new inmates at Nottingham that were to be the problem. I was generally left alone to get on with life and got on well with the other prisoners apart from one.

The animosity was triggered between me and a lifer due to my tough, two-footed challenge on him during a football match. He picked himself up off the ground and informed me he was going to kill me. This was no empty threat if the hateful look on his face was anything to go by. I reckoned I was a goner. My worries soon dissipated when one of my teammates who happened to be the hardest convict in Nottingham, came to my aid. He informed my adversary if he ever touched me, he would break his legs.

They say it's good to have friends in high places; once again, someone at the top of the prison pecking order protected me from a beating. I was grateful to Garth and told him so the next time our paths crossed. He assured me it was no problem but from time to time, if I had any contraband worth having, I would always express my thanks by sharing it with him. I never got any bother from the lifer on the receiving end of my Chopper Harris impression. A couple of dark glances of disdain were all he dare shoot in my direction.

It was also in Nottingham I met another prisoner whom I liked. He, too, was a troubled soul who shared my experience in suffering from depression and other dark demons. Like me, he was a self-harmer and often considered ending his own life. We would talk for hours, empathising with each other. It was nice to find someone who knew what I was going through, someone who understood the torment and pain. Another thing we had in common was we had both come to the unwanted attention of one particular guard.

This officer was a real nasty piece of work who abused his position of power to intimidate and torment us. His dirty tricks included banging on our cell doors in the middle of the night and standing there silently staring at us through the window. He would systematically abuse and bully us with mocking cruelty. He would refer to us as retards and then tell us we we're making up our mental health issues for attention and that we didn't need medical help when we asked for it.

I fell into a cycle of self-harming and found myself a regular visitor to the unwelcoming strip cells. Once, I was sent there when a noose was found in my cell. I'd made it with the intention of killing myself. It was an obsession that wouldn't leave me but thankfully something or rather someone was keeping me from going through with that final act that would have lead me to a lost eternity. It wasn't to be the last time God had to rescue me from this awful situation.

I wasn't thinking about God, let alone seeing the hand of the Almighty in my stark situation. God seemed a million miles away as I languished in that cold bare cell. It wasn't just me struggling; my newfound friend was experiencing the same serious mental health struggles. One night, I heard a commotion outside my cell. Officers were dragging my associate to a strip cell despite his desperate pleas to see a doctor. He kept asking over and over for all to hear. The reply he received was to be shoved into the cell and told he wasn't going to be seeing anyone. The door was slammed in his face.

It turned out it was to be a face I'd never see again. His cries ebbed away and the night slipped back into silence. I never heard the crunch of his glasses under his feet. I never heard the strangling sounds as the noose he'd made from his strip blanket choked the life out of him. It must have taken him hours to unpick strand after tightly woven strand with a shard from his shattered spectacles and create his homemade implement of death.

What I did hear, the next afternoon, was a guard on his radio asking for emergency response and the sound of running to his strip cell. A person in a strip cell was supposed to be checked upon every fifteen minutes for their own safety. This was often relaxed in the afternoon, as my friend knew. Seems he'd timed his suicide between checks, giving him the maximum time to complete his attempt. We all watched from our cells, hoping he was okay. He wasn't.

The black body bag that came up from that cell, carried by four guards, right past us, was a testimony to the tragic waste of life of my friend. It could have easily been me. But I didn't really stop to consider and ponder the futility and the awful final reality of our self-destructive urges. I was too angry with the officers who turned a deaf ear to my friend's pleadings. The officers knew they were at fault and that there would be serious repercussions if the facts were ever found out. They were fully aware that I was witness to what had happened, and wouldn't stay quiet about it.

A death in prison had to be investigated and reports made. If they weren't careful, someone was going to get into trouble. They were careful, very careful. I was prevented from talking to the investigators. They deliberately blocked my cell off with a dinner trolley. The last thing they wanted was for the facts to come out. How he'd been tormented for months and had medical attention refused. I felt revulsion at the fact this man had been pushed into such intense hopelessness. I hadn't known him long but I felt grief-stricken at his death.

It could so easily have been my cold lifeless body they had to zip into a bag and cart off to the mortuary. The time in Nottingham ticked past as slow as a broken clock and I slowly inched towards completing my sentence. My relationship with the officers didn't improve and neither did my mental health. I wasn't the only one suffering. One prisoner on suicide watch, ripped off his own toenail, then used it to slice open a vein and subsequently bled to death.

The death of my friend seemed to fuel my mental torment and I began to experience increasing bouts of paranoia. These weren't helped by the fact I was taking every drug I could get my hands on. Even though we were locked up, people still had access to drugs. Sometimes they were thrown over the wall or were smuggled into the prison. It was a great relief to me finally to be released.

Chapter 23

Sheffield

I made my way to Sheffield; the city that many years later was to become my home. It was the opening months of 1993 but I hadn't just stumbled into England's fifth largest city randomly. I had the address of a guy who lived in the steel city who I knew from Lindholme prison. He'd told me to look him up when I got out and now seemed as good a time as any. Once out, I carried on taking as many drugs as I could get my hands on. My old Lindholme buddy, Jez, knew a ready source. Of course, to fund our insatiable appetite for highs, I was again, on the rob.

This is where my friend was to come in useful. He had a car and so I asked him to act as getaway driver. He didn't take much persuading and we agreed to carry out a job the next day. Whilst hatching our plans, we'd been smoking cannabis. This was followed up by a snort of coke and a visit to the pub. We then rounded off our evening by popping microdots, a form of LSD. I remember someone coming into the pub toilet and standing next to me at the urinal. I just burst out laughing, hysterically caught up in the nonsensical, hollow high and much to the quizzical astonishment of the man next to me trying to wee. We went back to a woman's house, someone Jez knew.

The next morning, I felt as rough as heavy-duty sandpaper. I remember washing my face for about ten minutes trying to wash away externally, the internal heavy, hazy feeling of a pounding brain. This was hardly an ideal start to the day of our heist. My plan was to rob a city centre jewellery store. It was hardly an Ocean's Eleven strategically planned operation. It had no finesse to it at all. It consisted of me, a pair of gloves and a lump hammer. Jez was to be waiting in the car a few hundred yards away, in a place with no CCTV. We couldn't hit the store in the dead of night as the shop had metal shutters pulled down out of business hours. So, my smash and grab raid had to be carried out in broad daylight, as the city centre shoppers were swarming around.

Fuelling ourselves with a breakfast from McDonald's, we drove to a local B&Q to buy the things I needed to get me past the two-inch thick window. This was all that separated me from the glint of gold and flash of diamonds. After purchasing these items, we made our way to the spot where Jez would be waiting for me, ready to make a quick getaway. When I got to the jewellers, I slipped the lump hammer out of my coat and gave the window a good whack. To my surprise, the window didn't shatter but shook like a jelly. I hit it a second time, and again, it refused to yield to my brute force.

I was in full view of the shoppers and I'd obviously announced my intentions to the shopkeeper who was likely already on the phone to my friends at the local constabulary. Panicking, I hit it a third time with everything I had. This time the window shattered and the hammer flew from my hand and into the shop. I grabbed a tray of rings and made a run for it as fast as my legs could carry me. Running down the road, I didn't look back. I knew I couldn't have looked any more conspicuous if I wore a striped shirt, mask and carried a bag marked swag.

One guy obviously knew what I was up to because he tried to stop me. He just bounced off me as I was running as fast as I could. I rounded the corner and ran across the road. Not quite all the way though. Before I reached the other side, I ended up on the bonnet of a car that slammed on the anchors at the sight of a sweating scallywag pelting out into its path carrying a tray full of stolen rings. Like the have a go hero, I too just bounced off the car straight onto the hard tarmac. I picked myself up and sped off, bruised and confused.

I only had to round one more corner and go down the road to where Jez was ready to whisk me away. But I went in the wrong direction under an archway. I realised my mistake and spun around to double back. I hadn't got far before the police came into view. Cursing, I turned once again and legged it. As tired as I was, I knew I needed a new route to take me to the waiting car. Though outrunning the police was my first priority.

I was still in possession of the tray of stolen rings, minus two that had taken a leave of absence when the car hit me. At the next corner, I found myself heading towards another police car. I had no choice to double back; I was now a robber in a police sandwich. I was once again arrested. I'm not sure how long Jez sat in the car, waiting for me, sooner or later he must have realised something had gone wrong and driven off. I never mentioned him to the police.

The next day I stood before a judge who bailed me to a hostel in the Norfolk Park area of the city. It wasn't a good place to live. I would have people come into my room, asking for Rizlas at three o'clock in the morning. Often, petty disputes would break out that would soon flare up into fights. I hated it there but I would hate it even more in the next place I would call home. I pleaded guilty and was sentenced to eight months.

It turned out one of the two rings I had lost when colliding with the car had been handed in. The other one is still missing and is probably adorning the hand of some unsuspecting Sheffield lass, courtesy of my ill thought out crime caper. I was sent back to prison where my worst demons would surface. My mental health was about to nosedive as I heard news that would cause the foundations of my already tottering world to come crashing down.

Hull was to be the next port of call in my tour of her majesty's jails. Many people wear band tour t-shirts detailing the places played by their favourite groups. I would be unable to document the places of all my confinements on one of these, as there wouldn't be room. It was said of football manager, Tommy Docherty, that he'd had more clubs than Arnold Palmer, but he was no match for the number of nicks in which I had been incarcerated. Before I reached my 30th birthday, I would have been to eighteen different prisons, some of them, more than once. The sentence passed down on me was lenient; I would only have to survive eight months. That turned out to be easier said than done.

Chapter 24

Madness and Mayhem

Compared to my last stretch, it shouldn't have been too bad serving a few short months. But, I began to experience serious mental problems in Hull. I would hear voices in my head, saying awful, horrible things. These voices started after being cursed by a fellow prisoner. He was Rastafarian, and wasn't too pleased I'd relieved him of some cannabis; he then cast the curse on me. Whether you believe this was the cause of my subsequent severe mental issues, I'll leave up to you. The fact was my already serious problems got much worse shortly after.

I'm unsure whether sinister forces were responsible, I'd also been led to believe mental illness can be a product of our environment and circumstances, the experiences we go through. It can also arise from lifestyle choices and the chemicals you put into your body and it can also be an illness we inherit, genetically, from our parents. It's also a fact that my mental issues were caused by all of these factors. I was playing with a proverbial full hand and I began to find it hard to cope. The voices that suddenly started were the worst. They would command me to harm and even kill myself.

One time, these voices incessantly told me to go and smash the television and use the broken glass to kill myself. The television in question at the time was one being watched by a number of prisoners in the TV-room. I would argue with the voices who would tell me I was scum and didn't deserve to live. They callously reminded me I had nothing to live for and no prospects in life. These voices became a perpetual nightmare and I just wanted to shut them up.

I refused their request to smash up the television so they then said I should smash the fish tank in the same room. Tired of fighting these disembodied messengers of malice, I marched into the room full of lounging prisoners and punched the fish tank. The glass shattered and water poured out all over me and onto the floor, along with the floundering fish. Afterwards, I felt very sorry about the poor creatures but at the time, I didn't stop to consider the flapping death-throes of the fish. Amidst the loud cries and protestations of the other prisoners, I lifted the broken tank down and tore a shattered shard of glass from the remains. I stabbed myself as hard as I could, shoving the big jagged piece of glass into my midriff, feeling it tear my skin. My hand was bleeding as well as my stomach. The place was in uproar. Two guards came running, and one of them must have coshed me on the head with his truncheon to bring the chaos to a close. One second I was trying to gut myself like a fish and the next, my lights were put out quicker than a power cut.

I was awakened from my cosh-induced coma by the pinprick of a needle in my bottom. I was given Acuphase, a drug used for the treatment of acute mental disorders. This was no doubt administrated so I wouldn't be a danger to myself when I came round. When I did, I found myself lying in the prison hospital but, once again, the wounds I'd inflicted on myself were too deep and serious to be treated in these surroundings. They were also concerned I may have shards of glass left in my stomach so I was taken to the local general hospital.

My wounds were treated, they stitched me back together and after an overnight stay, I was returned to prison.

While my injuries got better, my mental health didn't. The voices were here to stay. Things got so bad I had to have two guards watch me shave, for fear I'd kill myself. That's exactly what I tried to do one day smashing a broom handle in two and jabbing the sharp broken end as hard as I could into my neck. The two guards had to restrain me and call for back up to stop me killing myself. After that, I wasn't allowed to shave and had a long beard. People would call me Sutcliffe, after the Yorkshire Ripper, the infamous serial killer in the late seventies - early eighties.

I was again placed in a strip cell instead of the hospital and would beg and plead for medical help but was ignored. I felt I was going insane in that small hellhole of a cell. Time crawled by and loneliness and lunacy began their silent scream. I started to imagine the guards were building a hanging tower to lynch me. I started to hallucinate, the guards faces would morph into the faces of people I knew from outside prison. It was weird to see my Uncle Peter as a prison guard, coming into my cell. But these weren't the only strange delusions I was experiencing. Many dark thoughts invaded my head. I imagined my cell was bugged and had hidden cameras watching my every move.

Three times a day, the cell door would open and my food was delivered, for the rest of the time I was alone. No one listened when I cried and shouted. Things got too much for me and I had a mental breakdown. I wanted to die and started drinking my own urine thinking it would poison and kill me. I stripped off and rubbed my own faeces all over my body. I would also defecate on my bed so I had my own waste ready to throw at the guards when they came in. I would scatter my food over my cell so the guards would slip on it if they tried to get to me.

In reality the guards didn't want to come anywhere near me when they opened the door in the morning. The smell of me caked in my own excrement, turned their stomach and they would order me to have a shower. I was desperately mentally ill and getting my body cleaned on the outside was only papering over the cracks because inside, my mind was in turmoil. Worst of all was the voices attacking and assaulting me. Imagine someone constantly telling you you're no good, worthless and you should kill yourself. That's what I was enduring all day, every day. It would be many years later that God finally delivered me from these constant heralds of hatred and self-loathing.

It became obvious to everyone I needed specialist treatment for my mental illness and thankfully, after what seemed an eternity, I was transferred to Delaport secure mental hospital. I remember one of the guards who escorted me to my new abode, telling me he was so glad I was leaving. He said I'd been a nightmare, the worst prisoner he'd dealt with in his forty years as a prison officer. He complained I'd caused him more paperwork than the rest of the other prisoners put together. While they were glad to get rid of me from Hull nick, the staff at Delaport didn't share their gratitude at my arrival.

In the first few days, my mental issues carried on unabated. I locked myself in the bathroom and started to smash the small window in the hope of being able to cut my own throat. The door was broken down before I had a chance to sever my jugular. Eating dinner one night, I tried to gouge my eye out with a fork and was jumped upon by the staff who eventually managed to wrestle the would-be skewer from my grip before I'd done any permanent damage to myself.

Despite my behaviour, I have to say the staff there were brilliant. They truly seemed to care. I will always remember one lady called Carling. She was beautiful, and was so gentle and patient with me. I was diagnosed with paranoid schizophrenia, borderline personality disorder, depression and acute anxiety. The doctors were so concerned at my condition and the fact I didn't seem to be responding to any medication, they decided to try a more radical solution. I was to undergo a treatment called electroconvulsive therapy.

I had a needle put in my arm and was asked to count from ninety-one to one hundred. The sedatives pumped into me meant I couldn't remember reaching ninety-four. Then electric probes were attached to my head and a strong current passed through, causing a seizure. The aim of ECT is to shock the brain into functioning properly. It's known as a last chance treatment, given only to those suffering from the most severe mental illnesses. Sitting outside on the grass in the afternoon sunshine, recovering from my ECT treatment and talking to Carling felt like heaven compared to my recent experiences. I would just sit there and listen to her talk. There was no chance of me escaping; I had to be helped to my feet afterwards. But that hour or so was like an oasis in the desert to me. Eventually, under the excellent care of the staff, I began slowly to improve.

Chapter 25

Doncaster

I was sent back to prison where I was given some devastating news. I received a visit from the prison chaplain who asked to see me alone. I knew something must be wrong as we were hardly famed for having cosy chats. He informed me that my mum had died. His visit lasted no more than a minute, but this news left me distraught. I struggled to cope with the emotions that engulfed me. I would never see my mum again. I ended up punching the door till my knuckles were skinned and bloody.

The next day, I asked a con who was serving life for murder if I could borrow his phone card. At first, he thought I was trying to blag him. When he saw the tears in my eyes and realised my predicament, he gave me all the phone cards he had, telling me I needed them more than he did. Thanking him for his kindness, I rang my foster mum and asked her to come to the funeral.

I was allowed out of prison to attend the service. There were just three other people there to say their goodbyes to Mum. The Vicar, my foster mum, and a prison guard. I wanted to see my mum one last time and to kiss her goodbye so I asked for the coffin lid to be removed. My request was refused as they said they didn't have the time. I remember feeling angry I was denied this last interaction with my mum. Perhaps it turned out for the best. I'm not sure what my mum would have looked like, laid in the coffin, at least I don't have to remember her as a cold and lifeless figure. My memories of her that I hold dear are her love and care and the little things she would say and do along with all her idiosyncrasies.

Inside, I was in agony, I stood next to that guard, engulfed in the raw grief of losing Mum. I was angry, frustrated and embarrassed all at the same time. The pathetic sight of the four figures in the empty crematorium was no testament to the kind of woman my mum had been to me. I will always treasure the memories of her. I was beginning to understand the illness she suffered because I was starting to taste the same bitter pill she had to live with. The paranoia and mental torments she endured were now plaguing her son.

Once back in prison, I fell into a deep depression. I was taken back to the prison hospital and I took to bed and didn't want to get up. The guards tried to make me get out of bed but I refused, wallowing in grief and self-pity. I was heavily medicated and spent a lot of time in bed. My days were spent lying face down in bed, hiding underneath the covers. At night, one of the prisoners would bring in cannabis he had hidden. Everyone would gather around my bed and the friendship and laughter of that group helped me forget my troubles and grief and put a smile on my face, for a few hours each night.

The days of my sentence drew to a close and I was ready to enter civilian life again. Was the death of my mum to prove a turning point in my behaviour? Was I able or even desirous to put a stop to the endless cycle of crime and imprisonment my lifestyle always brought? No, is the answer to that question. I was one leopard who wasn't about to change his spots.

The first thing I did was to return to my mum's flat. I didn't have a key but I had a time- honoured way of getting in that I'd used several times before. One window wasn't properly latched and I was able to open it from the outside and squeeze through. I searched the flat for mementoes of the woman I loved. There were no smiling, happy family photos beaming back from the mantelpiece. I eventually found the only photo I have of my mum. It fell from the loft when I opened the hatch. It was the most valuable thing that could have dropped into my possession. I treasure this precious black and white image. Along with my memories, it's the only thing I have to remind me of her.

I visited Mansfield crematorium to ask for my mum's ashes but was told they had already been scattered in the garden of remembrance. This upset me greatly at the time. Years later, I would comfort myself with the thought the most important thing is not where the person's remains are but the destination of our soul. I returned to South Yorkshire, but this time I made Doncaster my temporary home. The contacts and company I sought out did nothing to improve my prospects or keep me from, once, seeing the inside of a prison cell.

When I entered a town or city, I would often inquire to where the roughest pub in the area was. I knew that, frequenting these less than reputable watering holes would be people and characters more likely to purchase stolen goods. Sure enough, in the Turf Tavern, located near the city centre and next to the bus station, I found human crocodiles ready to snap up any tasty morsel I could offer them. By word of mouth, I was also directed to dealers able to keep me supplied with the drugs to fuel the fire of my highs. I wasn't fussy and would gorge on any I could get my hands on. In my mental condition, it would have been wise to steer clear of hallucinogenic agents but I wasn't interested in being wise, just living for kicks.

There was one pleasure I indulged in quite a lot in Doncaster. I met a man in the Turf who would buy any CD/DVD's he could get his hands on. This guy also just happened to be a pimp. I'm not proud to say, he would give me money for these stolen items, then I would give it back to him to sleep with the prostitutes he pimped. I slept in various places whilst in Doncaster. One time, I broke into a council depot and slept in a van. I thought I'd found somewhere to stow away when I broke into a building on an industrial estate that seemed empty. I would come back and sleep upstairs. One morning I heard someone coming up the stairs. There was nowhere to hide so I just had to brass neck it. The new arrival told me he was the owner of the building. I told him I was a poor homeless sap who was looking to get out of the cold and off the street; I reassured him I hadn't damaged anything.

All of this was true but the three empty money trays scattered on the floor betrayed my innocent lost soul fairytale. Seeing him eye up the stolen tills from various places I'd robbed, I half expected him to say he was contacting the police. This would have forced me into a confrontation. Thankfully, I was able to leave without any trouble.

When I began to make money, I would often stay in boarding houses. Of course, for me to acquire cash, meant taking other people's property. Some days, I'd rob two houses. I was always on the lookout for watches or gold. I'd learnt to check the most unusual places for these bounties, as people would stow their valuables in toilet bags or hidden in underwear.

Places they imagined were safe. But they weren't safe with my grubby greedy fingers about. I found jewellers near the post office where I could take all my gold to exchange for cash. I think he melted it down so he wouldn't get caught with recognisable goods if the police came visiting.

For the watches and other gear, I found a contact who was a bouncer at a city centre nightclub. He began to act as a fence for me. Some of the things I nicked, I took to him, he would sell it on and we would share the profits. Whenever I had nowhere to sleep, he would put me up in a house belonging to his mistress and her daughter, much to her dislike. I once heard him warn her I made him too much money to have me disappear.

While I was robbing one house, I spotted a small television on top of a wardrobe. As I reached up to take it, a gun fell on me. The bullets inside told me it wasn't a replica. Instead of putting it back and scarpering, I stuck it in my pocket and carried on searching for valuables. I took it away with me along with a suitcase full of loot.

I walked down the road and flagged a taxi. I told the driver I was in the process of moving house. I got him to drop me outside a block of flats, one of which was frequented by my fence. I knew even if someone reported me to my good friends, the police, they wouldn't have a clue where the brazen burglar who made his escapes in a hackney carriage was heading.

Finding the gun had got me thinking. I was running a risk each time

I robbed; sooner or later, I'd be caught and carted off back to prison. I'd recently jumped into someone's garden ready to rob his house only to see him walk past the window. I jumped out of the garden just as quick. He confronted me as I made my way down the road, telling me he'd seen me in his garden and wanting to know what I was up to. I told him I was drunk and trying to find my mate's house, despite being suspicious, he didn't try to stop me.

I made my way to the fence's flat. I asked if he could put me in touch with a getaway driver, I thought I'd swap my screwdriver for the gun. If I could do over a post office, I could get my hands on some serious cash. He told me he'd arrange one, and get back to me.

My one-man robbing spree had probably sent the local crime statistics soaring into the stratosphere. After hitting a house and taking cash and valuables, I took a short cut through the park. I think one of the neighbours must have seen me and called the police with a description. Given the frequency of my house burgling, the police were no doubt patrolling in plain clothes. Of course, I had no idea that this was the case and the cyclist that approached me didn't give me any cause for concern. That is until he grabbed me and introduced himself as old bill. As he tried to arrest me, I struggled; before I could free myself from his grip, another CID officer came to his aid. I was caught red-handed yet again.

One week before Easter 1994, I stood trial at Doncaster Crown Court. I wouldn't be celebrating new beginnings, just experiencing the old depressing reality my actions had brought about. I received four separate one-year sentences, all for burglary. Two of these were to run concurrent, which meant I would be serving two years. Another five cases were taken into consideration as well as possessing controlled drugs. It wasn't quite as thick as the phone book but it was a long list of misdemeanours. I was lucky the sentence wasn't longer. I was sent back to Lindholme but I had no intention of getting my head down and serving my time. I was about to escape from my third and final prison.

Chapter 26

Third-Time Unlucky

In a film, I don't remember the name of, a con boasted, "There wasn't a prison built that could hold me, I will make good my escape." Lindholme was to be the third and final nick from which I would abscond. It was situated ten miles north of Doncaster and used to be an RAF base. It was a Category C prison. Cat A was for lifers, murderers and such. Cat B was for similar, violent offenders who perhaps hadn't been charged with the worst offences like murder. Both Cat A&B prisons had a wall and a fence, while Cat C just had just the latter.

Unlike the boastful film character, there would have been no way I could have escaped from an A or B category prison. I wasn't the Birdman of Alcatraz or Andy Dufresne in Shawshank. I was Nigel Williams in Lindhomle open nick in South Yorkshire. I didn't want to be in prison and decided I was going to escape.

The only thing that stood between me and freedom was a twenty-four-foot fence with barbed wire on the bottom and top. As I wasn't Superman, the only way I was getting out was over that fence. To do so, I would need rope. Unfortunately, for me, they didn't leave such things lying around. I would have to make my own using bed sheets and blankets. To do this, I began to steal other prisoner's bed covers and I would hide them under a big wooden cabinet.

The other prisoners weren't too pleased to be relieved of the only things that stood between them and a freezing night. They complained to the guards, who searched for the missing items. They weren't stupid and probably realised someone was planning to use these sheets to attempt an escape. They just didn't know that someone was yours truly.

I had to wait until night came to make my rope. Telling all that were in earshot that I had a bad case of diarrhoea, I entered the bathroom, sneaking the sheets under my clothes and clutching my stomach.

I first of all tore the sheets into strips, tied three of these onto the taps in the sink and plaited them. When I had enough lengths, I knotted them together. Each new join, I tied together in three separate places. This strengthened and reinforced them; otherwise, the strips wouldn't have been able to take a sixteen stone prisoner doing his Tarzan impression swinging to freedom.

I'd shared my plan with two other prisoners from my dormitory. I felt I could trust them and would need their help. If anyone did visit the loo, my two conspirators would let me know by making a lot of noise, then I could hide my homemade rope under a pile of clothes and leave these on the floor asking whoever it was to hurry up because I'd got the runs. My ploy seemed to work, no one wanted to spend too much time in what they imagined a germ-filled bathroom.

Finally, when I figured the rope was long enough, I secured a small metal rod that had been part of my bunk bed and topped the whole thing off by tying my old jumper on the end. I hoped it would act as an anchor snagging on the razor wire at the top of the fence. All I needed now was the opportunity and enough time and luck to clear the fence without being ensnared in razor-sharp wire. It would have been embarrassing to get stuck on the fence like some giant fly in a spider's web.

All along the fence, dotted at intervals were guard stations. These were little boxes with a heater and a seat from which an officer would peruse the perimeter from his warm perch. Thankfully, it wasn't Stalag Thirteen and the guards weren't issued with rifles, only their observational powers. I picked out a place around the back of H block for several reasons. Whilst it was visible to only one guard, it was the least clear view of a section of the fence from any station. It was also well away from the entrance, so if I did manage to get over the fence, the guards would have to go all the way around to the front before they were on my trail.

I planned my escape to coincide with the afternoon exercise. It was October/November time, the early falling darkness giving me the cover I needed. The prison was surrounded by fields, providing me the chance to get far away. The day of my planned escape came around. At dinner, my two mates who knew of my impending escape attempt, shared their dinner with me, knowing if I was successful, it may be a while till I could find my next meal.

I'd been working on the potato production line; it was my job to remove the stones and soil from the conveyor belt. If any bad potatoes came by, I would remove them too. After checking no one was looking, I would sometimes launch them at some poor unsuspecting prisoner who would end up with a spud giving him a thud on the bonnet. When he turned around, I would be diligently at work, removing stones and trying to stifle a laugh, I hoped to have removed my last stone.

Feigning illness, my imaginary tummy troubles striking again, I asked to be excused work detail. I'd planned to sleep so I could be on the move all night. As I lay on my bed, I was too het up and on edge to sleep. Time crawled by. Eventually, I asked to take some exercise and get some fresh air. I made sure I wore two pairs of trousers and two tops, hoping these would give me some protection from the razor wire.

Wrapping my makeshift rope around me, concealing it under my donkey jacket, I'd managed to pull on top of the extra layers. I must have looked like the Michelin man. Thankfully, nobody paid too much intention. I sauntered towards the chosen place from which I was to make my bid for freedom. After a brief check, I slipped my jacket off, uncoiled the rope from my midriff and replaced my jacket. I swung the rope and launched it lasso-style upwards towards the razor wired fence top. I was pleased to see it stuck fast the first time, my old jumper catching on the barbs. Giving it a sharp tug did nothing to dislodge it, so far so good.

The hard part came next. I had no gloves and climbing into the razor wire at the base of the fence, I immediately got my trousers caught. Trying to free them with my hands came at a cost, barbs ripped into my flesh. Managing to get one leg free, I began to climb, the adrenalin masking the worst of the pain. But then I got my other leg entangled. Although the rope was taking my weight, I was only twelve inches off the ground, dangling like an acrobat on a tea break. My leg was stuck fast; to make matters worse I heard the cry of one of the guards. I'd been spotted.

With renewed vigour, I freed my leg. Just in time, I was released from the wire on the bottom of the fence and began my ascent. My hands and feet propelled me upwards, my heart in my mouth at the prospect of the rope breaking. My old climbing instincts, combined with the fear of being caught, gave my limbs Sherpa Tenzing ability and I was soon three quarters of the way up.

The guard had by this time, reached the bottom of the fence, taking hold of the rope and trying to free it from its anchor and shouting at me to come down.

I spat back at him, "If you pull me off I will kill you," my voice full of aggression.

My venomous threats must have frightened him because he dropped the rope for a moment; this gave me a chance to reach the top, almost. Once at the summit, I was faced with the two strands of razor wire. These two spiky, silver sentinels stood, barring my way from getting over the fence to taste the freedom I so desperately craved.

The guard resumed his grip on my rope and was shaking and yanking on it with all his might. I knew if his efforts proved successful in dismounting me from my homemade steed of cobbled together sheets, I would come tumbling down with a bed of razor wire waiting for me. I had no choice; I grabbed hold of the top strand of wire to steady myself. The barbs once again bit into my flesh. Scars from the lacerations are still visible today.

Ignoring the pain in my hands, I managed to get a foot on the lowest strand. All the time, I was peppering the guard with profanities, his efforts on the rope making me swing about like a sapling in a storm. I knew the rope wouldn't hold much longer, I threw myself over the top of the fence. I was so desperate to escape; I attempted to do a forward roll over the twenty-four-foot fence. I braced myself for a heavy landing.

It never came. My donkey jacket stuck fast on the razor wire. Once again, I was left dangling, this time on the outside of the fence. I struggled to take my jacket off, making every effort to jerk myself free because other guards were now arriving. Finally, the jacket gave way and I plummeted the final eighteen feet. The fall winded me but I was unscathed apart from bloodied hands and legs. I gingerly got to my feet and climbed over a smaller fence. I turned round to face the guards with a grin, gave them all a two -fingered salute.

"You won't be taking me down The Block," I shouted gleefully.

Of course, I interspersed my words with the foulest swearwords I could muster. I certainly wouldn't be challenging Captain Oates for the most poignant of farewell speeches. I would have loved to spend a bit longer gloating but knew the guards would be on their way round.

I set off running towards the fields. I'm no athlete but it makes for a personal best, knowing the authorities are hot on your heels. Eventually, the fields turned to woodland.

I didn't know where I was going and darkness was falling. The woodland turned into boggy marsh. As I began to wade in waist-deep foul and freezing bogs in the fading light, the thought passed through my mind that, if I stepped into a hole in this stagnant swamp, no one would find me. Prisons tend to be away from built-up areas. Having a nick at the end of the road would hardly be a selling feature for any prospective homeowner.

The terrain began to change and I knew there must be a road ahead when the gloom was pierced by the flash of car headlights in the distance. Reaching the road, I followed it for a short time, taking cover each time a car approached. It was too dangerous to stay on the road;

the police would be looking for me by now. I needed to hole up some-where safe, away from prying eyes and wagging tongues.

The sight of farm buildings coming into view was a welcome sight. A barn was no five-star hotel but it would certainly do for me. Freezing and fatigued, I made my way inside, deciding to get some rest before moving out in the early morning. Exhausted as I was, sleep wouldn't come. I lay on the hard ground, shaking like a leaf with the cold.

I awoke with a start. I must have dozed off. I set out again, knowing the news of an escaped con would have been broadcast around the area. I needed to get as far away as possible, and as fast as possible. Approaching some factories, I decided, unwisely, to call in and ask for directions to the nearest motorway. I had no clue as to where I was or which direction I was heading.

The quickest way to put some miles between myself and those seek-ing to reacquaint me with a prison cell would be via the M18. Asking politely at the reception area proved to be my undoing. A man in the reception area asked me if I had just escaped from Hatfield. I told him truthfully I hadn't.

Well, it was only truthful as far as the accuracy of his question. I didn't think updating him with the exact circumstances of my escape would be beneficial to me at that moment. Although I had absconded from one of her Majesty's correctional establishments less than twenty hours ago, it hadn't been that particular prison. Trying to think on my feet, I told him not to be stupid as I was over twenty-one, too old for a young offender's prison.

Now, it is obvious my attempt to divert suspicion gave me away; I had knowledge of the prison system. He didn't need to be Sherlock Holmes to realise that the man before him lost, dressed like a prisoner and talking like a prisoner was an escaped prisoner. He repeated his ques-tion accusingly, this time inserting the name of the right nick. I once again denied the obvious but the damage had been done, he'd twigged on to who I was. I didn't waste any time making my exit, I knew I had been rumbled and he would alert the authorities.

Sure enough, five minutes later the chorus of blues and two's confirmed my fears. I legged it as fast as I could; unfortunately, my pace was no match for wheels. I had to get off the road as quickly as possible, running through a stream then a shortcut through a park. By this time, I could hear the police and their dogs, this served as a renewed tonic to my tired legs, motivated by the desire to flee the fangs of the German Shepherds.

I managed to get across the park and into the back garden of a house. Picking up a slate roof tile, I hid behind a shed. My hiding place was never going to protect me from supercharged canine scent glands.

I could hear the police working their way towards my hiding place, garden by garden. Sure enough, the gate opened and the police dogs picked up my scent. I climbed on top of a wooden picnic table, hardly an Eagles nest but at least I was away from snarling dogs. Ignoring the advice of the boys in blue to give myself up, I swung the slate, trying to keep them at bay. I knew there was no way I could escape but decided to go down fighting.

It wasn't much of a fight to be honest; a resourceful officer found a garden spade. With other officers playing decoy, he swung the spade at my legs and knocked me down. I fell from my perch and came crashing down onto the table. I continued to receive a whacking with the spade and truncheons until I was in cuffs. At least I was kept away from the slavering incisors of their dogs.

My body was black and blue for days afterwards. The colour of my bruises seemed to mirror my feelings. The future looked black after my brief flirtation with freedom and this made me feel blue at the reality of being behind bars again.

Chapter 27

Stafford

Once again, it was back to prison life. There would be no more Category C nick for me. I was on my way to one of the most notorious jails in the land, Stafford. It was here I was reacquainted with Steve, the man I'd tried unsuccessfully to track down in Wolverhampton. He'd once again found himself banged up for his robbing exploits. Just like yours truly.

In Stafford, Steve was to fall victim to vile abuse. I was among the first to find out. I had signed up for educational classes, it wasn't my thirst for knowledge that led me to attend these but the fact they got me out of my cell, and mixing with other cons. Steve also joined up. My Black Country mate was always the life and soul of the party, cracking jokes and having a laugh despite the grim reality of prison life.

One particular day Steve was sullen and withdrawn, it was easy to spot something was wrong. He broke down in tears. When we asked what was wrong, his explanation filled us with horror. The night before he had been given a new cellmate, after introductions, they both went to bed and Steve soon fell asleep. He awoke suddenly with a blade held to his throat and his new neighbour on top of him. He was raped at knifepoint.

Steve decided to report the attack, which was very brave of him. Many other similar incidents would never come to light due to either shame, revulsion or embarrassment. The threat of violence, intimidation and retribution was used by the perpetrators to keep their crimes secret. Steve's cellmate was moved before any of us had the chance to exact revenge for what he'd done.

Prison life was callous and brutal. It wasn't just the violent cons that made Stafford a hellhole. The conditions, and in particular, the cuisine were appalling. I lost two stone during my stint inside Staffordshire's premium correctional institution. The food was practically inedible. An inquiry was held into the conditions and it was threatened with closure unless improvements were made.

I decided, unwisely as ever, to stage my own one-man protest. After my cellmate had gone down for breakfast, I barricaded myself in my room and started to smash it up. I pushed the bed against the door and then threw a three-drawer cabinet on top. It wasn't long before a guard called on me to see why I hadn't shown up at the canteen for the first meal of the day. When he couldn't get in our cell, he shouted for me to "Open up". I declined in a rather impolite manner. He warned me he would be coming back mob-handed and I would be removed forcibly unless I complied.

"Bring it on," I told him.

I knew his retreating footsteps would soon bring a host of guards to my cell. Sure enough, five minutes later they were back demanding I open up to them, threatening to use a door jack to gain entry. The jacks were slid into the crevices on either side of the reinforced door and attached to a winding mechanism that would force the door open. They were incredibly powerful and used only in emergencies. I shouted a warning at them that my legs were up against the door. I'd blocked up the spy-hole to my cell so they had no way of knowing if what I was telling them was true.

The appearance of the metal edges and the noise of the winding mechanism, told me they weren't too bothered if I was stupid enough to risk serious injury. They were coming in come what may and I was outnumbered. My only advantage was they would be in riot gear and only one or two at a time could fit through the door. I picked up a leg from a broken chair. A leftover from demolishing my cell, it would make a good weapon for me to inflict some damage. Only this time, it wouldn't be wood I'd be trying to splinter but skulls.

The door creaked and jerked under the pressure of the metal pincers. I positioned myself as close as I could and steeled myself to meet the onslaught. A few seconds later, the door exploded inwards and the first guard came through, baton in one hand and shield in the other. I started to swing the chair leg and sought to get over the top of his shield and crack his head like a walnut. I was swinging wildly and for a good few seconds kept them at bay until they eventually forced their way in and pushed me back against the wall. I was still wielding the chair leg like a battle-axe but the guards had been careful to protect their heads with their shields.

They fought fire with fire, using their truncheons to inflict painful blows. Despite these, I was determined to carry on fighting what was to be a losing battle. Eventually, they battered me to the ground, disarmed and handcuffed me. I was dragged out of the cell and taken down the block. As I was frogmarched away, I heard one guard tell his mate I was a "tough so and so."

I spent time in isolation and ended up with another fifty days added to my sentence. This was in addition to already losing my parole for escaping from Lindholm. I served out the rest of my sentence in a less dramatic fashion, except for one particular incident, a run -in with a convicted terrorist.

I got on well with Paddy at first. He was serving time for gunrunning for the IRA. I'm not sure what his real name was. He was known as Paddy due to him hailing from the Emerald Isle, not very original, I know. He seemed friendly enough, which I was glad about. He was a big tough bloke with a fearsome reputation. A lot of cons were scared of him. I never had a problem until one day when I popped into his cell on the way back from the canteen.

I had just spent all my money on snacks and other provisions, which I was carrying back with me in a cardboard box. Paddy, egged on by his cronies, decided it would be a good laugh to start rummaging through my box of goodies. He was throwing the contents around and putting stuff in his pockets. Of course, I didn't like this and let him know, in no uncertain terms, that he needed to put my purchases back. He said he was just joking and not to get upset, then proceeded to put some stuff back into my box. When I got back to my cell, I took an inventory and found some tobacco and phone cards missing. I reckoned the value of my missing goods to be about twenty pounds, a lot of money in those days, especially to a prisoner. It was plain to me it was Paddy's light-fingered foraging that had divorced me from my prized possessions. I went straight to his cell to demand my belongings back.

He denied stealing from me and told me to leave. I was furious. It would be dangerous to attack Paddy at the best of times but it would be plain stupid to launch an assault with his cellmate present, another big Irishman. I would be sure to cop a kicking. However, I wasn't about to let it go. I came up with a plan.

If I couldn't personally give out the first choice of retribution I had in mind, I decided to hire someone to do the job for me. I enlisted the help of a middleman to arrange the services of the hardest con on our wing, The Daddy. This term wasn't used as a term of endearment. He'd earned it by fighting his way to the top and proving he was the hardest convict. I explained the situation to a cleaner who I knew was good mates with The Daddy. I told him I was offering a reward of a percentage of the stuff he retrieved from Paddy. I made it clear if Paddy got beaten up in the process, then so be it.

My plan was doomed from the start. Unbeknown to me, the cleaner was also friends with Paddy. I found out I had been rumbled one day when I was lying on the bed in my cell. I was startled out of my slumbers by an angry pounding on the door. It was Paddy, telling me just what he thought of me trying to take a contract out on his head. He gleefully promised he was going to cut my throat and I should watch my back. I responded in kind returning his threats and profanities.

There was no way I was going to open the door in case the furious Fenian had come tooled up. Obviously, prisoners weren't allowed to carry knives but that didn't stop us cons fashioning our own weapons. We would melt a toothbrush, inserting two razor blades a short distance apart. This nasty weapon was designed not only to slash faces but to leave them a permanent mess. Doctors were prevented from being able to stitch up the wounds, as the double incision didn't leave enough skin for restorative needlework. I had no desire to end up with my face ripped open.

Later that day, I made my way to association and the television room. I refused to let his threats confine me to my cell. I knew if he was serious then sooner or later I'd have to face him. Little did I know it would be sooner, much sooner. I chose a spot in the middle of the room, figuring I'd be safe in the open with enough time to react if Paddy came in. I settled down to watch the television and the first I knew of my adversary's arrival was when he hit me as hard as he could.

It wasn't his bare knuckles that came crashing down on me but another homemade weapon popular in prison. A heavy PP9 battery used to power old radios wedged into a sock and then wielded lasso style with devastating effect. Paddy bludgeoned me with the battery that sank with a sickening thud into my temple.

The blow felled me from my chair and onto one knee as my head reverberated with pain and noise. My brain shook like a wonky washing machine on a full cycle. Dizzy, disorientated and without realising what I was doing, I rose to my feet to face him. My legs shook like jelly underneath me. I laughed in his face and shouted, "I'm still standing." Feeling like I wouldn't be standing much longer I managed to brazen it out. He turned on his heels and retreated, leaving me feeling as precarious as the last leaf on a bough in an autumn gale.

Thankfully, my bravado had prevailed. If he had called my bluff and launched a follow -up attack, I would have been in serious trouble; I was in no fit state for a scrap. Blood was flowing down my face from the deep wound. I've still got a scar visible on my baldhead where the battery connected with my scalp.

Of course, I wasn't going to let the authorities know that my injuries were down to another convicts handiwork.

"I've fallen downstairs," I informed them in the office.

The guard raised his eyebrows and dryly commented, "The number of people doing likewise in this establishment is staggering."

I was dismissed and sent to the prison doctor. As he tended to my wounds, I plotted my revenge. I wasn't sure if I could overpower Paddy in a fight. I knew that I would repay his cowardly attack and hit him with something heavy and hard. I intended to give him a taste of his own medicine, a headache that he wouldn't forget in a hurry.

My plans were foiled when I was moved to a different wing.

Time drifted slowly on until I'd served my time and was deemed ready to enter society. Along with my freedom came the news that all my mum's lifetime savings were now legally mine. This amounted to the sum of a thousand pounds. What could I use it for, a deposit on a property or a nest egg to see me through until I could secure employment? Nope. I decided on a trip to the pleasure capital of Europe where the illicit temptations of drugs and sex were on tap.

A thousand pounds was a lot of money in 1994. But as they say, a fool and his money are soon parted. That proved the case with me. I'm ashamed to say, I squandered my mum's money. A couple of weeks living what I thought was the high life would soon see me brassic and catapulted back into the sordid lowlife.

Chapter 28

Amsterdam

I said my mum's inheritance bought me a ticket to the Netherlands most famous city, but not literally. It was my thumb and my bravado that got me there. I had no problem finding junction twenty eight of the M1, located near Mansfield. Three days, many lifts and a ferry crossing later, saw me walking the cobbled streets of Amsterdam.

In some ways, it proved quite an adventure getting there. Thumbing a lift in France, a guy stopped and offered me the comforts of his front seat. He had one hand on the steering wheel and held a bottle of lager in the other. He also couldn't speak a word of English and I guess you won't be too surprised to learn my grasp of the French language started and finished with bonjour. At one point, he stopped the car, got out and opened the boot. He motioned for me to get out of the car and join him.

I didn't have a clue what could be in the boot of this stranger's car. I'd got in without a second thought. Could it be a gun or a dead body? For those ten seconds, my imagination ran riot, what sinister sight awaited me? I was relieved to see a large stash of bottled lager. He was only offering me a share of his beer. I laughed and gladly loaded my arms with as many bottles as I could manage. I remember thinking this is one trip I would enjoy. We resumed our journey and after much gesturing in which direction I needed to go, he eventually dropped me off on the motorway slip road.

Once again, soon after holding my thumb aloft to passing motorists a vehicle stopped to give me a lift, the police. They told me it wasn't a safe place to be and they dropped me around the corner on a quieter road. I waited until they left and walked back to the exact spot I'd just been.

Arriving in Amsterdam, I wasted no time in making my way to the most infamous attractions, impatient to sample all the dubious wares available to the tourist. The Red Light District, where the girls stood posing provocatively in their windows, bodies on show and drugs that could be bought so readily in every cafe pulled me like a moth to a flame. I was in my element and I plunged head first into the pool of vice and degradation. I'm ashamed to say, I squandered my mum's money on prostitutes and getting off my face. Armed with a grand, I blew the lot.

I lived only for the moment and that moment had now passed. I was alone, homeless and broke in a foreign land. I ended up sleeping in a back alley, behind a restaurant. One night, I disturbed a fellow resident, a giant rat. Attracted by the waste slops, we weren't much different, me and my rodent friend, both living on a diet of filth and rubbish, both seen as unclean and unpleasant by the world. The difference being the rat was only doing what his nature demanded, while I was there by choice not compulsion.

I was skint and back on the rob. Not content to pull low-key jobs targeting bags and rucksacks, I entered a jewellers just off one of the main squares. I asked the female assistant if I could see their most expensive watch. Looking back, I hardly exuded sartorial elegance in clothes creased and dank from my nights spent sleeping on the city streets. I certainly didn't fit the profile of someone about to purchase a top of the range Rolex.

My question must have raised more red flags than a communist party rally. Still, the woman delved behind the counter and produced three fine examples of Swiss timepieces. Snatching one up, I turned to flee but a man who had come up behind me grabbed the rucksack on my back. I had no choice but to let it slide off and get through the door onto the street. I was followed by the man who immediately started to shout at the top of his voice for me to stop. That much I could understand the rest of his words were lost on me as his angry protestations were bawled out in his mother tongue.

Unfortunately, they weren't lost on the shoppers and pedestrians on the busy streets of the square. As the man continued his loud protests, I carried on legging it. Fleeing aimlessly and knowing he had my bag that contained my passport and all my details.

My getaway would not prove successful. Ahead was a police van with officers stood around it. They saw me running and heard the shouting of the man pursuing me. It must have been one of their easier arrests as I dropped fly like into the spider's web. I was carted off to a local police station and began wondering how prisons in this country compared with those of my native land. I fully expected to be calling one of these my home for the coming months.

I shared a holding cell with five other men and the police brought us a cigarette to share. We took drags, passing it between us and although some of them didn't understand me, we bonded, drawn together by our common plight.

After a couple of days, much to my relief and amazement, I was released. I decided I liked the justice system much better in Holland. I had been told to behave myself, which in my case was akin to asking the sun not to rise. I was back on the city streets, homeless, broke and with a raging thirst for the illicit pleasures offered by Amsterdam. The police had even obligingly reacquainted me with my rucksack. I was mightily impressed by the liberal attitude of the cops but would my luck run out the next time I encountered Dutch law enforcement?

I was about to find out when I tried to steal a pair of jeans from a clothes shop. The staff must have suspected me and phoned the police. Before I had the chance to get on better terms with Mr Wrangler or Levi, two armed policeman entered the store and made a beeline for me. They laughed away my pleas of innocence. One policeman kept laughing at me and goading me. I should have just walked calmly out of the shop. However, he was getting under my skin and I felt my anger rising like a volcano about to explode. The shiny black gun holstered on his hip should have been a deterrent but the inner shouts of anger drowned out any voice of reason.

Before I realised what I was doing, I had punched the laughing officer on the jaw. He soon stopped laughing as he fell backwards into a shelf and the other policeman, who helped him stay on his feet. To my surprise, the officers backed off, sensing I was angry and they would have a fight on their hands. So we had a Mexican Stand Off in a Dutch denim shop.

There was no way I could get out or escape. I would have to pass the officers to get to the door. Their backup soon arrived in the shape of two policewomen. They approached me slowly while the two original cops stood by the doorway, their eyes burning into me. The approach of the two policewomen was very different. They spoke very calmly and gently and asked me to go with them. Explaining they needed to slip on some handcuffs, I meekly obliged. I had been charmed by their gentleness and let them lead me away. I expected a kicking once we got back to the cells but it never came. Neither did the prison sentence for ABH (actual bodily harm) on a DNP (Dutch National Police) officer. What I did get was deportation. Holland had had enough of Nigel Williams causing mayhem on their streets and I was put on a ferry, and sent home to England.

I was deported with another lad, a Scouser whose name I can't recall. He had committed some motoring offences and we were consigned to the same cabin. We were warned to stay in the room and not to cause any trouble. Before we had lost sight of land, we were making our way to the bar from which my newfound friend kept me liberally supplied with pints of lager. Scouse was minted and not only did he buy my beer, he managed to purchase some ecstasy from some Dutch blokes we got talking to.

That night we sang and danced and laughed along with the cabaret. The next morning, I felt lousy due to the excesses of the previous evening; the waves from the North Sea did nothing to help matters. I still managed a full English breakfast on board, again down to the generosity of Scouse. He even gave me a hundred quid to get home. Instead of using the cash to catch a train, it went straight into my back pocket and out came my thumb. I'd keep the cash for drugs and hitched home. Although truth be told, I didn't have a home. I made my way back to Mansfield and found a bed at the Stonham hostel.

Chapter 29

Mansfield

It was here I met a lad called David who was a recovering heroin addict. The problem was he wasn't recovering very well. He had been prescribed methadone to help wean him off the heroin. I started to share his methadone with him. He still craved heroin and would inject himself with it. I joined him a couple of times, thankfully, I much preferred speed. Addiction to any drug is bad but heroin is one of the worst. It soon begins to sing a siren 's song, which is almost impossible to resist.

One day, David asked me to go with him to his dealer's house. We caught the bus to a town in Derbyshire and made our way to the property. We were let in and told to sit on the sofa. The dealer was in the kitchen, cutting and bagging the drugs. David went in to see him and was told to go and sit back down. A few seconds later, we heard the dealer getting irritated. He'd lost some drugs, a substantial amount going by his shouts of anger.

He began throwing things around, looking for his precious horde, all the time becoming more and more irate.

Sensing danger, I told David that if he'd nicked the drugs while he'd been in the kitchen, then he needed to return them. He assured me he hadn't and repeated the same protestations of innocence to the dealer who came and demanded to know if he knew anything about his missing drugs. The man told us not to move and went upstairs to carry on his search, all the while swearing and shouting. I told David we were leaving. I envisaged his dealer coming back down with a gun or a blade. A happy ending between a dealer who thinks he's been ripped off and those he thinks have fleeced him was a long shot. I wasn't prepared to stick around and see how it would play out. Slipping out as quickly and quietly as we could, we made our way into town.

Feeling safe amongst the shoppers and businesses, we wandered around, killing time before the next bus back across the county border. However, we'd let our guard down too early and soon came face to face with the dealer who emerged out of an alleyway. He was on his own, which meant we had a two to one advantage. Well, not quite on his own. He pulled his coat back to reveal a machcte.

He made us march in front of him around a corner to a back street where he'd parked his van. He told us to get inside and he climbed in after us. This wasn't a good situation.

Should I reason with him or try to jump him? He didn't have much room to swing his weapon but I knew one thrust with the machete and it would be a bloodbath. Besides, he was a big bloke and by now very angry, never a good combination. He told us to strip off and pointed the blade at us to encourage us to comply. We reluctantly obeyed and he searched through our clothes. There we were, three men in a van, two of us naked and the other brandishing a razor-sharp, deadly weapon.

Protesting our innocence and complaining of the indignity of our situation fell on deaf ears.

Our embarrassment wasn't over yet, he insisted we bent over so he could look between our buttocks for his heroin. He wouldn't take no for an answer. He kicked us out of his van after it became clear we hadn't got his missing drugs secreted away in our cavities. Thankfully, he allowed us to get dressed first.

We caught the bus back, drugless. Balancing a feeling of relief that we'd escaped from a situation fraught with danger and the shame of our strip search. It wasn't long after this; I was allocated a flat in nearby Sutton and moved out of the hostel. I said my goodbyes to David, not knowing I would never see him again.

A couple of weeks later, I heard he'd been found dead, a pointless and tragic fatality. David had overdosed on heroin, the drug, just a month earlier I'd shared with him It could have easily have been my cold lifeless body they'd found. Instead of his death shocking me into a change of heart and life, it had no effect on me. I'd fallen in with a bunch of people who shared my addictions and habits. Soon they also shared my flat with me as I invited them to move in. And so my flat became a haven for drugs and stolen goods. I was taking more and more speed, which cost money I didn't have. Other people did though, good honest hard-working people whose houses I'd break into.

One time, I was robbing a house and just about to make my getaway when the homeowner returned. It obviously gave her a great shock seeing a villain like me lumbering out of her back door, my arms full of her most prized possessions. I threw them on the grass and ran off past the frightened woman.

It pains me to think of all the grief and misery I inflicted on people. I'm deeply ashamed now and wish I could undo all the things I've done. But, this is my life story and as much as I'd like to colour it with softer tones, my life was stained by the dark desire of self and to get high at any cost. I was hooked on speed, I had to have cash and didn't care who I had to trample on, to get it.

One particular incident pains me to remember. I planned to burgle a house I'd noticed was unoccupied in the daytime. Unoccupied that is, apart from a Pit Bull. Arming myself with a knife, I set off to rob the place. I knocked on the door to make sure everyone was out and thankfully, a woman answered, saving me from a possible bloody confrontation with the animal. I love dogs now and the thought of what I was willing to do, upsets me. If that robbery was foiled, there were plenty more I managed to commit. All the proceeds were wasted on getting wasted and so the cycle continued. Round and round, until one day, the only inevitable outcome came to pass.

I broke into one house smashing a small panel in a window to get in. In the process of gaining entry, I cut myself quite badly. It didn't stop me from robbing the joint but I left a trail of blood in my wake. It was a long wake too as I marched a mile and a half back to my house carrying a big TV. In those days, the TV's weren't lightweight flat screens. Certainly the one I was lumping home with me had a backside bigger than an East German shot putter. It weighed a ton, or it certainly seemed so. By the time I'd got it home, it felt like I had arms longer than an Orangutan. Someone probably saw me carrying my ill-gotten gains and rang the law. Either that or the police had followed the trail of blood right to my door. Within a couple of hours, they were knocking.

I stood defiantly at the door arguing with them and protesting my innocence. One sharp- eyed bobby noticed the deep, fresh gash in my hand and stated there had been a house robbery where the thief had cut himself. They wanted to know how I'd come by my wound. I told them I did it on a nail when I was fixing a fence. Of course, they weren't stupid and knew as well as I did, I'd been on the rob. Not only did they know they found the evidence when they forced their way inside. They had me bang to rights. The TV proved my guilt; they now could arrest me and take me off the streets.

This was just what Judge Matthewman had in mind when I stood before him at Nottingham Crown Court. It was the day after Valentine's Day 1996. There would be no love or leniency shown me, only the justice my persistent lawbreaking deserved. The Judge told me plainly I was a menace to society and pronounced me one of the most dangerous career criminals he'd come across. The next words out of his mouth hit me like a sledgehammer. He sentenced me to four years and said if I ever came up before him again, he would lock me up for a lot longer. I was, once again, about to be sent back to Lincoln prison.

Chapter 30

Back in Lincoln

As I sat in the back of the prison van (aka The Meat Wagon), which was careering me, once again, to my incarceration, the severity of the sentence bit hard into my mind. I sat quiet. The bravado of the other prisoners washing over me, lost in my own personal self - pity. I decided if I didn't get parole, I would top myself, as I didn't think I could hack four long years in the nick. Instead of four years, I would soon be looking at having my sentence increased dramatically and would be faced with the horrifying prospect of serving a whole decade for my actions.

Bosnia was the nickname of the wing on which I was placed in Lincoln prison. Back then, the Balkans was a war-torn area so this should give you some idea about the character of life on C wing. It wasn't cream teas and garden parties, that's for sure. It was here my skills as a fisherman came to the fore. Carp and bream weren't what I was trying to land though.

Prisoners would sometimes make deals with one another and pass their trades between cell windows because for much of the day, we would be stuck inside. At least we knew there would be no prying eyes and we could pass our packages to one-another. Most of the time, these contained drugs smuggled in. Cons would wrap these up in paper packages, making sure they were tied with string. They would then attempt to pass these through the outside window, which was a lot trickier than it sounds. They would throw them lasso style down to the waiting prisoner who would have a mirror and be watching to snare the precious package with an outstretched arm. Often these attempts were successful, at other times; packages would fall to the ground.

That is where I would come in if any of this contraband happened to be in the vicinity of my ground floor cell. I would strip the three green strands in the blanket, entwine them and add a battery on the end to weigh it down and finally attach a fork for a hook. I would then go fishing to retrieve the toppled treasure. I know fishermen are famed for their patience, sometimes sitting all day waiting for a bite. I too, needed the same virtue as it could take countless efforts of throwing out the line before the fork would snag on a package. Even then, it could be more frustrating than playing a seaside grabber in an amusement arcade, although what I was after wasn't some cute cuddly toy but hard drugs. If I was successful, I would then reunite the package with the rightful recipient and would be rewarded for hooking the hash or landing the loot. The only problem was I'd sometimes get into trouble when it came time to change my blanket. They would see the missing strands and know exactly what I'd been up to. I would sometimes lose association time, and this meant I wasn't able to play chess or watch television.

Spending so much time in my cell, led me to snare a pet or two. I would tie a string to the window and place a trail of bread on the outside of the window all the way to just inside. There were a lot of pigeons around and one would sometimes swoop in for a tasty treat of rock hard prison bread. When they got to the crumbs just inside the window, I would yank on the string and the window would close trapping the pigeon. I would then keep it for a pet for a short time. Sometimes, we'd sneak it out into the corridor and let it go, this annoyed the guards immensely when it would fly into the rafters and they wouldn't be able to catch it, much to our amusement.

We also cut off plastic bottle tops, put sugar and food in them and trapped mice inside. I would keep the mouse in a bedside drawer and feed it. Mice are much harder to keep than pigeons and they usually ended up scampering under the cell door to freedom. These animals weren't the only non -human living things in Lincoln nick. We shared our cells with creatures you wouldn't want as a pet, cockroaches. These would only come out in the dark and the first thing you knew of their presence was when they would bite you while you were sleeping. This left unsightly red wealds, courtesy of these little beasts. We tried to block up the air vents to stop them from getting in but somehow, they kept on appearing. We would crush them, not aware this in turn releases their eggs, and then we couldn't understand why there was an infestation of these foul bugs. I hated these unclean nasty little things.

There was one guard that showed the same dislike and disdain of all the prisoners. He seemed to especially hate me. He would stop cons on the landing and make them fasten up the top button of their shirt. He'd do it because he loved to assert his authority over us. Some guards were strict but fair and, although we didn't always take kindly to what they were asking, at least we could respect them. Not so with this one guard. He loved to wind us up and basically act like a complete cretin. I'm sorry, there's just no other way of saying it.

He made fun of the mental health problems that plagued me. I have to admit I didn't help myself because I developed a sideline in trading the drugs I was prescribed. I was on two Zimmer tablets to help me sleep, along with antipsychotic drugs. I would have to get my drugs from a hatch and take the antipsychotics whilst the staff watched. I became adept at putting the tablet in my mouth, taking a swig of water, and swallowing. As far as the staff was concerned, I'd taken my mind meds. In reality, I'd hidden the tablet under my tongue before swallowing fresh air. As I walked away, I'd retrieve the pills, dropping them into a tissue I had in my trouser pocket. I would then be able to barter these tablets for drugs, phone cards and food.

Of course, not taking these tablets messed with my mind and caused problems. It was the price I was willing to pay to get hold of the things I wanted in prison. The antipsychotics usually got quite a reaction with the prisoners who sought to take a trip using the drugs prescribed to keep me sane. They often expressed their surprise at the strong reaction that reverberated around their heads for days after. I'd always try to keep one of my Zimmer Frame tablets, as we knew them, because I still needed them to get some sleep. I'd barter the other one for a spliff or two, if I could get it. My one-man drug dispensary brought me to the attention of the guards but they were unable to prove anything. This didn't improve relations with the vindictive authoritarian guard who everyone hated. Little did I know it, by pressing the bell in my cell one afternoon, I'd put myself on a collision course with him that would end badly for us both.

This particular day, I was supposed to be attending educational classes, which I enjoyed. There had been some trouble on our wing and the prison had gone into lockdown. Lockdown was the phrase used for the procedure adopted by the guards when any serious trouble occurred. It's pretty much self-explanatory and does what it says on the tin.

No prisoner is allowed out of their cell until order is restored and, even then, they would keep you caged for fear of the fire of violence flaring up again.

Not knowing what was happening, and going stir crazy, I committed the cardinal sin of pressing the bell. This brought the guard who must be obeyed to my cell; to say he wasn't pleased was an understatement. Instead of explaining to me what was happening, he gave me a load of abuse and threatened me. I responded in kind and met fire with fire. He'd had enough of me and said he was going to sort me out once and for all. I told him to bring it on and added a few choice phases as he disappeared to round up reinforcements. My cellmate looked on nervously from the sanctuary of his bed, an innocent bystander, knowing he could be about to witness a ruckus.

I didn't care. Frankly, I was sick of the cruel mocking of this guard. I was angry and ready for a fight. I knew he would come back mob-handed, but even so, I was determined to go out fighting. If they were coming to give me pain, I would give out as much as possible in return. I picked up a water jug, ready to use it. Sure enough, my cell door opened and in rushed the guards with my antagonist leading the charge. I punched him as hard as I could with the jug, which shattered on his head and knocked him clean-out. Guard number two was just about to grab me when I hit him with an uppercut, the broken handle of the jug piercing his throat going right through into his tongue. He also dropped. Then I was engulfed by the rest of them who rammed me down onto my bed.

I used my feet against the wall to push myself away and they momentarily lost their grip on me and I was able to resume my attack.

I was soon overwhelmed; my rage was no match for the sheer number I faced. They got me in what's known as a chicken hold with my arms raised up and head pressed down. This hold is designed to render you compliant because of the pressure they could place on your wrists. I've known many prisoners who have ended up with broken wrists due to the infamous chicken hold. Unfortunately for one guard, I found my head within reach of his leg, I sank my teeth into him and bit him as hard as I could, almost taking a chunk out of his leg. The guards applied maximum pressure as they dragged me out of the cell and away down to the basement.

The room was notorious. A place they took unruly cons to teach them a lesson, a place in the darkest recesses of the nick. I knew where they were taking me and what I was in for. I'd left three of their colleagues needing serious medical treatment and it's safe to say they weren't best pleased. The pain they inflicted as they marched me towards my punishment, seared through my body causing me to cry out to God for help.

Throwing me in the room, they informed me God couldn't help me down here. I was theirs to do what they liked with, and I wouldn't be leaving. A few of the guards held me while the others began giving me a kicking. This went on for a couple of minutes, causing me to cry out to a higher power for deliverance again. Their response was to laugh and carry on. Again, they told me no one could help me and resumed their systematic pummelling. One officer told the guards holding me to wedge me up against the wooden bed. He gleefully told me of his plan; he was going to stamp on my head.

Before his size 9's had the chance to inflict any damage, which would have had very serious consequences for me, the door opened and in walked Mr Green. I'd always respected Mr Green and got on well with him. He'd been a guard who helped me with my spelling and my applications during my previous stay in Lincoln. Back then, he'd been a run -of-the-mill guard; he had now risen to Senior Officer. He told them

I'd had enough, and to stop. They had no choice but to obey him and I was carted off to the isolation cell.

Although my body was wracked with the pain, I ought to have been thankful my ordeal was over. Yet, the overriding emotion was one of anger and hatred towards the guards. I decided whoever came through the door of the cell would be leaving on a stretcher. If they wanted conflict, I'd give it to them. This time, I'd try to achieve a higher body count of injured guards.

When my cell door opened an hour later, it was the Governor along with five or six guards in full riot gear. I stood there stark naked, hands balled into fists ready to do battle. She told me there were two ways of playing this. One, I could come quietly and be led down to the hospital wing where I would receive treatment for my injuries and my mental health problems or, the second option, was to be left to rot in isolation. She disarmed my anger with her calmness and I chose the first option and let myself be led away.

After treatment, I was placed behind Double Door Lock. This meant I wasn't allowed physical contact with anyone, as I was considered dangerous. Even my food was delivered through a hatch. It was whilst I was there; I received a visit from a Christian who volunteered to talk to prisoners. The fact that I was a maniac behind two sets of bars didn't put her off from wanting to talk to me about God.

"There's no such thing as God," I interrupted. "If there's a God and He cares for me then why I am stuck in prison? He doesn't exist, He's not real."

Here I was, vehemently denying the existence of the God to whom I had cried out to save me from the guards, a prayer that had been answered with the intervention of Mr Green. I was like a lot of people who pray to God in times of deep distress, I soon forgot all about Him when the times of trouble and anguish had passed.

I vented all my despair and frustration on this woman and her God.

She listened patiently and replied calmly to all my protests, insisting God was real and we all needed to find forgiveness, peace and joy through Jesus Christ, God's only son. I told the woman it was easy for her to say because she could walk out of the prison gates, back home to a family that loved her. Looking back, it wasn't easy for her to say. To walk into a prison filled with the dregs of society and to tell them about the love of God, then face the scorn, anger and indifference with gentleness and a heart full of love. I wasn't ready to hear her words.

It wouldn't be in the bowels of Lincoln prison that the love of God would shine through the black clouds of my anger and despair. I was about to be shipped out to another jail. Once again, it was a prison I'd been in before. Wolds stands on the Humber Estuary and it was here small seeds of hope would be sown that would finally come to fruition and bloom into a glorious harvest of salvation.

Chapter 31

Pinpricks of Light

I was transferred to Wolds because I had attacked the prison guards. This time I would be charged with what my solicitor informed me, was a very serious offence. I could have easily killed the guard whose throat I lacerated with the shattered shard of the jug handle. If I'd sliced through his jugular vein, I'd be looking at a murder charge. As it was, my brief informed me I would be looking at another six years on my sentence. I was staring down the barrel of a ten -year stretch. I knew I couldn't hack another decade behind bars. Thoughts of the impending trial filled me with dread. I tried to dismiss them from my mind and settle into prison life, but they kept nagging away at me.

My cellmate at Wolds was called Nuzzy, a giant of a man, full of rippling muscles and colourful tattoos. He was serving a seven -year stretch for stabbing his girlfriend. He'd come home early one day and found her in bed with another man. Despite Nuzzy's intimidating appearance and the serious nature of his offence, he was one of the friendliest and gentle guys you could hope to meet.

The one exception was when he asked me to spar with him. It was a complete mismatch. What took place in prison would never take place in a professional boxing ring; it was like a Yorkshire Terrier going toe-to-toe with a Rottweiler. He ended up backing me into a corner, giving me a pummelling in the process. He had a punch like a mule's kick.

Generally, he and I got on very well, I considered myself very lucky to share a cell with him and call him my friend. You certainly wouldn't want him as an enemy I thought to myself, as I watched him doing his nightly push -ups. I'd always been good at this particular exercise but even I couldn't keep pace with the big man who would bang out a hundred without stopping. It helped me having him as a cellmate; it took my mind off my troubles.

Apart from my cell buddy, prison life at Wolds was much the same as the other nicks I'd been in. I was given the hated job of pot washing. These duties were allocated to new prisoners, who, without exception, always tried to get out of it at the first possible opportunity. It was the most knackering and was seen as the lowest ranking job. Pot washing for hours on end was laborious and left you with a bad back. Tackling the encrusted breakfast, lunch and dinner pots from every wing was both time consuming and energy sapping. The only silver lining to such forced labour was it was the highest paid job for a con at nineteen pounds a week.

During my first day on the job, I received the time-honoured and unpleasant initiation. I was welcomed into my new role by having a bucket of icy water that had been kept in the walk-in freezer, poured over my head. I had to complete my shift shivering with cold and my teeth chattering like crazy. When the time came for me to be relieved from my washing up woes, I thought I'd get even with the guy who'd subjected me to the ice cold drenching. Looking back, it doesn't seem the smartest of moves to dump a freezing bucket of water over a hard nut doing eighteen years for armed robbery. The opportunity presented to me seemed too good to resist.

He was on the loo at the time. The prison toilets were designed with low doors so the officers can check there is no drug dealing or suspicious behaviour taking place. On entering, I saw this man seemingly oblivious to everything around him. This was my chance to get even. He was a sitting duck. Or maybe not so much like a duck, they like water and this chap didn't seem too keen as I lifted the heavy bucket and tipped its freezing contents on him from above.

I made my escape, sharpish, gleefully laughing. My mirth a mixture of the hilarity of him there with his pants around his ankles, shocked by the icy water, and partly terror that this guy would straight up murder me. As I exited the cubicles at breakneck speed, I heard his voice boom out from behind me. For the sake of decency, I will paraphrase his complaint.

"I'm going to kill you. I've not even got any dry toilet paper to wipe my backside."

I asked the officer on duty permission to leave the wing, making some excuse. There was no way I was staying around a raging nutcase with a thirst for revenge. I'd let him cool off or rather dry off first. I have many memories of prison life, most of them grim. But even today, this one still causes me to laugh out loud.

It was at Wolds that I was allowed to bring something new into my schedule. I'd been there a couple of weeks when I received a surprise visitor at my cell door, the prison vicar, Dave Caswell, another person trying to tell me about God. I also received visits from two Christian ladies and played pool with a Christian lad who visited, called Shane.

Every Tuesday, another guy, Rob, would visit to talk to anyone interested in God. Rob was to prove a faithful friend to me down the years but back then, he was just another Bible basher. It seemed all these God-botherers were busy bothering me about God. I'd seen films where a band of cowboys had been surrounded by Indians. Looking back, God was surrounding me with his people.

Being a decent chess player, I know one way to win is to advance, piece by piece, until your opponent has nowhere to move and is boxed in. If it's not too flippant to say, God was moving His people in the same way around me. The latest of these was the chaplain. This time, I wasn't full of rage and didn't meet him with anger, just indifference. I'd always found the Sunday prison services tedious if I'm being honest but I wasn't averse to anything that would break the monotony of prison life and get me out of my cell. The man with the dog collar seemed nice enough and after a brief chat, he invited me to attend a Bible study group that met Wednesday mornings. I immediately told him I would come. My first reaction didn't spring from any noble spiritual desires, just the desire to be on my backside instead of working.

I was on laundry duties Wednesday mornings. Faced with the choice of sweating over dirty clothes or sitting in a comfy chair listening to someone waffle on about the Bible, I'd be stupid not to choose the latter. I didn't know what to expect but it had to be better than cleaning the prisoner's dirty clothes and sweat-stained sheets. The following Wednesday morning, I was issued with a gate pass to attend the Bible study group. It was my magic ticket; all I had to do was wave it at the guards on all the gates between my cell and the chapel. I walked through with a smile; feeling chuffed at myself for avoiding my duties. I also remember a vague sense of excitement accompanying those selfish sentiments. I had a strange feeling something good was waiting for me.

It was such an unusual positive feeling for me to have; it surprised me and stoked the fires of my curiosity. The first thing that struck me as I walked into the chapel was the lack of guards. On Sundays, the guards stood stationed ready to intervene at the first hint of trouble. Here was just the vicar and a bunch of guys, a mixture of inmates from all different wings. This was great; I could relax and chat with people.

It wasn't long before one of the other men asked me politely to stop swearing. He explained we were in God's house and it wasn't right to take the name of the Lord in vain, I should show some respect. Instead of this making me angry, it made sense to me and I tried to watch what I said. Although I didn't find it easy, bad language and cursing had become ingrained in me. It had been my native tongue almost all my life. My vocabulary was truly vulgar with profanities pouring from my lips every second word. It would require a great effort to mind my P's and Q's, or rather my F's and B's.

I was encouraged to open the Bible I'd been given and we all pored over the reading of the week. Afterwards, there would be a time for discussion and questions, led by the vicar. He wanted us to pause and reflect upon the meaning of the words we had read. He wanted to know what we thought and how it applied to us. I listened eagerly for a few weeks and enjoyed listening to the debates and the implications of what we were reading. But the words never really seemed to speak to me and I wasn't sure the Bible had anything to say to me. Then one week, we came to a passage that caught my interest.

The Gospels tell the story of how Jesus was being crucified along with two thieves. As they hung there in agony, both of these thieves reviled and mocked Jesus. Then something amazing happened. One of the criminals, on the cross beside Him seemed to have a change of heart. He rebuked the other thief for his taunt at Jesus, when he sarcastically asked why He didn't save them if He was The Son of God.

"Don't you fear God?" asked the contrite thief to his mocking companion. "Since you are under the same sentence? We are punished justly, for we are getting what our deeds deserve but this man (Jesus) has done nothing wrong." Then the thief said, "Jesus, remember me when you come into your kingdom."

To my amazement, Jesus answered him, Truly, I tell you, today you will be with me in paradise. (Luke 23:42)

Here was a man like me, a thief and criminal. The worst of the worst and Jesus had promised him forgiveness. He stole, lied and he had said harsh unfeeling words to Jesus. This vagabond, this scum of society, a robber and reviler was going to be with Jesus in paradise. I absolutely couldn't get my head around it. As far as I was concerned, if you have done something wrong, you were punished for it. There was no forgivingness when you break the law or hurt people. However, here was the Son of God, offering forgiveness to someone with whom I could identify. Could there be hope for me?

"But how could God forgive me? I'm a criminal, I don't deserve forgiveness," I asked the vicar incredulously.

"The Bible suggests otherwise," he replied with a smile.

The first pinpricks of light began to pierce the black ceiling of hopelessness.

Even though I needed a new path, I was still angry and mentally unstable. I was still on strong medication and still surrounded by dangerous people and dark surroundings. I was still enduring the horrible voices every single day. Sometimes there were times when the fog of depression lifted and I seemed to be able to think clearly. But there were times when the pain in my head was severe.

One day, a bunch of us were in the TV room, watching a soap. Another prisoner, called Danny, just got up and without asking anyone, changed the channel. No one said a word but with everything I'd been learning from the study about treating people well, his behaviour and lack of consideration for the people around him, touched a nerve in me.

"Could you please turn that back, I was watching that?". I spoke calmly, keeping the anger I was feeling out of my voice.

The room had gone quiet and everyone waited for his answer. Danny's reply was to warn me he would rip off my head and defecate down my neck. Only he didn't phrase it quite so politely. The guy was a bully and had acted up plenty of times, I was sick of it. I'd had enough and went straight down to my cell and put on my boots. I marched up and stood between Danny and the television blocking his view.

"No one says that to me," I told him. "Get your shoes on; I'm going to fight you."

The irony that I was going to knock someone out due to my newfound biblical convictions never occurred to me. Anger had climbed into the front passenger seat of my emotions and was driving me towards a violent confrontation. It wasn't one I should have been seeking, Danny was older and bigger than me but I didn't care. He was in front of an audience and wasn't going to back down. He rolled his eyes and walked downstairs to his cell with me following closely behind. I shut the cell door behind us and gave him time to pull his trainers on.

He repaid my politeness by running at me unexpectedly, catching me unaware, smashing my head against the mirror hanging on the concrete cell wall. As I fell, the sink gave my head a glancing blow for good measure. Before I could recover, Danny was on top of me and was pushing his thumbs as hard as he could into my eye sockets. I knew I needed to get him off otherwise my eyeballs would pop. He was heavy and I had to use every ounce of strength I had just to get him off me. Motivated by my desperate situation, I managed to topple him sideways onto the floor. I didn't hang around. I yanked open the cell door and staggered out onto the landing. I was in no fit state to carry on our ruck. My head was ringing like a fire alarm and my eyes were in a bad way. I could hardly see anything thanks to Danny's thumb gouging.

I would end up sporting two black eyes, which only matched my mood at having to back away from a fight. I may have lost this battle but at least I hadn't lost my sight. Another few seconds of extreme pressure could have ruined my retinas for good. I was given an eye patch to aid my recovery. I comforted myself I would have the opportunity to avenge myself and win the war with this bully.

Surprisingly for me, I passed up the chance to exact cruel revenge on Danny. A few days later, hanging around in a social area where we could iron our clothes, I ran into a con known as Macka. He was heating up an iron. Holding it up as it fizzed and sizzled with the heat. He informed me he was going to use it on Danny's face. I knew by his cold hard tone he was serious.

"Don't do that." I told him. I was grateful he wanted to stand up for me but something inside knew it wasn't right.

"Why not?" a confused looking Macka asked me, "He deserves it."

I couldn't explain the change in me. I wouldn't have thought twice about the chance of vengefully using a red-hot iron to straighten out the creases on my assailant's face. I knew I needed a new path, a new direction.

Not long after, a few of the guys jumped Danny in the TV room. Fed up with his bullying and arrogance, they gave him a kicking. My confrontation and fight with him had proved to be the catalyst that brought the other prisoners to take matters into their own hands.

Danny's reward for getting a beating, was to be hospitalised and then shipped out to another prison for being a troublemaker, whilst I was about to travel further down the road that would lead me to the salvation I so badly needed. It would prove to be a rocky road full of potholes, where I would often stumble and fall before I finally received the redemption God freely offers.

After attending the Wednesday morning Bible study for a while, the vicar asked me if I would be interested in doing an Alpha course. Alpha is a series of videos explaining what it means to be a Christian. Spotting another opportunity to skip out of sitting in my cell for an hour in the afternoon, and instead nibble on a hobnob and slurp tea, I said yes. Only this time, I wasn't only motivated by selfishness, I was beginning to have a real interest in spiritual matters.

If someone had told me two months earlier that I'd be eagerly attending a Bible study, I'd have laughed and sworn at them. I had always thought Christians were boring killjoys. Yet, Nicky Gumble, the man who spoke on the video, was surprisingly normal and spoke plainly. I began to get an answer to the question I'd posed to the vicar a few weeks earlier.

I learnt forgivingness was possible for me because Jesus had died on the cross. He died to pay for all the wrong things we do, think or say. Now, if we're truly sorrowful for those things and ask for God's forgiveness and believe in Jesus, if we turn away from all our wrongdoing, if we give Jesus our hearts and lives by following Him, we will be forgiven.

Not only did Jesus die on a cross, He rose again so we can go to be with Him in heaven when we die. I also learnt it wasn't just the worst people who needed forgiveness but all mankind. Those separated from God because of their sin would, one day, have to stand before a Holy God. All of us deserve judgement and hell but, because God loves us, He sent His Son so we can be saved from this fate through faith in Jesus Christ.

I began to realise God loved me so much that He sent Jesus to die for me. It was truly amazing. I was excited at hearing this good news and began to tell others. Most other people didn't share my enthusiasm. It must have been strange to them, a prisoner they knew who swore and fought, had serious mental health problems and abused his body. Yet, here he was now, spouting about the love of God. Many didn't want to know and weren't shy in telling me where I could stick my good news. Others were indifferent but some listened and wanted to know more. I didn't know much more myself.

One of the people I reached out to was my cellmate, Nuzzy. I came back from the first session and told him how impressed I was and told him he should come with me the following week.

"There's also tea and cake", knowing the persuasive powers of such luxuries and my cellmate's sweet tooth.

Needless to say, he was on board.

I remember attending a Bible study one week, feeling lousy. On top of my other troubles, I was starting with a bad cold. When it came to the time for us to pray, they prayed God would heal me. Amazingly when I awoke the next day, there was no sign of the heavy cold and sore throat. The headache and aching limbs had gone. My nose and throat that had been beginning to feel more congested than a rush -hour motorway were suddenly set free. I knew from past experience this infection would be making me miserable for at least a week and yet, it had vanished. I have had countless colds and illness since but looking back, I think God was encouraging me despite all my problems, letting me know He was really there. That He loved me.

Despite my setbacks, I was really starting to get behind the idea that God really did exist. From time to time, Christian visitors would come. They spent time with us, playing pool and talking. I didn't understand why they wanted to give up their spare time to fraternise with us convicts, the scum of society. While the rest of the world would probably cross the road to avoid us, these people sought us out so they could share the love of God with us.

I'd ply them with questions about God. They never got tired of answering them, no matter how stupid they were. Occasionally, I'd try to catch them out, but most of the time my questions were genuine.

"Why is there so much suffering in the world?" I wanted to know.

"Sometimes sufferings are the result of living in a fallen world that is in rebellion to God, a world where the devil is actively seeking to destroy. And sometimes, sufferings come as a result of the paths we choose and the decisions we make" they replied, frankly.

Running my fingers over the scar on my arm, I knew I couldn't continue to blame everything on the cards that life had dealt me. It was the way I'd played them and the paths I had chosen that led me to prison and self -harming. I needed a new path.

For all my evangelistic efforts and my excitement to share with others what I was, becoming convinced of, my life was far from being problem-free. Every night, I'd retire to my cell and the spectre of another six years haunted me. It was the last thing on my mind before I fell into a restless sleep and as soon as I opened my eyes in the morning, it was there, hanging over me like the sword of Damocles. I was told the prosecution had thirteen witnesses ready to testify against me. I was the solitary witness for the defence. If my hopes were pinned on myself in the witness box, coming up against a trained lawyer, ready to pounce on anything I said out of place, then I knew I was doomed. Besides, why would the judge take my word, a proven liar, robber and good for nothing that had spent almost all his adult life in and out of prison?

I knew he would believe the prison guard over me. And I knew the prison guard wouldn't be too keen to share his bullying, threatening ways in front of a courtroom of people. They would be seeking to apportion all the blame on my shoulders, a full six years of it. The thought of standing trial made me feel sick to the stomach.

One fitful night, when sleep refused to smile on me, I slipped to my knees and prayed to God. I told Him, if He got me through this trial then I'd follow Him the rest of my life. I began to pray every night knowing I was powerless to do anything in this situation but petition Almighty God, and ask for His help.

Shortly after, I was told I was getting a new cellmate, a posh rich bloke who was in for tax evasion. I pleaded not to be paired up with someone who I thought I had nothing in common. It turned out that this bloke was very clever despite him winding up in jail. In the long hours banged up together, he basically wrote out a defence for me.

There was also a former solicitor frequenting the dark recesses of Wolds with us. He was also doing time for tax evasion. I would take what my new cellmate had written and he would advise me on any changes needed. In return for the help of my new legal team, I would supply them with sandwiches and other dainty morsels; I was allowed to do this as I was now working in the kitchens. I passed all this paperwork on to my real solicitor who was suitably impressed. To be able to do something to prepare, helped me but it didn't stop the constant feeling of worry hovering over me.

The day of the court case came round all too soon. I waited in the holding cells beneath Lincoln Crown Court, sick with nerves. The Barrister representing me came into my cell and announced she thought we had a ninety per cent chance of winning the case. It turned out the prosecution had failed to hand in an important piece of evidence. Although this news cheered me, it did nothing to disarm the fear tightening my gut and making my head swim. I made my way into court and stood before the Judge, a silent prayer on my lips and trepidation in my heart. The Judge took less than five minutes to reach a conclusion.

First, he berated the prosecution for not producing the relevant evidence and then he concluded the guards had acted illegally in entering my cell during a lockdown. He announced he was throwing the case out and the prosecution had wasted his time and proceeded to dismiss the case. Relief flooded through me and the tension drained away like water through a sieve.

Normally, if ever a prisoner is vindicated in court against the guards, it would be the cue for a celebration. A victory show from atop of the tables in the dining room where taunts were shouted towards the guards. Mocking the prison establishment was the usual order of the day for anyone in my position. It gave the rest of the prisoners the chance to join in jeering at the guards defeat, rubbing their faces in it.

I had no interest in glorifying myself because, I knew, it was God who had brought about the verdict. I went straight to my cell and fell to my knees to thank the God that, as yet, I hadn't come to know. Even so, I knew He was real. My mind knew God existed but my heart was as yet unacquainted with Almighty God. I knew I wasn't a Christian, I also knew I'd promised to follow Him if He got me through the trial. The case against me had collapsed in such a dramatic way; it had to have been God. I prayed again, asking God to make Himself real to me. I didn't experience any blinding light as I slipped into my bed that night, tired, relieved and thankful. Yet it would be some time before I became to experience God as a reality in my life. I was still in darkness despite the first pinpricks of light shining through.

That darkness was once again about to become the blackest pitch as two things happened. I was transferred, away from all the Christian help and influence I'd begun to enjoy. This in turn, coincided with my mental health, once again, deteriorating.

Chapter 32

Dark Despair

I was moved from the prison where I had the first glimpses of hope and redemption. I was sent to another prison where for a time; I would regress and fall back into dark days. The irony was I was moved to a lower security category C prison because of my better behaviour. I had to leave all my friends and the people who spoke to me about God and prayed with me. All the things that were having a positive influence on my life suddenly stopped.

I didn't want to go but I was relocated anyway. Not strong enough to live the life I wanted to, I fell back to my old ways and my behaviour worsened. I was then sent to a stricter prison as a consequence. I was transferred to Nottingham nick and, yet again, my mental health spiralled out of control, like a kite without a tail.

The depression that had been knocking on the door of my mind came in uninvited and made itself at home. I began to self-harm again and was plagued by suicidal thoughts. Hopelessness consumed me and I couldn't see a way out. Urged on by the voices in my head, I wanted to die and end the torment I was suffering in my mind. Things got so bad with my self-harming; I was placed on suicide watch. I wasn't even allowed to shave without two guards being there to keep watch. Again, I tried to end my life, using a blade. This time I jabbed a razor into my neck, before I could finish the job, the guards were on top of me, rescuing me from myself and my bloody attempt to leave this life.

The penalty for being caught self-harming was to be thrown into a strip cell. It was an ordinary cell that had been stripped of everything but a bucket and a threadbare blanket, so thin you could see through it. In addition, an old blue mattress lay on the concrete floor. In the winter, it was hard to sleep it was so cold, dressed in shorts and a t-shirt, shivering beneath a measly strip blanket. Sometimes the window would be broken and an icy draught whistled through.

I hadn't been back in my usual cell long when, one night, I was sent back to the strip cell because I had pleaded to see a doctor. My suicidal thoughts were so intense I couldn't bear it. I needed help and cried out to the guards. They told me to go to sleep and shut up. Tossing and turning in both body and mind, I eventually drifted off into a troubled sleep, only to be awakened and thrown into the dreaded strip cell. For the crime of crying out for help, I was to be left in there over three weeks. It was like a prison within a prison.

Time seemed to crawl when I was alone with just my thoughts and memories. But, you can't have a conversation with a thought or embrace a memory. I was ill, forlorn and fearful. Solitary confinement only added fuel to the fire of my mental torments. I believe that all the times I spent abandoned and alone in strip cells had a profound effect on me. I live with the consequences, even today. Locked up alone, all day, every day, could damage any normal person never mind someone already battling serious mental illness. Loneliness, despair and depression joined the voices echoing in my head. They added their whispers, urging me to take my life. I don't know how long I would have lasted as the days merged into weeks, with no sign of me rejoining normal prison life. My mental health was deteriorating rapidly. I needed to be delivered from what had become a mental torture chamber. Help came, yet again, from the most unlikely source. I believe it was the unseen hand of God, unbeknown to me, even in the dark night of my soul.

Before being consigned to the strip cell, I'd begun writing to an old school friend called Jason. Jason's Mum, Rita, wrote to me as well, to encourage me. I replied and we began to exchange letters. One day, when I'd been in my dreary dungeon a few weeks, she turned up out of the blue to visit me. Maybe it had been the fact that my regular correspondence had ceased and she was wondering what had happened to me. When she turned up, she was informed I was in a strip cell and wasn't allowed visitors. She insisted on seeing me but was told bluntly it wasn't going to happen. She refused to take no for an answer and an argument ensued that became so heated the warden was called. She demanded to know what was happening to me and why I'd been thrown into solitary confinement. I'm grateful she went into bat for me. All the fuss she caused meant that the warden ordered that I be returned to my normal cell.

He no doubt realised I shouldn't have been sent there originally, never mind having languished for three weeks. I was sent back to the daily treadmill of prison life. I wasn't in any shape for anything as I was mentally very unwell. I kept self-harming and being sent to the hospital wing. They would patch me up and send me back to my cell. The same doctor would treat me every time. Another occasion, when he was tending to my self-inflicted wounds, sick of seeing me once again, he frustratedly asked me,

"You're going to kill yourself one day. Aren't you"?

"Yes" was my matter of fact answer. I thought one day soon I would.

Thankfully, my dire condition was recognised, perhaps they were keen to avoid any complaints from Jason's mum and decided to look after me properly. The fact was though; they couldn't look after me properly as I needed expert medical care.

It was decided I should be sent to a secure hospital where I could get the treatment I needed. The trouble was there were no beds available and I would have to wait. It took four long months. I spent this time in the hospital wing as my continual self-harming meant I couldn't be left in my cell. I actually preferred it there anyway.

My only problem was cigarettes weren't easy to get hold of. The guards knew this and some would taunt us by smoking in front of us, making sure they left nothing of their cigarette for us to forage. A couple of times, they forgot and would flick the discarded fag into the bin. We would retrieve it and use the tobacco inside to make a roll-up. It summed up the grubby existence of prison life, searching through the rubbish bins for a tab end.

Whilst in Nottingham, another prisoner attempted to take his own life. He barricaded himself in his cell and set light to paper, books and furniture. The first we knew of it was the smoke that snaked its way under the cell door. It stung our eyes and made it hard to breathe. I took some clothes, wet them and blocked up the bottom of the door to try to keep out the smoke. If it was this bad in our cell then the fumes must be horrendous in the poor soul's cell. The guards took a while to break into his barricaded cell and found him unconscious and badly burned. He needed CPR, but survived, just. The fire brigade was called and put out the fire before it spread to the rest of the prison.

Whilst on the hospital wing, I befriended a new prisoner on remand who was blind. One eye was blind and in the other, he wore a glass one. I felt sorry for him and would do my best to help him, bringing him things and leading him from his cell to the television room. Helping him seemed to take my mind off my own problems. This went on for a few weeks until one day when the two of us were alone. I was relaxing reading a book as he lay on his bed. He asked me what book I was reading.

"How do you know I'm reading a book?" I asked him.

I'd heard other senses become heightened when you have a disability and expected him to tell me he could hear me turning the pages. Instead, his reply shocked and angered me. He told me he could see through the centre of the glass eye as it was only a cover and his own eye underneath was fine. I was immediately furious with him.

"I've fetched and carried for you, leading you around these last few weeks and you mean to tell me, all this time you could see?"

He apologised and explained he wanted to influence the court so he wouldn't have to serve any more time and had come up with this scheme. I didn't stay mad at him for long and continued taking him everywhere, arm-in-arm so no one would know it was really the unblind leading the unblind. He also told me he was worried because the doctor had told him he would check his sight and was petrified not only of losing the sympathy factor in court but of life on the mainstream wing. He was in his sixties and experiencing life behind bars for the first time. I knew from bitter experience; the prospect of prison was frightening and could reduce big tough men to quivering wrecks.

It was also at Nottingham where the arrival of a new prisoner had caused quite a commotion. He'd no sooner been shown to his cell when he started shouting and crying and making a hell of a racket. I asked the prison guard what was wrong with him and if I could go in. The guard advised me just to let him calm down and it wasn't safe to intrude on this emotionally unstable new inmate. I somehow convinced the guard to unlock his door. The tall muscled figure was beating his fists on the wall while wailing loudly. I went straight over and threw my arms around him. He clung to me, sobbing, and I could feel my shirt becoming soaked with his tears. I tried to reassure him and he just cried like a baby for a good ten minutes. Finally, he composed himself enough to share his tragic story with me.

He'd been a bouncer in a pub when one evening, a group of youths had turned up looking for trouble. He'd refused them entry and things had kicked off. Turned out, they weren't too happy at not being allowed into their favourite watering hole and had become violent.

They'd attacked my new chum, who was named Tom. Tom had defended himself and punched one of them who'd gone sprawling, hitting his head on the curb. Other bouncers had come to Tom's aid and when order had been restored, an ambulance was called for the stricken youth. The lad later died in hospital and Tom was on remand, awaiting trial. Sadly, Tom was found guilty of manslaughter and would receive a long, harsh sentence. He was a married man with kids and had never been inside before. I took him under my wing and showed him around. He calmed down and settled into prison life. I was glad I was able to help him though I badly needed help myself.

Eventually, a place was found for me and I was transferred to Doncaster Gate Hospital, Princess Mary Ward, in Rotherham. It had been an old maternity ward that had now become an intensive psychiatric care facility. Instead of delivering babies, it concentrated on trying to deliver the mentally ill of their worse symptoms. These included people sent from the court and those from within the prison system who were experiencing acute psychiatric illness. It was a place most sane people avoid like the plague. God is not like people. It was here that I would come to know that there truly is a God who loves me despite all of the vile things I have done and all the turmoil, trouble and serious mental illness I was experiencing.

Chapter 33

The Breaking Dawn

For most people, a hospital is the last place where you want to find yourself. For me, being housed in the hospital's secure unit was a breath of fresh air compared to the harsh prison environment I'd endured for so long. The place was built to care for the mentally ill and housed both men and women.

It seemed strange to be around women after living in the testosterone -fuelled environment of a men's nick. I soon took advantage of this fact and would go and chat with the women on the ward. In some cases, it didn't end in just conversation and we would find quiet places in the unit to have sex. I was like a starving man at an all you can eat buffet. I fed my base instincts, sneaking into the bathrooms; we would put the taps on full blast to drown out the noise from our lusty encounters. It wasn't only the bathroom that witnessed my wantonness, anywhere quiet would do. I'd use any corner of the hospital for a place to copulate. I liked one woman in particular, a boisterous blonde called Clare. We soon struck up a relationship.

My mental health began to improve, helped by the specialist medical care. It felt like I'd been rescued and, once again, I felt a bloom of gratitude to God in my heart. Not only was I surrounded by less abusive people, but I also came into contact with numerous Christians. It seemed, once again, that God had arranged a small band of people who knew and loved Him, to help and talk to me. These included Stephanie, the occupational therapist, Julie, the hairdresser, and the regular Christian visitors. I would often talk with them about God and all the trouble and pain I was feeling. They didn't offer me any magic solutions but urged me to take the guilt, shame and anguish that tormented me, and take it to God, to ask for His help, to cast my cares on Him, because He cared for me.

I listened and started to talk to God, sharing my feelings with him. The frustrations regarding my mind and body were shared with Him who formed them both in my mother's womb. I found this hard at first and didn't get it right away. I knew I needed to ask God's forgiveness for the way I had lived and the things I had done. I knew it was God who had kept me alive and somehow, He loved me, Nigel Owen James Williams, despite everything.

One day, a group of Christians brought their guitars and put on a concert for us. I sat in a big easy chair, quietly listening. As the music played, I experienced a strange sensation. I was aware of God's care and love for me. This God I'd heard all about from numerous people, was here with me. I was a man who had lied, stolen and lived without regard for others. I had done awful, horrible things to people and their property. I knew I was a wretched miserable sinner, a man with serious medical issues, in a mental hospital, a man who didn't deserve love and mercy. Yet, it felt like God was putting His arms around me and gently rocking me. I'd never known an earthly Father and yet, at that moment, I experienced the wonderful love of the Heavenly Father. Joy, peace and love flooded my heart and I knew in that instance, I believed in Jesus Christ. I knew He was my Saviour.

Many people would just write it off as a psychotic episode but I knew then, and I still know now, over twenty-two years later, that God is real and men, women, girls and boys can come and find peace, joy and forgiveness in Jesus.

The Christians led me in the sinners' prayer. A prayer expressing a realisation and sorrow for living for ourselves and breaking God's laws and commandments, and at the same time, expressing a desire to turn away from living like this and being willing to follow Jesus, who died and rose again so we can be forgiven. Jesus, who took the punishment of all who will repent and believe in Him.

I prayed to ask for God's forgiveness and committed myself to follow Jesus for the rest of my life. The Holy Spirit had come to give me new life and this warm loving comfort was the greatest feeling I've ever experienced, stronger and truer than any drug or false high. I felt a pure unmitigated joy coursed through me, filling me with emotion. I couldn't stay still, I felt like I was going to burst. Leaping off the chair, I ran down the corridors and stairs. I had to share what I knew deep in my innermost soul.

"Jesus is alive. Jesus is real."

I'd been born again, forgiven, washed clean of all my sin. But only those who had been at the concert really knew what was going on. The concerned eyes of most of the staff followed me, along with mutterings of alarm.

"Could we get some more medication for Mr Williams please?" shouted one startled doctor dryly.

"I don't need any today." I shouted in reply, lost in praises to God who had saved me.

Even though I had become a Christian, life didn't magically get easier. Although I'd come to know God, I wasn't transformed overnight from prisoner to pious saint. Thankfully, something that left me immediately was those vicious voices that had spat their venom at me for so long. From the moment, I was saved, they moved out and God moved in.

Looking back, I'm ashamed of my behaviour as a Christian. I carried on having sex with Claire. I had no concept of the sanctity and purity that God holds sexual union between a man and his wife. In my defence, you have to remember the way I'd lived. My life was the only one I knew and I didn't properly understand the right way for a Christian to live. I had to change. I felt that God had started a change in me but I wasn't sure exactly what it should look like in reality. I certainly knew I shouldn't fight with people and yet, that is exactly what happened.

I was a baby in Christ. I'd been born again, and like a child, I needed those more mature to teach me the ways of Christ and to care for me. I had a feeling I wasn't behaving as one who claims to know Jesus Christ should. I still hadn't been taught about the things I should and shouldn't do. I'd been taken out of darkness. Just as the dawn breaks, diffusing light slowly creeps over the horizon and chases away the night. The transforming light of the Gospel crept slowly into my life. In many cases, the bud opens slowly before the flower is revealed, and so it was with me.

I have to hold my hand up and take responsibility for many things. However, the violence that marred the first couple of days of my Christian life wasn't entirely my fault. At least, I didn't instigate the trouble. I was involved in three fights in just two days with a guy on the ward, called Dan. He was really unwell in his mind. I was in the smoke room relaxing quietly; I'd slipped off my shoes to be more comfortable. There was no warning from Dan, he just breezed into the room and tried to stamp on my bare feet. He was wearing heavy shoes that would have done some serious damage. Motivated by self-preservation and trying to keep all my toes intact, I moved my feet quicker than a tap dancer on fast forward. My assailant redoubled his efforts to cripple me so I hit him as hard as I could. I continued hitting him but he wouldn't go down. This was the only thing I could do, to stop the stamping.

Staff came running to split us up. I got into trouble even though I was only defending myself. The next day, I had to rescue someone else from Dan. I heard Claire scream my name from the smoke room and ran down the corridor. Bursting into the room, I found Dan attacking my girlfriend. I laid straight into him, throwing him to the ground and punching him continuously.

The furnace of my anger had, above all, been kindled because a man was attacking a woman. So the fire became a blaze and burst out into frenzied attack on this man. I know it may seem rich, someone like me moralising, but a man assaulting a female to me was the lowest of the low. This compounded my dislike of Dan. I didn't listen to the staffs' attempt to bring peace but carried on walloping him. In the end, it took six or seven to pull me away.

When I'd calmed down, I felt bad for what I had done. I wouldn't have given it a second thought a week ago. Now I knew there had been a change, I belonged to God. I had to live for Him and knew I had to do better, but didn't know how. I realised I'd had to protect my girlfriend and knew also that the aggression and violence I'd used, was wrong.

The very next afternoon, who should I meet in the stairwell, but Dan. I was walking up and he was making his way down. I moved to the side to let him pass, not wanting another confrontation. He wouldn't let me pass and again swung at me. This time, I grabbed him and half-shoved, half-carried him up the stairs and through a door. Once again, staff had to intervene and split us up.

Despite the troubles with Dan, the whole first week felt like I was in a bubble of God's protection and love. I felt God was with me, watching over me. I no longer felt alone and was filled with a sense of peace. There were bars on the windows but my soul and spirit felt free at last. Here I was, still serving out a sentence in a secure mental hospital and yet, a deep sense of peace and love I couldn't explain, was with me.

My new Christian friends gave me an audio book of the Bible, which I started to listen to. Every night before bed, I would play it. I didn't always understand it, especially as the reading was taken from the King James Version, written in 1611. It uses language and words that are outdated. However, I was learning more and more about God. And unlike my first Bible studies, I knew these truths and promises applied to me and were not mere intellectual discussion points.

A couple called Keith and Andrea started visiting me once a week. I used to look forward to seeing them. On the same day, the inmates would bake cakes and buns, so at night, when Keith and Andrea would visit, we'd munch my culinary creations and read the Bible. They would pray with me and tell me stories of what God had done in their lives. They were a great encouragement and help in my newfound faith and relationship with God.

The months went by and the time came for me to leave. I'd served my sentence. Keith and Andrea helped me return to Mansfield and get set up in a homeless hostel. They found me a church to attend and contacted the vicar to arrange a time for him to visit me. He invited me to a Sunday service. I attended, not knowing what to expect. I was nervous because I can get uncomfortable around large groups of people and feel on edge.

I had no need to worry. The folks there made me feel welcome, and set me at ease. They were so loving and accepting of me, in spite of my past. I was very different to them and felt this sharply; it seemed to me I was the proverbial, fish out of water. I also struggled to understand the things spoken about in the church service. Most of what was said went over my head. I never would have believed I'd be in church, worshipping with mostly middle-aged, respectable people. The only chance of me seeing smiling faces like theirs was in photos on their mantelpiece, as I burgled their house. Now, here I was sitting in church with them.

Despite this new life, I was still struggling with the old habits of drink and drugs. I felt lonely despite my new church friends. I was still in touch with Claire in the hospital; the hostel would let me talk to her on the phone. I would still take speed at night. It sometimes took time to kick into my system and by the time it did, I had usually taken more, eager for the stimulus it provided. Then I would end up staying up all night, watching television.

I wanted and needed to change but it wasn't happening quickly enough for the hostel manager's liking. When I returned from the drug dealer's house, I would make a beeline for the hostel bathroom to sample the wares I'd just purchased. This aroused her suspicions and she would bang on the door, demanding to know what I was doing. I guess I was a poor liar and she didn't believe me. Eventually, I was thrown out and faced life on the streets.

Thankfully, I didn't stay homeless long. A man I'd got to know while living at the hostel invited me to live with him, his girlfriend and child in their newly acquired council house. I was glad to get off the streets and have a roof over my head. I wasn't glad, however, when I found out they expected me to go on the rob with him and his mates. They insisted it was the only way they could put food on the table. As I was their guest, I had no other choice but to join them. I hated what we were doing and knew it was wrong in God's eyes. Things were about to get worse.

One night, there was a banging at the door. The girlfriend answered with her tiny child in her arms. I didn't know who it was but could tell from the raised voices and profanities it wasn't someone dropping in for a friendly chat and a cuppa. It turned out it was a group of youths who were abusing and threatening the woman. I was the only other person in the house so I went to see what was going on. I tried to shut the door but these youths were trying to push their way in. I knew if it kicked off, I couldn't protect a vulnerable mother and baby against five yobs brandishing knives. After a struggle, I managed to get the door shut and locked. The youths sauntered away after peppering us with threats and abuse from outside. I breathed a sigh of relief, no one had been hurt and it was all over, or so I thought.

Five minutes later, the man returned home with his mates in tow and was less than pleased to hear of the visit we had received from the gang. Listening to the mother describe how they had threatened her and the child and watching the red mist of anger descend, I knew it was far from over. Deeply offended, the whole group set out looking for revenge. I prayed we wouldn't find the youths and everyone would have time to calm down.

Turning the corner into Brown Street, we saw a group of lads walking down the road. It was them. We'd found them, much to my dismay. My friends weren't seeking an apology; they were thirsting for revenge in the shape of broken jaws and black eyes. They just piled into these youths. I stupidly concluded, out of a misplaced sense of loyalty that I had to stand up and be counted. The fighting spilt onto the streets, bringing traffic to a standstill. I smashed one guy's head into the bonnet of a car, much to the shock of the elderly couple in the front seat. He tried to grab my leg so I booted him in the face and he picked himself up and scarpered down the road.

People were watching and coming out of their houses to look on, concerned at the unfolding violence. I think everyone was too scared to call the police, luckily for me, as I would have definitely been back behind bars. Looking across the street, I spotted one of our group taking a beating and ran swiftly to his aid, kicking his assailant as hard as I could in the ribs. He went down and my friend quickly jumped up, started to rain down blows on the prone youth. One by one, the gang took off bruised and battered.

We had won, but I felt no elation or pride. Instead, I felt sick. I remember going to bed feeling awful. I cried out to God in my desperation.

"I'm in a really bad place right now. I'm stealing and fighting again. I don't want to be here and I don't want to be living this way. If things carry on like this, I know I'll end up back in prison. Please help me"

The next morning, an answer to my prayer came through the letterbox.

Chapter 34

Back in the Steel City

After you leave prison, you get sent small amounts of money to live on. The letter I received contained one such payment, a cheque for £35. I immediately knew what I was going to do with it. It would be my ticket out of the life of thieving and fighting. I bought a one-way coach ticket to Sheffield.

Claire had been released from hospital and was living in Rotherham with her mum and dad. I figured that the Steel City, which I knew from my previous jaunts, was close enough for me still to see Claire. I also knew some Christian friends that lived nearby, Andrea and Keith, who'd been such a tower of strength and support to me already.

I caught a taxi from the bus depot and asked to be dropped at the Sally Anne Hostel. I'd stayed there before and thought it would be a good place to settle until I could sort myself out. There would be no hot food and bed there for me though as it was full, no room at the inn. I was in a pickle. Claire had already made it clear I couldn't stay with her at her parents. My only option was to turn to Andrea and Keith for help. As I picked up the phone, I felt my heart begin to beat faster. What would I do if they refused to help? Alone in a city where I was a relative stranger and no idea what to do? I was at the mercy of God.

After explaining my plight to them, they told me to stay where I was and they were coming to get me. Breathing a sigh of relief and gratitude to God, I sank onto a bench, offering a silent prayer of thanks. They said I could stay with them while they found me somewhere to live. It felt good to be in their home and I basked in the warm sunshine of their family environment. Soon they found me somewhere to stay and I moved out. I will always be grateful for what they did for me.

The new place was called St Anne's hostel. This was a place where temporary accommodation for homeless men was on offer. Together with support, advice and assistance in the hope a permanent place could be found for the future. It was here I became friendly with the woman who worked the night shift. She was also called Anne. I would stay up most of the night just talking and playing pool with her. Her kindness kindled sparks of feelings, and I'd be lying if I said I didn't develop a crush on her.

I'd seen Claire a couple of times but we soon realised it wasn't right for us and things fizzled out. It was at St Anne's I started to suffer badly with my mental health once again. Coming to know God and experiencing His salvation, had been a wonderful mountain top experience, a special time I would never forget. Now it seemed I'd have to descend the mountain into the dark valley of depression. The mental health problems I suffered had been with me for years and were deep-rooted issues, stemming from my childhood and my lifestyle.

Although God was already at work in other areas of my life, there was to be no quick fix or easy solution with regards to my illness. The Gospel does not contain a promise of a trouble-free life. No Christian can expect to be carried to heaven on soft beds of flowery ease; we must go through many tribulations before seeing the pearly gates swing open, and entering into the fullness of joy. Sometimes, we can't see the sun when the black rain clouds gather on the horizon but the fact is it is still there whether we realise it or not. If it wasn't, we would soon perish. God's tender love and care have been just like this in the dark moments of mental torment. I have, sometimes, despaired but I know the grace of God has been there to sustain me.

Alone in St Anne's one night, I began to suffer. My release valve was to self-harm but I went too far and bled all over my bed sheets and carpets. It looked horrific and they called an ambulance. I was rushed to hospital and was admitted to recover from my injuries. I was discharged after a couple of days. Instead of recovering, I nosedived into a pit of despair that proved to be a playground for my paranoia. I began to feel unwell and convinced myself that my drinks had been spiked. I took myself off to the hospital, knowing I needed some respite and help from my mental tortures.

They told me there was nothing they could do for me, and to go home. A mixture of anger, frustration and despair filled my senses. I couldn't face another night, alone, at the hostel. In fact, I decided I couldn't face another night, full stop. I locked myself in the toilet and consumed all of my tablets at once. I then hid the empty packets in the toilet cistern and sat down and waited to die. I didn't feel sorry for myself, I just longed for the mental torment and anguish to cease.

I'd been sitting there for maybe fifteen minutes when someone came in, looking for me. I refused to come out of my lair. I waited to pass out, expecting my last earthly sight to be the inside of a grubby loo. The police were called and they smashed down the door to get me out. I was handcuffed and walked to the police van. I kept expecting my legs to buckle and black unconsciousness to engulf me. I never told anyone I'd taken an overdose.

I was locked in the van by two Bobbies while the Sergeant talked with the doctors and nurses. They made the decision to drive me to the secure mental ward. While in that small mobile cell, I began to feel unwell. I could hear the two coppers hatch a plan to play a joke on their Sergeant that they had lost the keys when he returned. I didn't pass out and heard the returning policeman berate the officers for their careless behaviour, he swore at them as they broke out into laughter and produced the keys. I wondered if they'd still be laughing when they had to drag my corpse from their vehicle. I really thought I was going to die and the police van would become my coffin.

I have no recollection of the journey. They told me I was going to a secure hospital and not the nick. If I make it that far, it will be a nicer place to die, was the simple thought I had. Obviously, I didn't die; I woke up in a hospital bed in the Michael Carlisle Centre, Stanage Ward; a place that cared for those with acute mental problems. I'd been asleep almost twenty hours. As bad as my illness was, and even though I had planned to end my life, it seemed God had other ideas. Once again, it had been down to His kindness, care and mercy that I had breath in my lungs and a beating heart. Once I'd come round, I was deeply thankful to God.

The Christmas decorations were out, lighting up the room. They reminded me that although they celebrated the events in Israel some two thousand years ago, this same Jesus whose heavenly angelic anthems rang out into the cold Bethlehem night air, this same saviour who was laid in a manger, had saved not only my soul, but my life.

While recuperating, I began to share my faith with everyone around me. I'm not sure what people made of a self-harmer with mental problems telling people about Jesus. I hoped if God could use fisherman and tax collectors to preach the Gospel then he could use someone like me. It didn't matter what anyone thought. What really mattered was that I testified to the truth that salvation and forgiveness are only found in Jesus. Some wouldn't listen to what they perceived as the rambling of a crazy person. Some listened and I struck up a friendship with young woman called Sharon. We became close during the two weeks I spent in hospital recovering. In fact, we became too close and we soon embarked on a physical relationship.

When I was well enough to be discharged, I was sent back to St Anne's. It was the day before Christmas Eve. Once again, I was alone and living in a hostel. I hadn't been there long when I received a phone call from Sharon. She told me she had been offered a council flat and asked if I wanted to go and live with her. I can't pretend I was in love with Sharon but I was lonely. It didn't take me long to make my decision. Either I stayed in a hostel alone, with some shady characters, many of them destined to re-offend or stay in a proper place that offered me comfort and safety.

Having someone to talk to and live with was a big help for me with my illness and I improved. Although, I have to say, I didn't treat Sharon with the care, dignity and respect a man should have for his woman.

I let her fetch, carry and cook for me. One thing I did do though was help decorate the flat. At the start, we just had a blanket on the floor and no more. We soon begged and borrowed, but not stole, our way to furnish the place.

One lady I will be forever grateful to is my National Health Community Psychiatric Nurse, Helena Smith. She was instrumental in helping me furnish the pad, as well as spending hours with me, helping me fill out the benefit forms. She was so patient, kind, caring and compassionate. When I was being sent back to St Anne's all alone from the hospital at Christmas, she started to cry. She helped me with my bills and provided the support I needed. It felt good to be living in a proper flat and not being alone.

I joined a local church and Sharon came with me every Sunday. While my behaviour was far from that of a model Christian, I was committed to going to church every week. I wanted to be faithful to the God who lavished His grace on me. I wanted to learn and know more about the wonderful God who I knew loved me and had forgiven me such a mountain of sin.

Once again, it was an elderly congregation at the new church and I struggled to fit in. That all changed when Sharon received a visit from someone she had met in hospital. His name was Dave Goddard. He was a Christian who gave up his time to visit the sick and the suffering. He'd talked with Sharon in hospital about God and kept in touch with her. Now here he was in our kitchen.

I was in the living room, resenting the presence of this man who was a stranger to me. What I didn't know was God would use this man to save my life. We eventually got chatting, and Dave told us about a church he went to called Living Waters. It was actually closer than the church we were attending. He encouraged us to come along and assured us we would be accepted and welcomed. The next Sunday we did just that and found his promise held good. We were made to feel loved and valued and settled into church life. I now had a place to live and also a spiritual home.

It was here, at Living Water, that I would have my name in the headlines again. This time, it wasn't for the crimes I committed or a report of the sentence I'd received. The church produced its own magazine a few times a year and delivered it to local houses. In it were articles about God and what he had done in people's lives. The Pastor, another Dave, Dave Missing, suggested I put my story on the back page. He wanted people to read what God had done for me and testify that God is real, that He cares for people, even people like me. I agreed and helped deliver the magazine, enjoying my five minutes of fame after years of infamy.

I guess that little story was in a way a precursor for the first seeds of this book. One man suggested I deliver the magazines on my own to a certain area a mile or so from the church. I listened to his encouragement and advice and set about my task with zeal. What this man had failed to mention was the area he had suggested was a Muslim neighbourhood. It soon became apparent to me and it wasn't long before I was stopped by a man who had been one of the recipients of the magazine.

"What are you doing around here, delivering this?" he demanded to know, stopping in his car to confront me.

I then started to explain what God had done for me. He ended up driving away, telling me I shouldn't be around his area. Although I didn't meet with any obvious success, it would eventually lead me to put my story in a little booklet to hand out on the streets. This is something I continue to do and God willing will do for the rest of my life. As my story has grown and developed, so did my booklet. I still give them out and try to talk to people. I ask how they are and if any prayer or any help is needed. I enquire if they want to talk about God, and if they would mind me telling them about Jesus. So I guess I have a lot to thank that man who suggested it. At the time, I was just relieved to have survived the magazine delivery unscathed.

One morning before church, a new face pulled up on a moped. His name was Andy and I welcomed him and asked him all about his bike.

Little did I know this man would also have an impact on my life. Far from saving it, he was to cause me distress and heartache.

The months went by and I enjoyed church life and having a stable environment. The Pastor counselled us to get married explaining to us that sex outside marriage is wrong in God's eyes. Sharon moved out for a while to live with a Christian family.

The truth was I was too unstable to get married. I had all on caring for myself and dealing with all my mental health issues. I was also too weak to live apart from Sharon without a physical relationship. Platonic to me was more likely to be the name of an electronics company than a sustained attempt at celibacy. A short time later, she moved back in and we continued living together.

Although Sharon and I carried on living as a couple, our relationship went through ups and downs. One particular incident sticks vividly in my mind. It doesn't paint me in a good light but since the purpose of this book is to give an honest account of my life and to testify to God's grace, I will include it. One night, I was sleeping peacefully when I felt what I thought was a punch in the face. In reality, it must have been Sharon turning over in bed and elbowing me accidentally on my jaw. Before I knew what I was doing, my instincts had kicked in and I was on top of Sharon in the pitch black of the night with my hands around her throat.

I had been conditioned to prison life where attacks and violence could explode at any time, where you always had to be ready to defend yourself. As soon as I realised what I was doing, I released her and she fled, sobbing, out of the room. I felt just as distraught at what had happened and apologised profusely. The next day, I went and bought her some flowers to say I was sorry. In some ways, I did treat Sharon with love while at other times; I treated her like a doormat. I'm sure you must be heartily sick of hearing how much I regret my behaviour but the truth is I do.

Even though my life was still beset with problems and I was still living with my illnesses, the one sure anchor in my life was God. I desired above all that my relationship with God would grow stronger and I would grow in my faith towards Christ. I knew more and more I wanted to follow Jesus and know Him more but I was still drawn to my past life with its excesses and temptations.

One late summer day, I reached a watershed moment. Sharon had been visited by her support worker, Barbara. They had gone to get a coffee at a local cafe and to discuss Sharon's mental health problems in an informal setting without me interfering. I noticed a black purse sitting on the settee. I knew wasn't Sharon's. I sat down on the sofa and opened it. Much to my surprise, it was stuffed with twenty-pound notes. I took the money out and counted it, it totalled a whopping eight hundred pounds.

I knew it must belong to Barbara and I also knew that amount of cash would be very useful to me. I'd always had to risk life and limb in my illegal pursuit of riches. Now here it was next to me, singing a sirens song of temptation. I felt like it was unconsciously begging me to slip it into my pocket. I was arrested by the thought that a follower of Jesus needed to be honest. This thought came to me with such force and clarity; I knew it came from God. Even so, I was torn in two.

While I sat there weighing up my options, the phone rang. It was Sharon asking me if I'd seen Barbara's purse. She was upset because she was going on holiday to Spain the next day and had a large amount of cash in it. She asked me to look around the settee, as that's where they'd been sitting. She had no idea I was already on the sofa with the purse in my hands. I told her I'd go and look and lowered the phone to my knee. A couple of seconds elapsed where a battle raged in my heart and mind. I knew I could get away scot-free with this king's ransom but I also knew it was wrong in God's eyes.

"I've found it," I told Sharon, "come get it."

What would have been ordinary behaviour for most Christians was a step forward for me and my walk with God.

I'd like to say after this incident, I went from strength to strength but that wasn't to be the case. The truth is, I would stumble, slip and shuffle slowly forward. Sometimes even briefly slip backwards in my Christian journey. But this was a little victory for someone like me who'd been on the rob since I'd been a young lad. It proved I was walking the narrow road of faith even though many difficulties lay ahead. It would prove to be a steep and snare strewn path, but the Lord Jesus had walked the same path before and He promises never to leave or forsake me. He would be my guide through the valleys as well as the mountains of this life.

Chapter 35

Baptism and Betrayal

The Pastor talked to me and Sharon, telling us, "If you are serious about following God then you need to get baptised." I knew it was a big step, I also knew there was no turning back now. I no longer wanted a life of crime, I wanted to serve God. This is exactly what baptism is, a public demonstration of a new life. Baptism is an outward symbol to the world of the inner change that has taken place. I was to go under the water with my old way of life, when I lived selfishly. When I emerged, I would be spotless, a new person with all my sins washed away. A fresh start, a new life where I resolved to love, follow and obey God through Jesus Christ my saviour. It wasn't a decision I made lightly but I was sure and certain of my newfound faith.

I was thrilled that after explaining things to Sharon, she decided she wanted to be baptised. Just to put the cherry on the cake, Andy, the guy I met outside church with his bike asked to join us. The day of the service came around and it was a wonderful experience. Coming up out of the water, I felt so excited and grateful to God. It was made even more beautiful by the fact my girlfriend and friend were able to share it with me.

A couple of weeks later, I attended a Christian camp. I had decided it would be good for me to be around other Christians for a full week, to be able to mix with them and hear about the things God had done in their lives, to listen to sermons and Bible teaching and to be able to worship God without distractions.

One night, returning to my tent alone, musing on the teaching I'd heard, I lay down on my bed. I was startled to hear the most beautiful singing I'd ever heard. It only lasted a few minutes but the strange ethereal choir made my heart soar and filled me with revenant awe for God. At the risk of being ridiculed, I know in my heart what I heard that night was angels. The next morning, I excitedly asked others if they'd heard the singing too. No one had. Many may think I was dreaming or it was part of my mental illness but let me assure you that wasn't the case. There are many reasons I'm looking forward to paradise, hearing that heavenly choir once again, is definitely one. Why had no one else heard it? Maybe God was arming and encouraging me against the body blow I was about to receive.

I'd called Sharon a couple of times on my Nokia brick mobile phone whilst away at the conference, to see if she was okay. She seemed fine. I had no hint of the news that would be announced when I answered my phone the next afternoon. What I heard numbed me with shock. The call was from a member of my church, a guy called Kevin.

He too had had a dramatic experience of God. He was an ex-Army officer who fell on hard times when he left the forces. He had decided he had nothing left to live for and was going to commit suicide. Before he had the chance to end his life, he came across the church and heard the Gospel. He believed and found hope instead of despair, and chose life instead of death.

You may be thinking it's only the desperate and down -and-outs that look to God. This is not the case, people from all walks of life and professions come to faith. But often, due to human nature, we don't look heavenwards until we're compelled to, laid on our backs in the gutter. All mankind has a sin problem and it's usually those who are the worst in society that realise it first. In Jesus' time, it was the tax collectors and prostitutes, the immoral who heeded His call to repent, believe and follow Him. One reason for this is we naturally tend to think good thoughts about ourselves and hope we will be good enough to get to heaven. This will never be the case; the Christian message is that everyone needs a saviour. All need redemption, from the Prime Minister in his plush office in Downing Street, to the prostitute on the Soho street corner. But it's the latter that often sees this fact, and God also chooses the base things of the world to shame the wise.

I knew I was a base thing and I had also found a good friend in Kevin, another soul God had rescued from the pit of despair. I enjoyed our friendship and conversations but the one I was about to have with him would be anything but enjoyable. He had devastating news to share. After exchanging pleasantries, he asked me a question that would rip me in two.

"Do you know that Andy and Sharon are now together?" He asked.

My heart sank like a stone. After all, we'd been through. I felt betrayed and taken for a fool. Needless to say, the rest of the conference may have been in Mandarin for all the good it did me. The news had twisted a knife into my emotions and hit me with a sledgehammer, spiritually. I couldn't think straight, wondering how long it had been going on. Just how big a mug was I? I'd been a good friend to Andy, inviting him round to our flat and this is how he'd repaid me. I can look back now and clearly see Sharon and I weren't right for each other but, back then, the pain was real and raw.

Once back in Sheffield, I needed to go and get my stuff. I arranged a time to call round and pick up what little gear I had. I'd furnished most of the flat myself but I didn't want any of it as it felt tainted to me. Thankfully, the church had arranged somewhere for me to stay. They had recently purchased a local pub for the princely sum of one pound. The establishment had gone bankrupt and the church had the idea of turning it into a community centre. The logic behind it is, some people who wouldn't dream of darkening the door of a church, may be more inclined to attend this ex-public house. They could hold events like mother and toddler groups and other meetings. These would give the church the opportunity of not being just a help to the local community but also a place to share the Gospel.

My friend, Kevin, was in charge of making the place suitable for such pursuits, which would involve a lot of work. I said that as well as sleeping upstairs, I would help him with the renovations. Keith came with me to pick up my gear from the flat I had shared with Sharon. He advised me not to get upset and start shouting no matter how Sharon reacted because no good could come from it.

The way she did react was to act as if nothing had happened. She offered me a cup of tea and I drank it through clenched teeth. It took all my self-restraint not to pour out my heart in a bitter diatribe. Self-restraint and I were hardly bosom buddies. Somehow, by Gods grace, I was able to leave on civil terms without world war three breaking out. Andy had more sense than to be there. He'd recently broken his leg in a motorbike accident and I would have struggled not to have rearranged his features or broken his other leg. I was a Christian now and knew that wasn't the answer or how God would want me to react. I'm not sure I could have lived up to those high standards though, if I'd had seen his face grinning at me from my settee.

Living at the old pub was only a temporary measure. After a couple of months, Val and Pete, a couple from church, offered to put me up for a while. Of course, I accepted their kind offer. Home-cooked food and being around people was too good to turn down. I repaid their kindness by meeting up with an old prison buddy I'd shared a cell with at Wolds. On the day of his release from a stretch for armed robbery, we celebrated by going on a bender. Although I'd stopped robbing, I still drank too much,

I was eager to tell everyone about Jesus but the people I knew didn't sit sipping cappuccinos in coffee bars. They were usually found propping up a bar in some spit and sawdust pub. I wasn't a strong or mature enough Christian to avoid getting drunk with them. As I sought to convert them to Christ, the reality was the only conversion taking place was me going from sober to inebriated.

The Bible warns that bad company corrupts good character. (1 Corinthians 15:3) Whilst I couldn't claim to be a virtuous saint, the work God was doing in me was being compromised by the company I kept and my following their lead. I hated being on my own with just me and my thoughts.

I enjoyed the company of my newfound Christian friends but most of them were busy with families. I knew if I attended certain pubs, there would be people there I knew. I'm still the same today, a restless soul wanting to be out of the house. Long spells spent in solitary confinement from my prison days have left their mark on me. I soon feel lonely, isolated and anxious if I'm on my own. The taproom of a rough pub was clearly not conducive to me living a holy life for God, a young and inexperienced Christian, prone to the temptation to get drunk. At this time in my life, it was a better option than sitting in a bedroom staring at four walls.

I remember returning to Pete and Val's half cut, late at night. I only have fond memories and good things to say about this hospitable couple. I'm not sure they'd remember me in the same positive manner. They had two young children at the time and Pete would get up at four in the morning to deliver potatoes to the local markets. I'm grateful to them and, if by chance they find themselves reading this book, then I'd like to say thank you.

I've been told Val still prays for me and I'd like them to know God has answered her prayers. There are still many areas of my life that need work, although I've matured from the man showing the stealth of a baby elephant, creeping and crashing around their house in the small hours of the morning after returning from the pub full of beer.

Maybe it was living with a loving family that brought it home to me that I had no one. I loved living with these people but I knew I'd never be part of theirs, or anyone else's family. I'm sure most people naturally take their family for granted. Just take a moment to be thankful for yours.

I'm not naive enough to believe families are perfect or never have issues. Despite this, they have a bond of blood. They say a family loves you despite your imperfections and failings. I had lots of these but I didn't have kin to care for me. At times, this reality comes forcibly with all the subtlety of a sledgehammer to remind me I'm alone in the world on a human level. I know it's part of my depression and illness.

The darkness, once again, began to fall on me, living with Pete and Val. It's like a thick blackout blanket, which obscures all light and hope. I knew I needed help and took myself up to the Northern General Hospital. My head was a mess and throbbed with pain. I was feeling so low. I longed to feel God's loving presence but the blackest night seemed to fill my soul. I couldn't discern God's light and love even though, underneath me, was His everlasting arms, holding me back from the edge of insanity and despair. And it was despair I felt after waiting several hours to see a Psychiatrist. When he came, he listened to my symptoms and bluntly told me there was nothing wrong with me. I'm not sure if he was annoyed at being summoned to A&E, to see this strange man, or whether that was his professional opinion. Either way, I was sent out of the hospital without the help I needed.

Chapter 36

On the Move

I felt I needed to get away; it wasn't fair to burden Dave and Val with my problems and to bring my mental issues into the heart of their family home. The only trouble was, I needed to go straight away and my next giro payment was a few days away. I called into a petrol station as I was walking past and offered the owner my entire book of giros. His apprehension at buying a book of giro cheques from a passing stranger was soon outweighed by the prospect of being able to cash a cheque every two weeks for the next two years. He gave me £50, and whilst that would pay for my food, it looked like my lodgings would have to be under a canopy of the stars.

After two weeks, I ended up cancelling my giro payment so the garage owner couldn't keep milking the cash cow. I sometimes still walk past the garage where I sold the giros and often wonder if the guy is still there and if he remembers me. I took off, once again, hitting the road with a few belongings and my thumb as my travel ticket.

I hitched a lift south, leaving the north behind and hoping my problems would be left behind too. Of course, that wasn't the case and my impulsive flight wasn't thought through properly. I had no plan and nowhere to stay. When I reached Essex, I just started walking, a slower version of Forest Gump. Whereas he attracted a crowd following him, I didn't. It was just me, alone, with my thoughts. The shoes I wore weren't ideal for mile after mile of endless plodding. Rough was the way I was feeling and rough was the way I was sleeping. I walked so far, my feet protested with blisters and the pains in my head were soon matched by the ones from my feet.

One night, I decided to break into a church to bed down for the night. I smashed a window and, once again, cut myself climbing through it. I found a first aid box and used the plasters to patch my tired toes. I also helped myself to some biscuits and tea and enjoyed sleeping under a roof. Lying in the church, I cried out to God. The next morning, I woke knowing I couldn't keep walking away from my problems and needed to seek help. I made my way to a hospital and hoped this time they could help me. After explaining how I felt and my history, I was admitted to Colchester Hospital. I was there two days before being driven back to Sheffield. A place had been found for me in the Northern General Hospital.

A couple of weeks before, I'd been sent packing from this hospital and now, here I was lying in a bed and receiving treatment for my mental illness. I hadn't helped myself by not taking my medication. A plane that runs out of fuel will surely come crashing down and similarly, I too suffered the same fate. It wasn't just negligence on my part. I hated the way the tablets made me feel. Along with the drowsiness, came a numbness and life often felt like I was wading through a river of treacle. I wanted to be well. I knew God had the power to cure me with just a word.

One of my favourite quotes is, one touch from the King, changes everything. (Godfrey Birtill 2007) I would pray for God to heal me from the mental illness that tormented me. I knew He'd healed my soul but struggled to understand why He hadn't chosen to heal my mind. I prayed for Him to take away this thorn in my flesh and, because I'd prayed, I thought I had the faith to stop taking my medication. If faith alone could have healed me, I would have been restored. Although faith can move mountains, it needs to find its source in God's will. God has done so much for me, He loves and forgives me but He has never chosen to heal me.

Down through the years, I've struggled with this fact and will never fully understand why. One day, I will have all the answers and see that God's providence was perfect. One day, when I stand before Him perfected and have every tear wiped away. That day seemed far too distant amidst the torments. I wanted a quick fix and I wanted to be whole. I know now God's grace is sufficient for me although I still have days when the winds of mental illness come in gale-force nine, to torment my troubled mind.

I was discharged from hospital and a place was found for me in a boarding house in the Pitsmoor area. This would be the start of constantly moving home. Hover flies stay in one place longer than I did. Some of the places I lived in were hospital wards, hostels, council properties, and others were the spare beds and sofas' of Christian people trying to help me. I would return to one particular B&B several times.

I remember being there at Christmas and having to share a room with a homeless alcoholic. The empty cans of cheap lager that littered the floor were testament I'd found a new drinking buddy. Across the hall from us was a woman with five children. I knocked on her door on Christmas day and gave her some bags of sweets for the kids. They were overjoyed and the woman was so grateful someone had shown her a bit of kindness. I was able to see that there are many other broken and lonely people, hurting, in the world, people who were far worse off than me, despite my illness and lack of my own home and family. At least I had Jesus Christ as an anchor in my life to stop me from sinking. The tempest raged and storms beat against me, smashing into me, wave after wave, but God was one constant source of help through difficult days.

I sat down with my social worker and we agreed I needed a stable place. She reeled off the places where I'd lived over the last year or so and the total was eighteen. If I was going to get better, I needed stability. A place was found for me at 911 South Yorkshire Housing, residential care for the mentally ill. It was a place where people were given their own rooms but where help was still at hand when needed. It was here that two major things took place. The first incident resulted in me once again, standing in the dock, while the second sickened me and once again drove me to the edge of suicide.

Chapter 37

911

I had better start by telling you about Meg. She was a woman living in 911 when I got there. I introduced myself one day, not long after moving in. She was as lovely as a summer's day. I was immediately attracted to her. Meg had had a rough life, although it hadn't embittered her. Shyness had never been a problem for me. Although I doubted Meg would even think about going out with me, I wasn't going to let that stop me from asking her out. To my surprise and delight, she agreed and we started to see each other.

One afternoon, I was looking out of my bedroom window when I saw two smartly dressed men approach the back entrance to 911. I just sensed they were Old Bill and the thought ran through my mind that they'd come for me. The sound of their walkie-talkies confirmed my suspicions. I briefly considered legging it. I immediately dismissed the thought, knowing God expects me to face up and be accountable for the things I'd done. Sure enough, a minute later there was a knock on my door. It was Joanne one of the staff members. Before she could speak, I said, "The police are here for me, aren't they?" "Yes," she replied. "What have you done?"

The truth was she wasn't the only one eager to know the answer to the question. I went downstairs to face the music, hoping it would be more lullaby than thrash metal. After introducing themselves as CID detectives from West Bar Police Station, one of them told me he had some good news and some bad news. He asked me which I wanted first. I chose the latter and was informed I was being arrested for the breaking, entering and robbery of the church in Essex.

The grubby fingerprints I'd left behind had given me away. Although I'd been miles from home, I may as well have left them my name and address. My own fingerprints betraying me via the Police Database. Hardly the crime of the century but those few biscuits I pinched would cause me to appear in the dock at court once again. They weren't even Hobnobs. I know it's not really something to joke about, as the window I broke needed replacing.

It turned out the apparent good news was they were taking me to the local nick to charge and bail me instead of having to make the long trip down south to be arrested. When I got there, they took a DNA swab and I was placed in a cell with a police officer for company. Because I was a resident at 911 and had a record of being a self-harmer, the risk of me trying to take my own life, was high. I wasn't allowed to be on my own, hence the attention of one of the boys in blue.

We started talking and I told him all about God and what he'd done for me. The officer seemed quite interested and began to ask me questions. I imagine when the officer got out of bed that morning he'd never have guessed he would have the Gospel proclaimed to him.

The cell became my pulpit. I was a preacher with mental health problems, on suicide watch and nicked for breaking and entering.

I was eventually sent back to 911 to wait for a summons to Essex to stand trial. Before the letter came through my letterbox, I would find myself being questioned about a far more serious offence. Although I had nothing to do with it, it would turn my world upside down. Things were going well between Meg and me and I would often tell her about what Jesus meant to me and all God had done for me. She said she wanted the same and began to accompany me to church. Things were about to take a dark turn that would eventually lead to us parting ways.

One particular night, I'd been out with Meg for a drink. She wanted to go on to a nightclub but I needed to go back to 911. I had to take my medication otherwise; I knew I would soon start to feel ill. I encouraged Meg to come back with me but she was adamant she wanted to stay out longer. I didn't like to think of her out on her own, late at night. She promised me she'd be okay and would call her brother to give her a lift home.

Reassured, I caught the bus home while Meg headed for one of Sheffield's nightspots. I returned to 911 and, after taking my medication, called in on Stuart, one of the other residents. We stayed up talking and watching television as I awaited the return of my girlfriend. Time ticked on and I began to wonder where she was. At four in the morning, she finally walked through the door. Her presence didn't release me from my anxiety for her well being because she was not only accompanied by a policewoman but also her mother. I knew immediately something was wrong. It turned out things were very wrong.

To my horror, it transpired Meg had been raped on the way home. The police wouldn't even let me see her. In fact, the first thing they did was to take a statement from me. They wanted to know where I'd been and if anyone could verify my story. I can understand now that the police were just doing their job, but at the time, I felt appalled at the thought of being accused of the rape of my own girlfriend. I wanted to comfort her and find out if she was alright but I wasn't allowed access to her.

Stuart confirmed my testimony and I went back to my room, my head a melting pot of emotions, and none of them good. Anger, remorse and guilt reverberated round and round my brain and caused me to pace back and forth like a caged tiger. When I finally got to see Meg, the truth turned out to be more horrible than I could imagine. She'd set off walking home and on the dark quiet backstreets of Sheffield, had fallen prey to the most heinous of assaults. My beautiful girlfriend, Meg, had been brutally raped by five men.

She was distraught and I didn't know how to help her. She wasn't the only one finding it hard to cope. I blamed myself; I was her boyfriend and should have been there to protect her. From that day on, things were never the same between us. We were in a terrible state and Meg couldn't cope. She would turn up at my door, dripping with blood having cut herself. We'd either call an ambulance or take the bus to A&E,

depending on the severity of her self-inflicted wounds.

For myself, I was trying and failing to help my girlfriend but the truth was I needed help myself. It felt as if I couldn't sink any lower. Pain seared through my mind, my heart and head felt broken. Depression settled on me like a silent blanket of snow, covering everything. I decided I no longer wanted to live and resolved to take my own life in a gruesome and bloody manner. I planned to slice open my stomach, running the blade across and upwards to ensure I inflicted a fatal wound.

At 911, we had our own bedrooms but shared a communal kitchen. That night, I went downstairs and broke the lock on the knife drawer. Forcing it open, I picked out the biggest knife and scurried back upstairs after replacing the drawer. I hoped that no one would notice until it was too late and they found the missing knife beside my cold, lifeless body. Once in my room, I began trying to drive the knife through the soft skin of my belly. To my frustration, my self-destructive plan was thwarted by the fact that the knife wasn't sharp enough, I couldn't get the blade to slice through skin let alone get near my organs. I headed back downstairs and back to the knife drawer, mumbling in frustration.

This time I choose the sharpest one and made my way back to my room. Sitting on the bed, I held the knife over my belly. Gritting my teeth, I plunged the cold sharp steel into my belly. But at that very moment, just as I was about to use the knife in the gruesome act of self-disembowelment, the phone started to ring. It was twelve a clock at night, who could be ringing me at this hour? I paused from my gory job long enough to answer.

"Hello" I sullenly grunted.

"Hey, Nigel," said the familiar voice of Dave Goddard my friend from church. "I know this might seem weird but I had a strong feeling God wanted me to call you. What are you doing right now?"

"I'm stabbing myself" was my blunt but truthful reply.

If Dave was shocked, he didn't let on. "I'm coming over. Put the knife down and tell the staff what you've done. I'll be there in ten minutes," he said calmly.

I put the phone down and looked at the blood pouring from my stomach and wondered if I'd bleed to death before he arrived. I lay down on the bed and waited, my mind swirling and my body beginning to feel the pain. Dave rarely phoned me and never at the dead of night. He couldn't have known that, at that very moment, I was about to end my life. But God knew. He knows my ways, thoughts and words even before they are on my tongue. His love for me astounds me, and I was amazed God would intervene. It was as if God was saying to me that He saw my pain and knew how I felt and loved me, even though I would do stupid and sinful things.

My thoughts were interrupted by Dave coming into the carnage that had become my room. He ushered me out and into his car making a light-hearted comment about not getting blood on his seats. He rushed me to the hospital where I was immediately seen by a doctor. I noticed the man had a cross around his neck and I asked if he was a Christian.

He told me he was, although I can only guess at what he made of the fact that the guy with the gaping self-inflicted wound in his gut was telling him how much he loved Jesus.

His brotherly action was to put his fingers into my wound and have a good poke around which hurt like hell. He told me I was very fortunate that I'd missed all of my major organs. He sewed me up but I was kept in overnight because of the amount of blood I'd lost.

The next morning, I left the hospital. I was grateful to God, for His care and love. I knew God wanted to keep me around and my life was precious in His sight. If it hadn't been for Him, I would have been dead. But sadly this wasn't the end of my troubles and it wouldn't prove to be the last time I thought death was the only way out. Now, I'm able to see clearly this isn't the answer, but back then, I was enveloped in a fog of depression and despair. I had a desire to escape the nightmare of paranoia and fear, which filled my head and would drive me once again, to the edge of the precipice.

Chapter 38

On the Manor

A flat was again found for me. It would be a place of my own in a support housing development. These flats were for people like me, needing a bit of extra help. It was on Eden Hall Road, on the Manor estate. At the time, this was one of the roughest estates in Sheffield. Cars were robbed nightly from better areas and then driven to the Manor and set alight. Sometimes, the fire trucks would be pelted with rocks when called to attend to the flaming vehicles. The quickest way to get to my flat was down a ginnel but local youths who were dealing drugs, would prowl around these cut-throughs like lions stalking a waterhole.

People had experienced bother with these youths. A friend of mine, called Colin, had been involved in some trouble with them and also been pelted with rocks. I had a choice of walking the long way around or running the gauntlet. I chose the latter and was expecting the worst. They never gave me any bother though; I just looked them in the eye and nodded. Whether it was anything to do with me being covered in tattoos and scars or if they'd heard I was an ex-con, I'm not sure.

It was more likely the Lord, going before me to protect me, as life on the Manor estate could be dangerous, sometimes. My friend, Colin, had been beaten up and sexually assaulted returning late at night, inebriated. Colin's was to be a heartbreaking tale, as he was an alcoholic. I would often share the Gospel with him and tell him of the hope and forgiveness found in Jesus Christ but he never listened. He became deeply depressed and troubled. I once found him with twenty packets of paracetamol with which he was planning to end his life. Although I managed to avert his tragic death at that time, it sadly proved only a temporary respite.

Two weeks later, he committed suicide. Once again, death claimed the life of someone I knew, leaving me to wrestle with sadness and the incredulity, I was still living and breathing, although I knew, it was only through the grace of God.

Although Eden Hall Road wasn't the most desirable residence to move to, I was grateful to get out of 911. I was finding it hard to cope with my relationship with Meg. She'd stopped coming to church with me and we began to argue. I couldn't shake the feeling I was to blame for what had happened to her and somehow I should have been able to protect her. She was a mess and her self-harming had spiralled out of control. Things between us weren't good and I saw the move as a way of making a clean break. It wasn't a healthy relationship for either of us, so we parted ways.

I still see her around from time to time but she doesn't talk to me. Maybe she blames me for leaving her when she needed me most, but I can put my hand on my heart and say I did try to help her and, at that time, wasn't fit to support anyone. I had all on just keeping my own head above water. Again, I can look back and see the unseen support and help of the Lord, which kept me going. I have been through deep waters and without the Lord; they would have swept me away.

About this time, I left Living Waters church and joined St Thomas's congregation. When Rob, one of the prison visitors from my time banged up told me about a church that had started meeting at Pond's Forge, a large leisure centre in the heart of the city, I grew excited. I was even more enthused at their next endeavour. St Thomas's was a grand old traditional church building about a mile outside the city centre. They came up with a plan to hire the Roxy nightclub in the city, and hold services there.

Attending one week, I listened eagerly as the leader, Mike Breen, was talking about the crucifixion of Christ. He described in detail the agony and sufferings Jesus went through. He told us how Jesus had been beaten and men spat in His face. How the soldiers twisted sharp thorns into a makeshift mock crown and forced it onto Jesus' head. How they then beat him over the head with a reed given to him as a pretend sceptre. How they flayed the skin from His back by whipping Him. How they stripped Him of His clothes. How they drove nails through His hands and feet, nailing Him to a wooden cross. And how, while He hung there gasping for breath, they laughed at Him and mocked, offering him vinegar for His thirst. As the preacher spoke about the death of Jesus Christ, I began to cry. That the Son of God would suffer and die a shameful death for someone like me moved me to tears. Tears tinged with sadness at what Jesus suffered and tears of joy that through the cross, my sins were forgiven.

Looking around me, I wasn't the only one crying; tears were coursing down the cheeks of everyone around me. I joined the church and offered my services as a handyman to anyone that needed me. It was my way of serving God. I painted the interior of the church and helped out where I could. I had made some good friends at Living Waters but felt it was a time for a fresh start and the Roxy church plant, fired my imagination. I was eager to play a part. A new church wasn't the only new thing.

I met a local woman from the Manor whose previous boyfriend was a local hoodlum. He'd been arrested for a serious offence. She had to visit his flat and dispose of a gun he kept hidden there before the police found it. She ended up taking it down to the local pond and throwing it in. The relationship didn't last long; she left me for someone else.

Talking about guns, I'd heard shots being fired at my windows and had found a bullet embedded in the window frame. When I reported this, the lady on the reception desk asked me if I was taking my medication. She thought I was imagining things, that my paranoia was the thing being set off and not an air rifle. She soon changed her mind when I showed her the bullet marks on the windows. As we were surveying my window, we actually saw a youth in the bushes with an air rifle. He soon legged it when he saw us gawping at him and the police were informed.

I'm not sure if they ever caught him but I had my own date with the court to worry about. The time for me to attend court in Essex was fast approaching. The problem was I didn't have the funds to get all the way to Colchester and no idea how I was going to get there. It was my tramping my way south without money that had led me into trouble in the first place. I had no desire to set off hoping to get there on a wing and a prayer. I didn't possess any wings but I could certainly pray and God was about to answer, the Lord was to provide.

God's provision didn't fall from the sky but from the kindness of a friend's pocket. I'd started playing football with a group of Christians, one of which was a lad called Zach. Giving me a lift home from football one night, he asked about my impending court case and I shared not only my trepidation of any possible prison sentence but how I was struggling to finance my trip south. Zach promptly drove me to his house and then disappeared upstairs. He came down and thrust a brown envelope into my hand. This turned out to contain £90. I was grateful to the Lord and to Zach and decided to ask Keith and Andrea if they would consider driving me down to Essex and supporting me while I stood before the court. They agreed and I gave them the £90.

We used it for petrol and to stop for some breakfast on the way. I managed to eat something, not knowing if it would be prison food I'd be tasting for my next meal. While I knew I hadn't committed the crime of the century, I was aware someone with my record could easily be given a custodial sentence. So on 23rd of November 2000, I stood in the dock and received a fine of £250. We celebrated by stopping for a meal on the way back and they gave me a tenner, leftover from the ninety quid I'd given them. I used it to buy cigarettes and groceries as my cupboards were bare. I hadn't known if I'd be coming home or doing time. I was thankful I hadn't been incarcerated.

I vowed the next judge I would stand in front of would be the Lord Jesus Christ on that great day, when all will have to stand before God's judgement seat. While the judge in Essex had found me guilty, I know on that final day I won't be condemned but pronounced not guilty because I believe in Jesus Christ who lived, died and rose again for all those who believe in Him. I hoped to hear Jesus' words say to me, well done good and faithful servant enter into the rest prepared from be-fore the foundation of the world. The truth was, at this time, I was far from behaving like a good and faithful servant of Christ.

While my words seemed to improve, my behaviour didn't. Although I was no longer given to stealing, I had another vice, I found harder to stop. One area the Lord enabled me to improve in was my dialogue; I began to swear much less. For years and years, cussing had been my native tongue. Expletives were second nature to me and peppered my speech. This could be embarrassing when a swear word slipped out while conversing with people. That language wouldn't have raised an eyebrow in prison but in private and especially in church circles, it could shock and offend. God gave me a breakthrough and the swear words melted away from my lips. Of course, I can't say I don't ever swear.

Sometimes, in stressful situations, I can fall back to bad language to express my distress.

It may seem like God was taking a speck out of my eye and leaving the log when I confess to you what I was up to while living on the Manor. I was lonely and craved company. But if I'm being totally honest, which is very painful for me, it's wasn't just loneliness that fuelled my desire. It was another word beginning with L, lust. I started to hire prostitutes that would come to my house.

This is a sin that the Bible gives a stark warning about and one of the worst sins possible. I didn't really know much about the Bible back then, and I still don't know enough now. I'd attend church on a Sunday and be encouraged at the worship, teaching, preaching and fellowship of other Christians. But I neglected the basic principles of the Christian life of praying and reading the Scriptures. A car that only puts a small amount of fuel in once a week will soon cough and sputter its way to a halt. This seemed to be a good metaphor for me at this time.

Sunday became Monday and by the time it melted into Tuesday I was spiritually running on empty and not living the life I should, not only ignoring all Biblical teaching but I was ignorant about what the Scriptures taught. I decided it would be good if I could meet some Christians who lived near me, from whom I could find friendship and support. I rang a local church and explained what had happened to me that I had been in prison and suffered from mental health problems. I told them I was now out of jail and living on the Manor, I asked if they could send someone to visit me or put me in touch with any Christians living in the area.

The man who I talked with said they'd try to help me; he took my address and assured me someone would call on me. A few weeks went by and I thought they had forgotten all about me, until, one day, a knock at my door revealed a rather nervous and timid looking bloke named Peter. He explained he'd been sent by the church and I invited him in and put the kettle on.

What I didn't know at the time, was that Peter's wife, Frankie, had been filled with fear at the prospect of him visiting an ex-con with a long list of mental health issues. She'd actually told him that if he wasn't back in two hours, she would call the police. Peter's fears soon began to melt as he asked me about myself and I began to pour out my story. We had a long chat and I was able to ask Peter questions about the Bible. I felt at ease with this man and after a rather cautious beginning, Peter soon opened up and spoke freely about God. All of a sudden, he jumped up, saying he had to go, remembering Frankie's words and no doubt, imagining her dialling 999. Peter was to become a good friend and remains so to this day but it wasn't until sometime later, I found out the reason for his hasty exit.

I continued my double life, one that to some may seem a contradiction in terms. I was a Christian, on one hand, I loved God and on the other, I was still struggling with the sins of drugs, drink and lust. My lack of knowledge of the Scriptures was no excuse. Back then, I wasn't so stupid that I didn't realise I was doing wrong. I knew full well Christians, and indeed all mankind, were urged to be pure and holy but the urges that raged inside me were strong. I had the new life of God inside me and yet, I still had the old me, a man of sin. I should have endeavoured to live for the new nature and to turn away from my former life.

But whilst I loved God, I still lusted after things that would be pleasurable for a moment but ultimately of no lasting spiritual good. It's probably not a great analogy but if you have two dogs, one tame and the other rabid, whichever one you feed will become stronger. The Bible urges Christians to seek to live for this new life and to reckon ourselves dead to sin and living selfishly with no thought to God. Nowadays, the rabid dog of my sinful desires is, with the Lord's help, kept on a much shorter lead.

But if the truth were told, I didn't try hard enough to resist the temptations to satisfy my base instincts by paying for sex. I used women's bodies for my own selfish desires instead of respecting and cherishing them. Instead of saving myself for someone special that I could marry and make love to, I made lust with these women.

I ask you not to give up on me. God never has, despite my awful actions. I know you may find it hard to stomach some of the things you have read about me. The road of redemption God has had to lead me on has been long, narrow and difficult and many times, I've veered off, slipping into the sewers and gutters. But the Lord has always led me back, with His kindness and grace. I would soon need His support and care once again, as my vow not to stand before another judge was left in tatters.

Chapter 39

Edge of Eternity

I failed to keep up my bail condition of reporting to my social worker as my mental health again, took a nosedive. A warrant was issued for my arrest. I was kicked out of Eden Hall Road so once again, found myself homeless.

I was sent to Doncaster prison. I thought I had finished with the harsh prison environment and was devastated to be locked up again. After a week, I was summoned before a judge. The fact I'd been unable to keep my vow is probably no surprise to you. There was no place suitable to which I could be discharged so I was sent back to prison and ordered to appear the next day before the judge. This happened for almost two weeks. Every morning, I'd be carted off to the court, and every afternoon, sent back to the nick. It was like Groundhog Day.

At this point, I was still beset with the addictions to drink and nicotine, in prison, I would be denied access to both of these. Not if I could help it though, I came up with a plan to change this. I got my solicitor to bring me some Rizlas, tobacco and a lighter. Having acquired this contraband, I was then faced with the problem of smuggling it back into the nick.

All prisoners were searched on the way in, so there was only one place that I could hide my prohibited items. Fitting all three of these things in that small crevice proved both challenging and painful. A silly phrase I've sometimes heard people say is that something is up my bum on the second shelf. In my case, that wasn't far off from being factually correct as I wrapped these items in the cellophane from my sandwiches. I then proceeded to push them as far as they'd go into the dark nether regions of my rectum. At the time, I thought it worth it to be able to relax and smoke in my cell at night. Later on in life, after two bowel operations, I would hold a very different opinion.

After two weeks of being a human yo-yo, bouncing from clink to court, a place was found for me in a bail hostel. I walked out of the prison doors for what I hope and trust will be the very last time. It was 2002 and my life was to get better but not before it got worse.

Soon, I was on the move again, getting a place at The Thursday Project, a facility that housed mentally ill people and offered counselling for three years. They also gave advice and tuition on budgeting, money management, cooking and other life -skills all of which would benefit me.

Although I appreciated the help, it couldn't stop the horrible torment in my head on the bad days. I sought the support of the mental health experts. The psychiatrist I saw seemed to be dismissive of my symptoms and the torment and pain I was experiencing. I also probably upset him by talking about Jesus. I've always shared my faith with basically everyone I've come into contact with, including the support workers and mental health professionals tasked with my care.

A friend of mine recently advised me to concentrate on my illness when talking with my psychiatrist. I understand this advice and I know he wants me to receive the best possible care, but asking me not to evangelise and share my faith, is like cutting off my right hand. Even back then, when I wasn't walking the walk, I was always talking the talk. I guess it was questionable how effective my witness was when I got upset and angry that the medical professionals were unable and seemingly unwilling to help me.

The professionals and I had our mutual frustrations. Once, when I told the manager of the day centre that I felt like jumping through the window, his retort was, "Well, why don't you then?"

Things weren't great between us and they didn't seem to understand. I needed help to cope with my paranoia. Round and round my brain like snowflakes in a storm, these thoughts could last for days before subsiding.

One day, I felt that everything had become too much. Ignored by the medical profession and even worse, my own muddled thinking, I felt like God had abandoned me. I knew the devil wanted me to kill myself. I came to this misguided conclusion and also that God wouldn't care if I ended my own life.

God had always been my rock, my shield and song in the darkest of nights. In the short time I'd been a Christian, if I set up a monument stone every time God had helped me it would have dwarfed Stonehenge. I was indebted to God's kindness but now I did not only doubt Him, but was deeply deluded. I climbed up to the roof of the multi-storey flats where I lived, intending to throw myself off and end it all.

I almost achieved my intention on the way up to the roof. With my feet precariously perched on the balcony rail, I had to haul myself up by swinging from the rickety old guttering. How it managed to take my considerable bulk without giving way and sending me crashing to the ground, I can only wonder. I made my way to the rooftop in one piece, but I wasn't planning on keeping it that way for long.

Once up there, I felt something or someone stopping me from jumping to my death. A battle was going on in my mind as I paced up and down the rooftop. Just feet away, was the edge and a drop of a hundred feet. I tried to ring Sky News, this may seem bizarre but I wanted to highlight the plight of the mentally ill and to explain the despair of those suffering its torments. I wanted my death to make a difference. I didn't want anyone else to suffer needlessly, having medical professionals tell them nothing was wrong. I also phoned Dave Goddard, to say goodbye. He tried to reason with me but I hung up on him. This time he wouldn't be unable to help, or so I thought. I made my way to the edge of the roof and stared downwards. The hot sun beat down on me and the sweat from my brow started to run down my face, caused by a mixture of the agony I was feeling inside and the hazy heat.

It wasn't long before I could see the emergency services arrive below. The fire engines, police cars and an ambulance waited below, ready to scrape up what little would be left of me. This is what I thought I wanted. Somehow, though, I couldn't manage to jump. I knew it wasn't fear, I'd abused my body for so long and was used to pain. It was the reality of the final small step out into the fresh air that would lead to oblivion that would propel me into the presence of my maker. What would He say to me? I only heard what the fireman that clambered up the ladder said. He tried his best to talk me down, so did the police officers.

I wouldn't come down; I felt I couldn't return to all the pain. My head was a mess and it wasn't getting any better. Minutes ticked by and the torments continued. My life remained in the balance and my dilemma deepened. Another figure came up the ladder, this time it wasn't a faceless uniform who didn't know me, it was my friend from church, Danny Smith. Dave Goddard had phoned him, as he knew Danny could get to me much quicker.

"What's going on Nigel? asked Danny. His calm voice and familiar face were soothing, I began to feel a little less stressed.

"Danny, I've had enough, I feel so done in. I want to throw myself off this building. I can't stand the thoughts in my head and I want to end it all", I told him honestly, the emotion in my voice bearing witness to my inner turmoil.

He asked me, "Whose thoughts are you listening to Nigel, the devil's or God's?" This immediately made me consider what God would really want me to do and what He had already done for me.

"The devil's", I replied honestly.

"Well, he's a liar and has been from the beginning. You need to listen to God and what He's saying."

Danny told me afterwards that as soon as Dave rang him, he had begun to pray for me. The Scripture that came forcibly into his mind was Psalm 118.

I shall not die but live, and declare the works of the Lord.

Whilst I didn't know the Lord had spoken that verse to Danny, I did know He'd already rescued me from suicide before and seemed to be doing it again. At that moment, the fog of depression lifted for a moment. I was able to think clearly. I knew God still felt the same towards me. People may desert you in your hour of need, the darkness of my mental illness may consume and overwhelm me but God remains the same, always righteous and holy, full of goodness, light and love. I knew He cared for and loved me. His will for my life was not to plummet to the pavement but to climb down and face my fears and problems. Thinking about God, everything became clear and I came down from the edge.

The police took me to the hospital where I saw a psychiatrist. I broke down while trying to tell them about the pain and turmoil in my mind, ending up in floods of tears. I know it may be difficult for those who have never experienced mental health problems to understand what I was going through, I couldn't just pull myself together, and I felt like I was being torn apart. I had been diagnosed with five separate mental illnesses. I remember around this time, coming out of a meeting with my health care workers, I returned to ask to borrow a pen to fill in some forms. As I did so, the team were still talking about me; I heard one of them say he didn't think I was going to make it. He wasn't the first to think my mental health would one day drive me to take my own life. Indeed, in the blackest moments, I shared his sentiments myself.

Coping with my illness was sometimes very difficult and trying. If you ever stand watching the clothes in a washing machine being thrown around, it will give you an idea how my head felt sometimes. Some days were much better than others. I was given an injection every two weeks of a drug called Clopixol. It was used on those suffering from chronic psychoses. Some days, I certainly felt chronic alright. Back then, if my memory serves me right, you could have up to 500mg of Clopixol. I was given 200mg fortnightly but I often told Laura, my community psychiatric nurse, to give me the full dose in one go. Looking back now, I know Laura was a good woman who did her best to help me, but I became distrustful of her due to my paranoia. I hope to meet her again so I can apologise and tell her I was in the wrong. This is the case for a lot of the people I met back then.

I used to attend Howard Road day centre. Here, I would tell all the staff about Jesus, I know I got on their nerves quite a few times. I know people don't want: what they see as religion rammed down their throats and that we have to be sensitive, gentle and kind in sharing our faith. Admittedly, I haven't always lived up to these standards in preaching the Gospel. But at least I can say, hand on heart, it was from a motive of care and concern for the welfare of people's souls that I told them about forgiveness and eternal life, that comes through faith in Jesus Christ.

Imagine if someone was walking towards a steep cliff edge, with the sharp jagged edges of the rocks waiting hundreds of feet below. Would you be happy to let people continue on until it was too late and they tumble over the precipice, to be dashed to pieces on the rocks? Of course, you wouldn't, not if you're a kind and caring person. How then could I not warn people about eternal punishment? One way I used to do this at the day centre was to leave out Gospel tracts and flyers on a side table so people could read them whilst waiting.

I would often find these dumped in the rubbish bin by the staff and would fish them out and leave them again. I was called into the office and given a warning. I wasn't going to let that stop me. They could rip up my tracts but they couldn't rip up my desire for people to read about the great God of love.

It was there that I met a wonderful lady, called Christine Dunwell. She was very kind and caring but always told me I was wrong about God. I thought all my words and prayers weren't making a difference but God had other ideas. A couple of years later, I was in a church meeting and in walked Christine. She came over and told me she'd become a Christian. I can't tell you how happy it made me. It gives me a renewed hope to pray for people even if they reject and rubbish the good news about God.

I'm aware some people think my faith is a symptom of my mental illness this is simply not true. All people need God and it's no different for those suffering mental health problems. Many stigmatise people like me, God doesn't. He loves all mankind and desires they come to a knowledge of the truth and be saved. Yes, I suffer mental health problems, even to this day, but it doesn't disqualify me from walking and witnessing for God.

I still need help and treatment for my illness and I'm grateful for the medical professionals that God has provided. Some I haven't got on with, a clash of personalities, and others have been kind, patient and caring. One such lady was my support worker from this time, her name is Marianne. She was such a good listener. The Bible says we should be slow to talk and quick to listen, I know this isn't like me. I open my mouth sometimes before engaging my brain. I tend to jump straight in with my size 10's where angels would fear to tread. I can't have been the easiest patient to deal with down the years and I appreciate all the care I've been given. I pray my testimony bears fruit with all these health service professionals.

Chapter 40

'Philly'

At this point, I decided to move to a new church, St Thomas Philadelphia. The decision to move wasn't just down to me being restless and desiring the new and exciting. The church did a lot of work with the homeless and recovering addicts. Not only did I think God could help me through this church, but I also wanted to help others like me. I loved learning about God and meeting new people. The thing about Christians is they generally accept and love you for who you are. There can be an almost instant bond of brotherhood. Of course, in the church are a rich variety of people from different places, classes and personalities. In life, we all get on with some people more easily than others and it's no different in the church.

No doubt, some people in the church would have little or nothing in common with me and perhaps, were wary of a rough -looking ex-con. Others may not have known what to say to me or could have just been quiet or shy. When I met brothers and sisters in the church who didn't seem to want to talk to me, I struggled. I have to work hard with my feelings and paranoia, not to start resenting them. God calls us to love one another and this is especially true of fellow Christians. And I'm happy to say, although there are exceptions to the rule, there is usually a warm welcome inside God's church. This is born out of the fact that, no matter what the differences are, age, sex, or where you come from we, have one thing in common. We are all saved by God's kindness and mercy by believing in Jesus Christ. I didn't have any family in Sheffield but I knew there were many Christians who I could call brother and sister because we'd all been adopted and become children of God.

It was at Philly I was introduced to a Christian organisation called

Streetwise. They held meetings every morning. We had many homeless people and ex-convicts, people who were struggling with life. A warm welcoming atmosphere of love was offered to all at these meetings. Through patience and care, much good was done. As well as help with the practicalities of life, the Gospel was shared. It was here they tried to teach me how to cook.

I'm sure if you had tasted anything I produced, you would have said tried was the right word. I won't be appearing on Masterchef any time soon but what little culinary skills I possess are down to Streetwise.

Whilst cooking wasn't my forte, I once again, used my DIY skills around the church. I also remember helping a friend Phil Kelly gut his house in Crookes. Gut was the word, as I remember standing in the rubble of his front room looking upwards at the attic ceiling. It was hard graft but we put the house back together. We would spend all day working on it, breaking off only to grab a fishcake butty special. If you've never tried one, let me recommend the famous Sheffield delicacy.

I also remember waiting with Phil for the plumber, he told me when the plumber arrived, he'd be singing the song, Yellow Submarine. Whilst we were waiting for him to arrive, we had to break up an old cast iron bath to get it outside. Phil said I'd have no chance of smashing it into pieces as they were built to withstand anything. Two blows of my lump hammer later and we were carrying it out in three pieces. Lo and behold, when the plumber turned up, he was singing the Beatles classic about a colourful underwater boat. I looked at Phil, opened-mouthed and he started laughing. He wasn't the prophet of pop though. When he'd met with the plumber that morning Phil had been singing Yellow Submarine. He told me he knew the song would have stuck in the plumber's brain and he would, subconsciously, be singing it all day.

Along with Phil, I made many good friends at Philly. One particular fruitful one from this time was with one of the leaders, Paul Maconachie. He would spend time with me and had a genuine heart of love that manifested itself in caring and praying for me. He's long since moved to America to pastor a church, but he still checks on me today.

Back then, I would come to the church every morning at 9am. We had a time of prayer and sang worship songs. One day, when I was waiting for the service to start I put Phil's theory to the test and softly began to sing and hum my favourite hymns. Pete James, who was in charge of choosing the music then, would unknowingly pick the very ones I'd been singing. This went on day after day, it was like a request show but without having to ask, just hum. Of course, Pete had no idea but thought he was choosing the songs himself without my coercion. Until one day when he caught me laughing at the songs he'd chosen and the penny dropped. Luckily, he saw the funny side.

While God forgives all our sins, we still have to live with the consequences of our past actions. One of which saw me hospitalised once again. This time it wasn't my brain that was the problem but my bowels. Well, I suppose it was my lack of brains that caused it in the first place. I'd better warn you first, if you're reading this book with a coffee and about to munch a sweet treat, this next bit may see you lose your appetite for your piece of carrot cake.

One morning, I started to suffer from terrible pains in my stomach. My friend, Tom, was coming round to see me later that day but I'm afraid, I wasn't much company. All I could do was lie on the settee, clutching my gut in agony waiting for the pain to subside. Instead of easing, things got worse and along with the excruciating pain in my breadbasket, I started to vomit. At first, my sick was alarmingly bright green in colour. Once I started to spew, I didn't stop and the colour of the stuff I was puking up, turned to dark green. I lay there all day waiting to feel better and when I couldn't take any more, I rang the doctors and explained the way I was feeling and my symptoms. The doctor said she would co me and see me. As I was waiting, the bucket next to my settee was continuing to fill up with stuff being hacked up from what felt like the deepest innards of my being. The colour once again changed, from dark green to brown. I couldn't believe there was anything left inside me but it wouldn't stop coming. The doctor took one look at me and rang for an ambulance. I rang my friend, Tchad Western, and he came to pick up Tom, who had stuck with me through my groans and gagging all day. Tchad and Tom followed the ambulance to the Hallamshire Hospital.

Once there, I was given a room on my own as I was still bringing up brown gunk. We developed a chain to dispose of this unpleasant regurgitation. The doctor would pass the paper bowl full of my upchucking to Tchad who, in turn, gave it to Tom. Finally, the nurse would deposit my vile vomit into the toilet. To say I felt awful was an understatement and I remember asking the doctor if I was going to die. She said I wouldn't but the look of concern on her face, failed to reassure me. It may seem a bit melodramatic but that's how bad I felt. Tchad was there praying for me and assuring me everything would be alright. Eventually, my Vesuvius of vomit died down and I was given a respite.

The next morning I was made to drink a massive bowl of chalky white liquid. I think they used it to give a clear picture on the x-ray. The scan revealed part of my bowel had been damaged and I would need an operation to remove seven inches of it that no longer functioned properly. Me using my rectum to secretly store contraband, was now coming back to bite me, almost literally, in the bottom. The pain I had suffered was no laughing matter and I had to wait a few months for my operation. That too, wasn't without its drama thanks to me telling a lie.

I remember coming round after the operation and Phil was sitting with me, holding my hand. I thanked him for being there and tried to move. I was in agony and even lifting a cup of water involved me suffering. They had to administer morphine and I was away with the fairies in la la land for a while. Gradually, I was weaned off the morphine as the pain subsided. I had been in hospital a couple of days when they told me I could go home when my bowels opened. I was eager to go back home, not least because I needed a drink. My body was reacting now to the shock of alcohol withdrawal. The doctors, however, wouldn't let me leave until they knew my bowel was working properly. I got fed up waiting and told them I was fully operational again in this department. I figured I'd put so much stuff up in that area, not only would I be able to pass stools but I probably manage a table as well.

I left the hospital and, after alighting the tram, the first thing I did was purchase a twenty- four pack of lager. I'd almost ruined one organ and was now showing no concern for another, my liver. The truth is I did care but had tried and failed to stop drinking on numerous occasions. I went home and cracked open a can. But that's the only thing I managed to open, as my bowel refused to work of its own accord. By the next day, I felt as bloated as a helium balloon. Twenty-four hours later, I started to suffer pain and had to return to the hospital and explain the situation.

I was re-admitted after being admonished by the staff and spent another couple of days enjoying the hospitality of the NHS. Finally, after some prompting, my bowel gave up its industrial action and normal service resumed. I would go on to need a further operation. I'm so grateful to the medical staff that I was able to be operated on and get things put right. I'm hoping I'll never have to endure that pain again, that my actions brought about. I guess the moral of the story is, don't put things where they aren't supposed to go.

Chapter 41

Growing in Grace

I found out Nicky Gumbel would be speaking at a meeting at Philly. Nicky Gumbel is the man behind the Alpha course that I'd watched in prison. God had used this man and his gospel message to soften my heart and set me on the path that eventually led me to become a Christian. Before the meeting began, I went up to Nicky as he was preparing his notes. I told him excitedly how I had completed the Alpha course when I was in prison. I explained that I used to rob houses and was a violent man but now, I belonged to Jesus. To my shock, Nicky asked me if I would repeat what I'd told him in the meeting. I said I would and made my way back to my seat. Before sitting down, I sought out one of the leaders and asked him to pray for me. I felt so far out of my comfort zone, my legs felt like jelly.

When I sat down, the nerves got even worse. I began to regret agreeing to address a room packed to the rafters. Every seat was taken and people were standing at the back. There were over 800 there that afternoon. Who was I kidding? I was no elegant speaker. I prayed, asking God to be with me and that everything I said would bring Him glory. When Nicky introduced me, my heart was pounding louder than any policeman's knock I'd ever heard. I've stood in many docks in my life but was never as fearful as that day I stood in the pulpit. I looked out, surveying the sea of faces waiting for me to address them and felt numb with fear. Please Lord Help was my silent and succinct prayer. The Lord answered my prayer and touched my stammering lips, enabling me to tell of his goodness and mercy towards a criminal like me.

Afterwards, Nicky thanked me and offered me his hand to shake. Being the man I am, I ignored it and pulled him towards me giving him the biggest bear hug he'd probably ever had. Here we were embracing, a well spoken, and well to do vicar and an ex-con who had only one thing in common. We both loved Jesus. I think I embarrassed Nicky with my over- exuberant greeting but I couldn't help it, I was so grateful for how God had used this man in my life. Instead of waking up in jail, I'd wake up and go to church every day. Every day we'd sing and worship and every day, the Pastor would pray with me.

Over the years, God answered many of his prayers on my behalf. I committed myself to daily get up from my bed and seek God's face. God is no man's debtor and rewards those who ask, seek and knock. God brought about two minor miracles in my life. I only call them minor because to most people the two things God freed me from wouldn't seem so important or hard to give up. But let me assure you, these two habits had been with me for years and were part of my everyday life. They'd long become ingrained and had become part of my obsessive personality.

The first was chewing gum. I was spending a few quid a day on it. My mouth was often dry with an unpleasant taste due to the medication I was taking. The other habit was biting my nails. I used to rip off toe and fingernails in prison and chew and swallow them. I'm sorry I know that sounds disgusting but it's what I did. I found the physical pain of pulling out my nails an escape from the mental torments I experienced. Even when God had taken away my desire to self-harm and I found fulfilment in Him, I would still constantly bite my nails. I had to be doing something and if it wasn't chewing gum, it was my nibbling on my nails. God took these two obsessions away and it was a wonderful answer to prayer. Yes, I still had more serious addictions and habits to break but I took great encouragement and it gave me hope. If God had taken away these two things, He would also deliver me from drink and drugs. Another thing God took away at this time was the pain that would shoot down my neck. God did this by healing me of the neck injury I'd sustained all those years ago, tussling with the police.

Slowly I began to change. Bit by bit, God was doing a work in my heart and soul. I began to learn to take care of myself better. Since becoming a Christian, I'd desired to live a holy life. To live in a way that would please my heavenly Father. But now, that desire was gradually becoming a practice. Of course, I still had so far to go, I still seemed to get things wrong and I knew that, as the apostle Paul stated, in me was nothing good. (Romans 7:18)

Paul called himself the chief of sinners (1 Timothy 1:15) but I'm not being flippant when I say that if he was chief, I felt myself to be king. Thank God for Jesus Christ because of whom my sins will never be counted against me. Nevertheless, I began to grow in grace and when I did mess up, I had Christians around me to keep me from going off the deep end.

They were needed in one such incident. We were driving away from a church meeting and hadn't gone far when we saw a youth stealing a bike from a smaller child. We stopped the car and rescued this kid from having his bike nicked. Once back in the car the older boy started mouthing off at us. My friend who was driving got out of the car, asking me to stay inside. He assured me he would handle the situation. By this time, others had walked the short distance from the church. It was soon clear that, try as he may, my mate wasn't handling the situation. It was escalating to the point that the youth jumped onto his car.

Of course, the first thing I did was try to get out of the car. People stood in front of the car door to block my exit. I didn't want to force my way out of the car and push them but I wanted to get this youth down from surfing my friend's car and, no doubt, damaging it. I wasn't planning on beating him up but I also wasn't planning on pleading with him. I know my friends only had my best interests at heart and knew very well, with my police record that any trouble would probably see me, once again, residing at her Majesty's pleasure behind bars. I suppose it was for the best because if the youth had lashed out at me when I was toppling him from the Toyota, I would probably have given him a slap. Thankfully, the situation finally came to a halt when the local landlady came out of the pub. The youth jumped down and my friend got back in the car and we drove away. As we did so a police van came round the corner, someone must have phoned them. We drove away and although there were dents in my friend's car and in my pride, no one had been hurt or injured, and the child got his bike back, so I had to be thankful.

Chapter 42

On the Streets

It was also while at Philly, that I started going out on the streets of Sheffield to tell people the good news about Jesus. A group from the church would meet up every Saturday afternoon in the city centre. There is a little garden area at a place called Barkers Pool and we'd set up camp there once a week. Every Saturday, I'd visit the local Christian bookshop and purchase string and brightly coloured balloons emblazoned with the message, Jesus Loves You. I'd tie them to the railings in the garden area. If any of the children wanted a balloon, I'd untie one if their parents said it was okay. We also brought a big banner to display, proclaiming just a single word, healing.

There'd been a movement all around the country called healing on the streets. Christians would offer to pray for people who needed healing. Our church was one among many that took to the streets. It was my job to ask people if they needed prayer and to lead them into the garden if they responded positively. I enjoyed being a soldier for Christ on the front line. I'd found Jesus Christ who is the way, truth and life and it felt wrong to withhold from others this wonderful message even if many that walked the streets of Sheffield, didn't want to hear it. We prayed for many people and saw God do amazing things, healing many from various ailments. After praying for people, we'd talk to them about God.

One of the most effective and fearless at sharing the Gospel was a young girl called Sophie. She had only just become a Christian and was so delighted and full of joy at what God had done for her, she came with us to share her faith. Sophie was the girlfriend of my friend, Roger's son, and had been looking into Islam and becoming a Muslim at the time.

Her boyfriend was going away on a holiday he'd booked before he met her, leaving her alone and with time on her hands. I asked Sophie if she'd like to come to church with me. She agreed and I arranged to meet her where she got off the tram, in the town centre.

We got to church an hour before the service started. As we were waiting, I shared my story with her and told her all about what God had done for me. She listened quietly and didn't say a word. I thought that perhaps I'd said too much. I hoped my witnessing hadn't been too pushy and put her off. I prayed for a good gospel message to be preached, a simple talk about why Jesus died on a cross. I hoped the speaker would explain to Sophie why she needed forgiveness, and how to become a Christian. I was disappointed as the preacher only spoke for ten minutes and said nothing I thought to which a non -Christian would relate.

As the service finished, I was thinking, what a missed opportunity this was and that I'd wasted my time asking this young woman to church. Thankfully, God had other ideas. Much to my surprise, Sophie turned to me and told me she wanted to become a Christian, asking me what she needed to do to believe in Jesus and be saved. My heart nearly jumped out of my chest and I asked her to follow me to the front of the church.

We found one of the leaders, Toby, and I repeated what Sophie had told me. He asked to be excused and said he needed to talk to someone and would be back in five minutes. I couldn't believe it. Here was this girl, wanting to come to Christ and Toby had swanned off to chat with someone. Thankfully, he was as good as his word and did return in a few minutes. After chatting to her and making sure she was serious and knew what she was doing, Toby led Sophie in a prayer that expressed her sorrow for ignoring God, breaking His laws and commandments and living for herself. She committed to follow Jesus for the rest of her life.

That night Sophie found fulfilment and forgiveness in God. She found the pearl of great price, Jesus Christ in whom is hidden all treasure of wisdom and assurance. She knew she was now a child of God. Sophie still loves and follows Jesus Christ today. She's still as passionate about sharing the Gospel as she was back in 2002 when she first came to know the Lord. Needless to say, her boyfriend got quite a shock when he returned. They didn't stay together but I'm delighted to say that I attended her wedding in the spring of 2020.

Another story from the Saturday street work is Richard. Every Saturday, I began to notice the same man walk past us at the same time. The man always fixed us with a steely stare without a hint of a smile. He was a big, rough-looking man with a shaved head and goatee beard. Every week, I'd offer him a flyer and he'd walk by without taking one or saying a word. I would tell him, every week that Jesus loved him as he walked off into the distance. I never let his silent rejection put me off and always said these same words as he passed me by. Roger told me that I was wasting my time with this man.

After one morning service at Philly had finished, I headed off for the city centre and attended a church called Charis that met in the afternoon. One day, sitting on the back row as usual, I looked across and saw a man I recognised. It took me a few seconds to realise that this was the man who had walked past me for months on end. I went over and shook his hand. He told me his name was Richard. He'd come to church because his best friend had been telling him about Jesus for a long time, as well as being pestered by me every Saturday.

I'm pleased to tell you, Richard gave his life to Jesus and is still serving Him years later. What's more, Richard and I became good friends and I learnt that he too had experienced a troubled childhood, ending up in Borstal. His life was transformed by God. I never know what's going on in the lives of those I'm talking to on the street, and who else God is using to speak to people. A seed planted needs tending and watering. My intervention with people may be the first time people come into contact with the gospel and I may be planting a seed. Or it may be that others have told them the good news about Jesus before, and my witness to them is the watering of the seed that others have planted. Whatever the case, it's only God that can bring life and causes the flower of faith to form, bloom and grow. I'm only one of God's messengers of mercy, a herald proclaiming the Gospel of the King and it's wonderful and encouraging to know that God uses a fool like me, to open the spiritual eyes of men and women. He used me despite all the challenges and problems I was wrestling with back then.

Although I was faithfully attending church and loving God, I was still battling drink and drugs. I continued to meet with my non -Christian friends to drink. I remember a woman in the church calling me over and talking to me about giving up these friends. I didn't want to give them up because they needed Jesus as I told them regularly.

"But Nigel, they will lead you astray because bad company corrupts good character," this lady informed me.

But, I hated being alone. I told her I needed the company and it wasn't good for someone like me to sit alone night after night. This is when the fear and paranoia would fill the vacuum in my life. She replied that, if I gave up these friends who led me into dark places and bad environments, God would provide people who would care and love me. At the time, I wasn't willing to listen to this good and godly advice.

Now I can see that I was like a man trying not to get burnt and then continuing to place his hands into the flame. My friends' habits of drinking and recreational drug use were a fire that my tinder-wood defences shouldn't have been around. As hard as I'd try to be free from these things, a spark from my friends' bad habits would ignite my addictions. I refused to let my friends go but God would cause us gradually to grow apart. The lady was right; God has given me some very special people in my life to take their place. Friends who instead of trying to get me to partake in ungodly living, encourage, support and show me unconditional love.

Back then a group of us would meet up at each other's places to drink cans of lager or go to various pubs for a pint. I would sometimes invite Rob, who had been my prison visitor. Rob has been a faithful friend down through the years and is an outstanding Christian. He is patient and kind, he would sit and talk about God or just hang out with our little gang as we drank and smoked. When he returned home, his sister used to make him put all his clothes in the wash and get in the shower, because they reeked of nicotine after being in our presence.

I remember one particular night, four or five of us had caught the train to Mexborough, a suburb of Rotherham. After a few pints, we fell into a disagreement with some local youths who far outnumbered us. One of these youths was particularly aggressive and argumentative. I managed to persuade our lot to relocate to another pub. Making our way back to catch the last train, who should we run into but the youth that had been the ringleader. Now he was on his own, probably making his way home too. One of our crowd, Big Pete, told him just what he thought of him and offered to fight him one on one. To give the youth his credit he didn't back down, it looked like it was all going to kick off. This wouldn't have been a happy ending for the youth, despite his bravado; Peter's nickname wasn't ironic like Robin Hood's, Little John. Big Pete was so called because he was built like a brick outhouse. He wasn't someone you'd want to meet down a dark alley, which is basically, what this youth had had the misfortune to do.

I could have shrugged my shoulders and decided that this mouthy bloke deserved all that he was about to get. Frankly, I had seen enough violence and bloodshed in prison to last me a lifetime. I knew that I had to intervene otherwise this youth would be carrying his teeth home in his pocket, if he made it home at all. A hospital bed would have been his likely destination as Big Pete could handle himself. Thankfully, I got between them and managed to diffuse the situation. We caught the train home without a punch being thrown.

Also out with me that night, was Jim. I've changed his name as the story I'm about to tell is quite disturbing. At the end of the night, he told me he'd lost his keys, so of course, I offered him the chance to stay at my place on the sofa. Being paranoid, I always used to push my wardrobe up against the bedroom door when anyone stayed over. This particular evening, I forgot, went straight to bed and drifted off to sleep.

I woke up sometime later with a start. Jim was standing over me with a kitchen knife in his hand. His eyes were open and he was staring at me. I flew out of bed and screamed at him, "what are you doing?", or words to that effect. He apologised then turned to leave the room. I closed the door behind him and barricaded it with the wardrobe. I can tell you it took me a while to get back to sleep that night. He'd given me a terrifying shock. The next morning, I woke him up to find out what had happened. His story was that he'd been sleepwalking. I told him he needed to leave and he magically found his keys that he'd lost the night before.

Needless to say, I didn't bother hanging around with Jim after that. I'm sure that incident would be enough to put anyone off, never mind someone who suffers from paranoia. Perhaps it was the Lord's providence towards me, that I should break my ties with Jim. At the time, I was trying to stop drinking because, if truth be told, I was an alcoholic. When out with Jim, I would start off on pints of cola but he'd always encourage me to have lager.

He was most insistent, telling me that I wouldn't sleep without it.

Drugs and drink had been a part of my life for such a long time and were addictions I couldn't get free from. I would go to church, worship God and then at night get drunk. When living at Upperthorpe, I would walk up to the shops and carry a pack of twenty-four cans back with me. Sometimes, I'd catch a taxi back, nursing my alcohol on my knee like it was my baby. I needed to be free from alcohol because it controlled me. This would have been very difficult with Jim in my ear hole; constantly encouraging me to taste, what for me, was forbidden fruit.

Some Christians can enjoy a pint or two or a nice glass of wine, which of course is not wrong. Jesus drank wine and his first miracle occurred at a wedding in Canaan. He famously turned water into wine. Probably the finest that anyone had ever tasted. But for me, because of my past and personality, I needed total abstinence. It was a battle I would never win alone; it would take a miracle for me to kick these habits. Thankfully, God is in the miracle business. He would do a great work in my life, but this would be another year or so later.

Another source of temptation, stemming from the company I kept, was my friend, Brendan.

Brendan was a good-looking bloke who had the gift of the gab. With these two deadly weapons in his arsenal, he always seemed to score direct hits. He had ginger hair and a silver tongue that were able to propel him into the affections of the fairer sex. Often when we were out, he would go up to a group of women and just start chatting. In his case, the evening usually finished with something much more physical than talking. If it was just him and I out, I would have to talk to the girlfriends of whichever woman Brendan was charming. As you know, this was an area of weakness for me, although I didn't possess Brendan's looks and linguistic abilities, I was still vulnerable to the temptations of the flesh. I should have been wiser and more like the Biblical character, Joseph, who ran away from sexual temptation instead of like Brendan who sought it out. Sometimes, he would bring women back to my flat and the sights and sounds that I'd witness didn't help me in trying to live a holy life.

Chapter 43

Mary

Living alone, I decided I needed some company. Two girls that I'm happy to say came into my life at this time, were Joy and Lady, a cat and dog. They had both been mistreated and I sought to give them a new home and some tender loving care. It wasn't easy. At first, Joy would hiss and spit at me. I spent a lot of time and patience trying to tame this morose moggie. In the end, she would follow me home for her milk and afterwards fall asleep on my lap. Things weren't so easy with Lady. I would take her for a walk and if ever I let her off the lead to have a run around, she would just leg it into the distance. I would have to try to catch her. There would only ever be one winner in a race between the two of us, and it wasn't me. I had to stop letting her off the lead. She would also bark continually when I was out of the house, causing the neighbours to complain. In the end, it was a choice of letting Lady go or being lynched by the neighbours. I sadly said my goodbyes to Lady and it wasn't long before I was back on my own. Joy disappeared and, try as I may, I couldn't find her. After all the time I'd spent with Joy and the changes I had seen in her character, it was a heartache to lose her. I hope she is curled up in front of someone's fireside purring away contentedly.

Back on my own, I faced the daily battles with my mental health, sometimes depression would seek to coil itself around me like a snake trying to squeeze the life out of me. When the black storm clouds of depression were gathering on the horizon, I would take measures to keep myself safe from harm by my own hand. I would pass over the balcony all my sharp knives to Mary, my next-door neighbour.

Mary was a lovely woman who would soon receive some tragic news.

She was dealt a cruel blow in losing her only daughter. This poor girl, once so respectable, had become a drug addict and sold her body to pay for her habit. It's a dangerous squalid existence and tragically, Mary's daughter was stabbed to death. There was an appeal shown on Crimewatch UK but I don't think the killer was ever caught. Mary never recovered from the brutal blow of losing a loved one in such a horrific manner. I would talk and pray with Mary and tell her that she needed to forgive the person that had committed this horrendous crime.

I'm aware that to forgive someone for callously killing your loved one is almost impossible and some readers will not agree with the advice I offered Mary. Forgiveness like this can only come through God's grace and His miraculous work. To harbour hatred and bitterness in our hearts will only damage and poison our own lives and do us harm. This is what happened to Mary. The last time I saw her, she looked like a shell of her former self, being all hunched over. I'm so sorry for what Mary went through because I liked her and she got on well with me. Why had this happened to her daughter? I didn't have any answers for her.

It's a question a lot of people ask. Why, if God exists, does He allow evil things to happen? What I do know, is that we live in a fallen world, in rebellion to God where terrible things happen because of the evil that resides in the heart of mankind. I also know that a loving God exists, and we can find forgiveness, comfort and hope in Jesus. We will never have all our questions answered in this life but let me tell you that God is a God of love who is holy, pure and righteous.

My desire for Mary was that she would turn to God by believing in Jesus. In her grief, she needed the loving comfort of God but she wouldn't heed my pleadings. Before I tried to help her, she had helped me by storing my sharpest blades until the worst shadows of depression had passed, I was very grateful.

I bought her a big rubber torch because the outside of her flat was dark and she felt unsafe. The torch could have a dual purpose to chase away the night's shadows and to be used as a cosh on the heads of any would-be assailants. As well as taking practical measures to keep safe when I was unwell, I would also seek prayer for my depression. On one such day, I was sitting at the back of the church and a friend could see that I was suffering. He prayed for me and the joy of the Lord flooded my heart.

Despite my ups and downs, I know that God cares and loves me and I wanted to share that love with others. Because of this, I had no hesitation in volunteering and helping a friend who worked for a charity, delivering furniture. One day, we delivered a sofa to a woman who lived in an upper story flat. This lady had lots of problems, one of which being she had little or no furniture. I believe she used all her money to feed her drug habit. I certainly couldn't recite Shakespeare's sonnets or tell you the capital of Botswana but boy, can I lift things, very heavy things.

I'm more Atlas than Einstein, brawn than brains. I had earned the nickname Thor when helping my mate, Dave. We were removing some concrete footings from his garden but one piece stubbornly refused to budge. We had both hit it several times with the sledgehammer, without success. Sticking out of the unmovable object was a metal rod. I lost my patience with the proceedings and attempted to become the irresistible force. Grabbing the rod, I twisted it from side to side with all my strength. It suddenly came free and I was left holding it triumphantly aloft. Excalibur it wasn't, but it did resemble a certain superhero's weapon as it had a pole with a massive concrete chunk sticking out of both sides. So Dave christened me, Thor.

Another time, a group of us were out walking and there was a massive brass bell about five feet high that was stationed in the grounds of a stately house. I was challenged to lift it off the ground; nobody thought I would be able to manage it. This made me determined to try and, lo and behold, after bear hugging the bell, I managed to wrestle it off the ground for a good few seconds. Long enough to silence the good-natured taunts I was receiving. So I had no hesitation in offering my services for lugging furniture about.

My friends, Jo and Pete, came to pick me up with the van containing the sofa. I thought that Jo was one of the most beautiful women I'd seen and what's more, she was single. I harboured hopes of us becoming more than friends at that time. Sadly, this turned out to be a branch of my imagination that bore no fruit. I never knew if she could tell how I felt but I didn't want to spoil our friendship or cause her to feel awkward around me. So I stayed schtum and my affections were kept hidden in my heart. Anyway, enough of my unrequited love, back to the story.

When we arrived at the third floor flat, it soon became apparent that it would take more than brawn to deliver the sofa. The stairway up to the flat was narrow and twisting. I took charge, directing Pete, but it was like trying to put a round peg in a square hole. I asked the woman if she minded me taking out part of the banister. She said that was fine so that's what I did. Annoyingly, we were still a couple of millimetres short of being able to manoeuvre the sofa to fit. Pete was struggling because it was getting heavy. We finally admitted defeat and I told Pete we'd have to come back the next day with a rope and winch the sofa up, and get it in through the balcony.

Whilst taking the sofa back to the van, we passed a police car with two officers in the front. I'm nothing if not cheeky and have a real brass neck. I tapped on the window and they opened it. I explained the situation and asked for their help. I expected them to tell me that they weren't allowed to help me but to my surprise, they both got out of the car and offered their services. The long muscly arm of the law came in handy that day. With their help, we managed to lift and manoeuvre the troublesome sofa, finally getting it into the house, although not before I'd scraped all the skin off my arm.

Bringing up the rear, the first thing I saw when entering the flat, was some sliver foil and a stash of drugs. I couldn't believe that I'd brought two coppers into her house and, in trying to help her, I was going to get her nicked. I asked the woman where she wanted the sofa placing, trying to keep the officer's attention on the job in hand and away from the illegal narcotics just a few feet away. The woman sheepishly guided us into the living room. I thanked the police for their help and told them of my less than illustrious past, I gave them each one of my flyers.

I shepherded them out trying to use my body as a shield to obscure their view of the drugs. I expected at any moment they would clock the stash on the side. They ended up walking straight past and the woman we had helped sat on her new sofa that night instead of the waiting room of the cop shop. Afterwards, we broke down laughing. I know only too well that drugs are no laughing matter and she needed help but I would have felt bad if she had been arrested on my account. She needed Jesus and not the hollow high of substance abuse. Often telling people this is not enough, as they have to see that you're real and genuine. I don't know what became of her or if she's still living there. My prayer is she's off the drugs and that God has transformed her life. I hope she didn't have any more close shaves with the law like the day when a couple of Christians gave her the gift of a sofa and the good news of the Gospel.

And so, the seasons passed and the months turned to years with me living in Upperthorpe and worshipping at Philadelphia church.

Chapter 44

Giant Steps Forward

In 2008, I would experience a major breakthrough in my ongoing struggles with drinking, smoking and drugs. When Neil Armstrong landed on the moon, he famously declared that it was one small step for man and one giant leap for mankind. For some people, deciding not to do drugs or stopping drinking or smoking is easy and a small step. For me to be free of these monsters that had plagued me since the age of twelve years old was massive.

Most people, when they wake up, stick the kettle on and have a cuppa. I, however, would reach for a can of lager and a cig as soon as my eyes opened. I often woke early and would stand on the balcony welcoming the dawn with nicotine and lager at 5am. My alcohol addiction came to an end in an unexpected and un-dramatic manner. Martin Garner, a man from church, came round to visit me one afternoon. He was a lovely Christian man who has since sadly died from a brain tumour. We were having a cup of tea when Martin's eyes were drawn to the empty cans of lager on the side. He looked at me and asked me a poignant question in his gentle manner.

"Aren't you sick of drinking Nigel?"

I told him that I was, and told him of my struggles to be free from alcohol, and how I'd been battling it for many years.

"Let's pray," was Martin 's reply.

I closed my eyes and waited for Martin to begin his intercession. To my surprise and disdain, Martin's prayer was only six words long. "Lord, deliver Nigel from alcohol, amen."

I'd expected him to carry on praying for me for some time but he was done praying and carried on chatting. When it was time to go, Martin asked if I had any alcohol in the house. I told him I had some lager in the fridge. He went straight over and removed a nicely chilled four-pack. I asked him what he was doing and he told me that he'd prayed and asked the Lord to take away my drinking addiction, and so he was taking the lager, as I wouldn't need it any more. I don't mind admitting that I was annoyed. Martin's prayer had been simple and brief and now, here he was, disappearing out of the door with my precious booze.

In an hour or two I would need to crack open a can, and now that meant me traipsing to the shops. I'm sure Martin meant well but I could have done without the hassle and expense he was about to cause me. But two hours went by without me desiring to wet my whistle with cheap lager. That night, I retired without having my beery nightcap. Usually, it was lager that sang me a bedtime lullaby, but this particular night, I closed my eyes and enjoyed a good and restful sleep. When I woke the next morning, I couldn't believe it; I had no desire for alcohol. The cravings had held me vice-like for years. Day after day, they controlled and tormented me and now they were gone. The Lord had answered Martin's prayer; the Lord had set me free. I felt ashamed at being annoyed at Martin and at having a negative attitude towards his short prayer. My overriding emotion though, was joy and amazement. I asked the Lord's forgiveness and thanked Him from the bottom of my heart.

It was a case of one down, two to go, as I still smoked and dabbled with drugs. Smoking was the next addition to melt away and came about as follows. I was desperate to stop smoking. It felt wrong to me to have this awful habit. It was a drag that I had to have a drag fifty times a day. It made me feel dirty and made my clothes reek of nicotine. My morning can of lager had been taken away but I was still smoking first thing every day and wasting my money on cigarettes. I would spend most of the money I received on funding my addictions, leaving me with little left over to buy food. My standard meal at this time was the cheapest beans on bargain bread. My skinheads on a raft were of the impoverished kind.

Now I had stopped drinking, I badly wanted to quit smoking too and use the sixty quid a week I would save, to bless others, instead of poisoning my lungs. I couldn't stop in my own strength and God hadn't taken away this addiction. So, I had started looking into acupuncture to help me quit smoking. Shamefully, I'm reminded of an old King of Israel, Asa. Asa prayed to God when a vast army of a million men had come against him. The Lord had answered him marvellously and miraculously, delivering him from the hands of this vast marauding mob.

The next time Asa was faced by an enemy army, instead of praying to the God who had been his help and deliverance in similar circumstances, he hired foreign troops. He ignored the Lord God who had been a rock and a refuge to him and sought help from those who didn't know God. (Read 1 Kings 15) This was just like me, who after experiencing Gods kindness and deliverance, was now turning to acupuncture.

At the time, I had no idea what was involved in this process and how it is based on eastern philosophy. I had even gone as far as phoning up and enquiring about a course of acupuncture. They quoted me two hundred pounds and assured me of complete success in getting rid of my nicotine addiction. I was seriously considering paying the money and having the treatment. One night, around this time, I visited a church on Duke Street, which was a gospel church just outside the city centre.

I thought back to my days when I was horrified and afraid to be on the black and Asian wing in prison. Those feelings were long gone as Christians were Christians and, therefore, my brothers and sisters. It didn't matter what colour or nationality they were. Speaking that night at the church, was a man whose name I cannot remember but I will never forget the words he spoke to me. After he finished preaching, he asked if any people present were struggling with addictions and wanted prayer. This was me, so I responded by going to the front. I didn't care who saw me. I greatly desired to be set free from smoking. I didn't say a word to the man about my situation and he didn't ask me what my addiction was but the words that came out of his mouth shocked me to the core.

He looked straight at me and told me that acupuncture doesn't work but God does. Now this man didn't know me, I'd never met him before and, besides which, I'd told no one that I was considering having this treatment. But God knew. God knows all things. He prayed for me and I left the building amazed.

I'd like to say that I never smoked again but the fact is that I continued to smoke after that night. However, I knew that acupuncture wasn't the way to go. I had to do something so I made an appointment with the doctor. Explaining things to the doctor, he told me that I needed to see the nurse before he'd prescribe nicotine patches. I insisted on seeing the nurse there and then, and he told me that wouldn't be possible, so I insisted a bit louder and then a lot louder. He again refused to let me see the nurse.

I had to be free of smoking and I couldn't wait another two weeks. He left the room and I didn't know if he'd gone to get the nurse or the police. Thankfully, it was the former and they prescribed the nicotine patches. That night, I stuck one on but when I awoke found that it had come off. Again, I was disappointed but then I realised I didn't want a cigarette. I prayed and once again, asked the Lord to set me free from this vice.

I didn't put another patch on and as the day went by, I didn't reach for the cigs. I would always have one, or five, after a meal and yet, here I was, going about life without the nagging desire to smoke. God had set me free without acupuncture or nicotine patches. The preacher at the gospel church had been right. While other people can quit using these methods, the only way for me was for God to take it away. I was free from alcohol and nicotine and knew it was time to give up drugs once and for all.

Now that I wasn't smoking, it was easy for me to stop using cannabis. Although I'd took speed and various other drugs for a long time, off and on, I knew it was time to turn the dial to off, permanently. And so it turned out, by the spring of 2008, I was free from drink, drugs and smoking. There was no open -top bus parade but it meant a lot to me and marked a milestone in my life. A stone carved and crafted solely by God, and I was thankful to Him to be free from these addictions that had snapped at my heels like hounds that wouldn't give up my scent. I resolved never to go back to what God had delivered me from, and with God's grace, I've been as good as my word on that. I'd like to tell you that was the end of all my problems but I'd be lying if I did.

Chapter 45

Crookes

Shortly after this, I was offered the chance to move up to the Crookes area of the city. It was only a couple of miles up the road but was a much nicer and sought after area of Sheffield than where I was currently living. I'd been at Upperthorpe for a good few years and got on well with all my neighbours. I was sad to leave them but I thought I'd be silly not to move. I have to say, that instead of praying about the move, I just decided that it would be common sense to grab the chance with both hands. In hindsight, it turned out to be the wrong move but I wasn't to know that at the time.

Some friends from Philly had a flat in Crookes and asked me if I would like to move in. I knew them well and had been working for them for a while, voluntarily. With my illness, it wasn't possible to have a proper job. I know some people would just write me off as a scrounger who had blown all his money on drugs, drinks and cigs. I have to say, I agree that I shouldn't have been buying these things that were no good for me. The truth is that I often went without food, or bought whatever was the cheapest and often nasty option, to be able to have these things.

I never knew when my paranoia and the pain in my head would strike. My illness never announced when it would visit and when it did; it rendered me unable to leave the flat. At times, it was a struggle just to keep my head above the waterline of sanity. I'm no scrounger, and would like to be working when I'm able. I much prefer to be active than to sit on my big backside. So, I would wash my friends' burger vans, help replenish stock and assist them with deliveries. I also worked as a gardener, keeping the outside spaces at their rental properties, looking nice.

So, when they offered me the opportunity to upgrade my postcode, I jumped at the chance and moved from S6 to S10. I soon missed my neighbours and contacts. It was further to Philly church too, which previously had just been round the corner. I hadn't been there long when I began to get ill. It could have been down to the stress of moving, a fish out of water complex. I may have suffered the attack anyway, I'm not sure. Either way, I didn't help by not taking my medication regularly and the outcome was a severe attack of paranoia.

I couldn't cope and I felt like I had to get away. I caught a train, and ended up in Bournemouth. I had drawn out all of my money but I didn't feel safe staying in a hotel. So I slept al fresco in the bushes or the beach with the foxes for company and the stars for my canopy. I had no blanket to keep me warm and, although it was summer, the nights were cold and the sea breeze left me shivering. I was there a few days, but instead of feeling better, I got worse. I was all alone far from home with a pain in my head and paranoid thoughts shooting around my mind, making me fearful and restless. In the end, I went to a hostel and broke down, crying in front of a member of staff. I poured my story out between sobs and she phoned my support worker up in Sheffield. Arrangements were made for me to catch the train back home. I remember being in a train carriage at St Pancras, the heat stifling, I sat there feeling like my head would explode. The train was delayed and I was anxious and agitated. Finally, we started to move and the train made its way north.

As soon as I was back in the steel city, I made my way to my friend's house, Bruce and Coleen. I almost collapsed outside their door, as I hadn't had anything to eat for a few days. They fed me and looked after me, taking me home and making sure I took my medication. What awaited me when I got home did nothing to improve my illness. The property I was staying in had an iron gate on the outside of the door that had been installed by the previous tenants. As I walked up the path, the owner's son and his mate were going at it with an angle grinder. I asked them what they were doing and explained that I needed the extra protection because it gave me peace of mind and helped with my paranoia. I asked him if they were trying to evict me and he reassured me that the property would be mine to rent for as long as I wanted.

Sadly, that wasn't to be the case but I was thankful to get home and try to recover from my woeful wanderings. It would be the last time that I took to running away because of a bout of illness, but my depression and paranoia would soon push me once again to the edge of a precipice. My recovery was fleeting and it wasn't long before I again, contemplated taking my own life.

I was very ill and wanted to throw myself from a city centre bridge, under the wheels of the vehicles speeding past below. It's a strange sensation, knowing the actions that I was about to take were wrong but being swamped by black tides of depression. It's like being in a deep dark pit with sheer sides and no way of climbing out. I phoned my friend, Abigail, praying she would answer. Abigail is a lovely, gentle, kind and caring Christian. She seemed to exude peace, calmness and tranquillity. I remember sobbing so hard, I couldn't catch my breath and the tears were cascading down my face as I stood all alone on the bridge. The phone rang out and Abigail's voice greeted me. I couldn't compose myself to tell her about my problems and what I was about to do. She could hear my anguished sobs but, if she was shocked, it didn't register in her voice.

"It's okay Nigel, let's pray," she said, in her softly spoken tones.

She proceeded to ask God to strengthen and help me. As she prayed, I managed to control my breathing and bring my sobs under control. The God that she prayed to, her God and my God, that day, as on many other days, answered her prayer from heaven. The peace that passes all understanding fell on me, covering me like a warm fleece blanket descending on a cold naked body.

It wasn't the first time I turned to Abigail for help and support and it wouldn't be the last. I remember one time, when I was attending a Christian conference, I hadn't slept all night and my eyes were red, sore and burning. I was beginning to feel increasingly anxious and paranoid. I phoned Abigail and asked for prayer. She amazingly prayed that my eyes would be healed. I hadn't told her that my eyes were hurting and yet, God had told my friend. God ministered healing to my eyes and peace to my soul, answering my friend's prayer. She's always been there for me down through the years and is still a precious friend to whom I'll always be grateful. She's had some tough times in her life through no fault of her own and yet, has faced these problems with quiet dignity and unshakable faith in Jesus Christ. I've absolutely no doubt that, along with many other people, God has placed her in my life. She was the voice and hands that day on the bridge that God used to dry my eyes and turn my feet away from climbing the railings.

I still suffer these attacks but have developed a strategy that helps me cope. When my illness comes on me, I put a worship song on and try to pray and praise God. If the feeling doesn't subside, I phone a good friend and ask them to pray with and for me. I chat with them and find that sharing my problems helps me. There's no magic solution but just to know someone cares and is praying for me, helps. My friends also help me put things into perspective and try to help me see that everything and everyone isn't against me. Often I will take some Diazepam or sleeping pills and retire to bed, getting my head down for the night. Most times, things will seem a little better the next day and the frowning skies don't seem so bleak. Sometimes, the pain and torment is still there but I comfort myself that I've made it through another night, and am another day closer to being with God. James Montgomery, the hymn writer, declared that nightly he pitched his moving tent a day's march closer to heaven[1]. That destination was still a long way off for me and before then, I would be flying halfway around the globe.

---

1 Forever With The Lord by James Montgomery

Chapter 46

New Zealand

My friends, Bruce and Colleen, had come halfway around the world to help the church at 'Philly and the time came for them to return home. If Colleen was called Sheila, you might guess that they hailed from Australia. Well, you wouldn't be too far wrong, they were actually New Zealanders. They promised to invite me over as soon as they were settled and they were as good as their word. In fact, I would visit them twice.

So it was that I found myself nervously boarding a plane at Manchester airport bound for the other side of the world. The journey proved problematic on two fronts. I was paranoid that I would lose my passport and papers. I was constantly worried and on edge. This had the unfortunate effect of stopping me from sleeping. I was so very tired, but sleep wouldn't come. I tried counting sheep as I thought it would be good practice for when I got to New Zealand. It didn't do the trick. I finally took some diazepam and a sleeping tablet only to be woken up by the bloke behind me who informed me that I was snoring like a pig.

So, it was a bleary-eyed and frazzled Nigel Williams who disembarked to meet my two friends waiting at the airport to pick me up. When we got to Bruce and Colleen's house, it was midday. The advice to combat jet lag is not to nap but stay awake until night falls. I had to ask to be shown to my room though, as soon as my body hit the bed, I was asleep and I didn't reappear until the next morning.

My trips to New Zealand are ones I will never forget. The stunning scenery and places we visited were spectacular. The sunshine and the warmth of my friends company shone brightly on me. I was able to relax and enjoy the holiday and the weather. It was winter in Britain so down under it was glorious summer. I celebrated my birthday whilst there with dinner at the Auckland Sky Tower, a revolving restaurant. It was an amazing place with a wonderful view and, as the name suggests, is a huge building. At 328 meters high, it's the tallest freestanding structure in the southern hemisphere. After filling my stomach, I then proceeded to very nearly empty its contents again as I jumped off the building. I completed the famous Skyjump from the top of the tower making it a birthday I certainly won't forget in a hurry. I have a video to prove my vertigo-busting leap, not for viewing by the faint hearted.

That wasn't the last of my daredevil feats in New Zealand. I also bungee jumped, head first, from a platform suspended over the Kawarau Gorge. I have a t-shirt, photo and certificate as a memento of my bravado. My hosts showed me the coolest places, museums, hot springs and beaches. We spent Christmas Day at a beach barbecue and then dived from a nearby bridge into the sea. It was also at the coast that something wonderful and unforgettable happened. I was sunning myself on the beach and Bruce was on the cliff-top looking out. Suddenly, he shouted that dolphins had come into the bay. I jumped up and ran towards the sea. I wasn't sure if the sight of a portly Englishman splashing his way towards them would cause these wonderful creatures to retreat. To my great delight, they seemed as interested in me as I was in them. They swam and leapt all around me. It was a truly breathtaking moment that will live with me forever.

This wasn't the only time I got up close with the wildlife on that trip, only the next encounter wasn't so enjoyable. One day, at the beach, we were eaten alive by swarms of sand flies; they seemed to like the taste of me especially. I didn't let it spoil the trip though. I remember writing in the sand the words friends forever for Bruce and Colleen to read from their cliff top perch.

They took me everywhere and gave me the time of my life. They even asked me to speak at their church and share my story. Bruce had pre-warned me to keep my testimony to under ten minutes so he would have time to preach. Thirty minutes later, I was just finishing speaking. I honestly can say that I hadn't planned to disobey Bruce's advice. It was just that the Lord gave me incredible liberty and freedom to share my story. Many in the church seemed to be moved and encouraged at what God had done in my life and Bruce wasn't mad at me. Even though, I felt bad that a couple of people said that I'd been the best speaker at the church for the last year. It was a good job Bruce is a humble man because he had been a regular speaker since returning.

One person who did get annoyed at me on that trip was a friend of Bruce's, called Neil. We'd bumped into Neil's friend who wasn't a Christian so I shared my story and the Gospel with him. Driving back in the car, Neil told me that I'd overstepped the mark and shouldn't have talked to his friend about Jesus.

"How will he ever come to believe in Jesus if no one tells him?" I asked. He curtly responded that I should have left things to him. The next time we saw Neil, was a couple of days later. He said his friend had texted him and told him he was looking into Christianity after what I'd said, and Neil apologised for his outburst. In both of these cases, I know it's not down to me but to God alone, His power and grace. Whilst it was thrilling to experience positive responses to the Gospel, it often isn't the case. Indifference and being ignored are commonplace, together with the occasional outburst of hostility.

On one such occasion, I was handing out tracts outside my local supermarket in Crookes. A chap in a wheelchair came out with his shopping balanced on his knees. He began to shout at me when I offered him a flyer, proclaiming the Gospel. He continued ranting as he crossed the road, twisting round in his chair to give me a last blast of verbal. As he did this, his shopping bag fell to the floor and got caught in the wheels of his chair. He was stuck fast, unable to move forward or reverse. Traffic had to stop for him and he became even more agitated and angry.

I tried to help him but his cloth shopping bag was entangled in the wheels. The easiest way to solve it would have been to lift up the whole caboodle, wheelchair and all, but he wasn't having that. By now, people were stopping to look and curious faces peered out from the cafe to see what the commotion was. I had to tear his shopping bag to free it from the spokes of his wheelchair. Needless to say, he wasn't too pleased when I gave him his shopping bag back in two pieces, and his loaf of sliced bread that had been sliced a bit more.

I pushed him safely to the other side of the road, allowing the traffic to start flowing. If you think that my help was appreciated by this man, you'd be wrong; he proceeded to blame me for the state of his bag and supplies. I apologised and went back to the supermarket to buy him another loaf of bread. I'd sought to share Jesus who is the bread of life and here I was giving him earthly bread instead of heavenly. Sadly, the Hovis failed to placate him. He took it from me with a grumble and wheeled away into the distance, seemingly oblivious that I'd rescued him from a busy road and his own bad temper, which had caused a traffic jam.

It was on that same road that I was nearly splattered, myself, on another occasion. I was waiting to cross one day, and looked to see if any traffic was coming. The coast was clear and I was just about to step out when I hesitated and looked the other way. I was just in time to see a group of youths in a car on the wrong side of the road, and definitely on the wrong side of the speed limit. I had to jump back as the car sped by me. I'd literally been one-step from being knocked down and it would have been game over, with the speed they were going. I later found out that they were joy riders. I'm convinced it was God's intervention that caused me to turn my head at just that moment. One second later, and I would have been toast.

Chapter 47

Two Kitty's

I have much fonder memories of a different wheelchair user. My downstairs neighbour, Kitty, was in her eighties. I would pop in to see if she was okay or needed anything. At first, she was a bit wary of me and rather reluctantly accepted my offer to make her a cup of tea. But Kitty soon got to know me and I'd make her a sandwich and a brew. Kitty wasn't good on her feet and couldn't get out much, so I came up with an idea. I asked to borrow a wheelchair from the day centre and Kitty was delighted to get out in the fresh air.

Sheffield is a very hilly city. It has seven major hills, just like Rome, and I'd push Kitty all the way up to the Bolehills, a nearby beauty spot that looked out over the surrounding countryside. While my adopted metropolis is known as the Steel City, it's not all industrial and grey. We'd sit, enjoying the afternoon summer sunshine, gazing out over Stannington Edge and the countryside beyond. Kitty would tell me stories from when she was a girl, which were much more pleasant than tales from my own past. One thing I did share with her though was my story of salvation and Kitty listened eagerly. This elderly, fragile woman, who in all probability didn't have long left in this life, came to have an assurance of eternal life through faith in Jesus. On our walks, we'd pass an ice cream van and I'd get Kitty a cornet. I remember one time, buying Kitty a 99 but by the time we got to our destination, it had become a 38 at best. It was all around her mouth and nose. They were lovely afternoons that I'll never forget. The time came when Kitty had to move into care but I still fondly remember the time I spent with her.

I had two other female friends at this time, whose lives were tragically both cut short. One of them was also named Kitty. This Kitty was much younger than my neighbour. I met her at the day centre, we were both attending, both suffering from mental health issues. I offered to do her garden and paint her flat, she agreed but only on the condition that she cooked me a meal and cleaned my flat for me. Of course, I accepted her terms at once and it was the start of a close friendship. I remember ringing Kitty one day while I was out at the chemist picking up my prescription. I was checking what time she was coming to make my place spick and span. When I got through to her, she said that she was ill in bed with flu -like symptoms. After telling her I was sorry to hear of her illness, I prayed for her. I then made my way home and had been back for half an hour when there was a knock on the door.

I gingerly approached the door, shouting, "Who's there?" I wasn't expecting anyone, and my paranoia made me naturally suspicious. I opened up when I heard Kitty's dulcet tones greeting me from the other side of the front door. I couldn't believe she'd got here so quickly, not only because she had been ill but because she had to catch two buses to reach my flat. She told me that after I prayed, she immediately felt better and so here she was, raring to go and completely healed. I rejoiced to see her, thanked God for His goodness and went to put the kettle on for a cuppa before she put on her marigolds.

Kitty's health wasn't always as good as that day though. She suffered from terrible depression and it finally caused her to take her own life. One day, she left her flat and never came back. I've often tearfully wished that on that day, she would have knocked on my door, but she didn't. She caught a train to the seaside and flung herself off the cliffs.

The coastguard and air ambulance were scrambled and Kitty was pulled alive from the sea. Sadly, she died on the way to the hospital. Her death hit me hard, and it was compounded with the loss of another lady who I'd become friends with, called Susan.

Susan had found a lump in her breast that turned out to be cancerous. She had a mastectomy but the cancer, sadly, returned. I accompanied her through her treatment but eventually, there was nothing they could do. I tried to help and support her and she told me she was so thankful for my friendship and she didn't know how she would have coped without me. It was hard watching Susan die, after losing Kitty.

It may seem to you that my life is a tale primarily about tragic characters. Whilst anyone can get ill and die, you also have to remember, I was mixing with people with mental illness, ex-prisoners and addicts. I also spent time with many people whose lives were a testimony of God's goodness. But their stories don't feature because it's the sensational, not steadiness, that interests readers. It's the unhinged and not the unremarkable that captivate the imagination. But for every Kitty, there are Abigails and Robs, whose lives had been miraculously transformed by God but without the thunderstorms of a broken life. I often wish that I had a past and a story like theirs but I am who I am by the grace of God and I can't change my past, I can only share it with you honestly.

New Zealand wasn't the end of my travels during my time living at Crookes. I would also cruise the high seas. It was my first time on a cruise ship and was a far cry from the ferry that I'd returned from Amsterdam on, years ago. I loved every minute of the holiday. I remember taking my Bible with me on deck early in the morning as the ship sailed into port. I sat reading the Book of Acts that tells how Paul had visited Ephesus and a riot had ensued, as the first rays of sunlight highlighted the stunning coastline of Turkey. I would be walking in the footsteps of the Apostle as we visited the self -same place. Thankfully, we didn't encounter a riot that day but were able to marvel at the sights and smells of the ancient city.

It was a time of adventure I really enjoyed. I couldn't quite believe that I was enjoying this lifestyle, if only for eight days. The food served aboard these floating palaces, was nothing like the prison slop I'd survived on for so long. Yet, here I was, a bloke like me from a small town near Mansfield, cruising the azure waters of the Mediterranean. I would have another adventure on a much smaller boat, in very different circumstances to the calm tranquil seas that we sailed on that summer.

Chapter 48

God Speaks

Francis was a good friend of mine from church. He was an experienced sailor and was a member of a sailing club down south. This meant he had access to a boat at Lowestoft, at certain times. He invited a group of us from church for a trip on the boat. The wind and waves began to pick up whilst we were on the high seas. Such were the conditions that our entire group apart from me and Francis, began to feel seasick and were throwing up. Francis took them below deck to the sleeping quarters, leaving me alone at the helm. Not the smartest move, leaving a land-loving paranoid person like me, at the helm. Although I wasn't feeling ill, I was feeling terrified and began to panic. I can't do this, we're all going to drown, I thought, fear striking me with paralysis.

It was at this particular moment, all alone on the deck of that little storm-tossed boat that I heard something that I'd never heard before or since. I heard the audible voice of God speak, telling me that He was in control. I heard the Almighty declare with love and authority that He was in control of the sea, of the boat and of me. The sound of God's voice is hard to describe. It's gentle and yet, powerful at the same time. The same peace that I'd felt before when standing on that Sheffield bridge, flooded my soul. The waves were still beating against the side with the same ferocity but inside me, all was calm. My storm-tossed heart assailed with the waves of terror was suddenly filled with calm and serenity. I knew for sure at that moment that God was in charge of everything from vast planets down to tiny plankton. Underneath the frowning skies, God was smiling upon me.

His peace had once again fallen on me in the most marvellous manner, stilling the voice of fear that had been shouting in my head. I'm aware that many people will think either I'm deluded or dishonest. I know that even some Christians will have their reservations about what I'm saying, but I know what I heard and the effect it had on me. I can put my hand on my heart and promise that I'm telling the truth.

I'm not trying to encourage people to seek after signs and wonders. To be constantly seeking the supernatural is unhealthy and can lead people into unbiblical practices and false teachings. God's normal way of speaking to His people is through the Bible. To seek to run after the miracles of God and major in the Ministry of the Holy Spirit, may lead Christians to become unbalanced in their faith. The Word of God, the Bible, is the sword of the Spirit and if we would hear God speaking to us, we need to be reading the Holy Scriptures. It's this practice, along with prayer, obedience and faithfully attending God's church in which Christians should be engaged. These are how God shapes, directs and speaks to us. But occasionally, in times of great trouble, and at various times, God can and does, use the supernatural and miraculous to speak, protect and comfort us. The problem comes when we replace the everyday means of grace by constantly seeking the mystical and miraculous.

That day, on the boat I heard God's voice tell me He was in control. I have no reason to lie.

I'm sure you'd agree that I haven't left anything out about my life story. I've revealed painful and personal information; it's been a real warts-and-all revelation. I've laid myself bare before all reading this book. This is my story, a real story about my life and I'm duty-bound to tell you everything that happened, the good, the bad and the ugly. I've been honest with you about the bad and I'm being honest with you about the good.

And let me tell you, it was good. If heaven is just listening to God's voice for the rest of eternity that would be enough for me. The voice that spoke creation into being, spoke on a small ship to a sinful man, and it was glorious. I long to hear that voice again and know that one day, when my eyes finally close for the last time in this world, I will hear words and see things that are above and beyond our imagination. Jesus was once in a boat with his disciples when they encountered similar conditions. Possibly the wind and waves on the Sea of Galilee were even worse than the Suffolk sea. The disciples were terrified like I was and woke Jesus who had been sleeping in the stern. The Son of God immediately calmed the waters with just a word, "Be still", He commanded and the raging waters became as calm as a millpond. God had worked the same miracle in that little boat and said to my heart, "be still and know that I'm in control." I've accompanied Francis on his sailing trips multiple times since then. But this memory is one that I will carry with me to my dying day and I try to remember what God said to me that day, every time I encounter challenges and difficulties. I am in control.

Chapter 49

Evangelism and Eviction

We held weekends away with the Streetwise project where we invited those suffering from mental illness, ex-prisoners, drug addicts and homeless people. Ian, a local businessman from the church, funded a lot of these trips. They were brilliant and helped provide a bit of sunshine in the lives of those who needed it most. We would do archery, horse riding, raft building, caving, fishing, quad-biking, rock climbing and many other activities and sports.

At the start of the weekend, the new people would often be quiet and withdrawn. Often, I would break the ice by arm wrestling the entire group one by one. It gave everyone a chance to bond as the banter flowed on who was going to beat me. No one managed to though, even those who were a lot bigger than me. I enjoyed winning, but my main aim was to integrate the new people as quickly as possible. It seemed to work and they would begin to relax, and always seemed to have a good time.

Being a Christian charity, we would often finish the weekend by stopping off at a church on the way home. The sight of a gang of rough-looking blokes coming through the doors of a church would often cause quite a stir. I remember one weekend; I'd taken my hair clippers and had ended up shaving everyone's hair off as a laugh. The elderly congregation at the church we visited on the way home, seemed especially alarmed at the sight of sixteen slap-heads. But we weren't a bunch of ruffians out for trouble or even members of a Kojak convention, and once they got to know us, we were made welcome.

A conversation at one such church provided me with the opportunity of appearing on camera. I told a church member about my old life of crime and addiction before becoming a Christian. He listened intently and asked for my contact details. He told me about a friend of his, called Tim, who made DVDs about people like me, about rogues, ruffians and ragamuffins who found redemption and had been transformed by the power of God. A few weeks later, I sat in front of a camera, making a short film. I'm more armpit than Brad Pitt and yet, here I was, committing my testimony to the silver screen.

Another opportunity to share my story transpired during a visit to my friend, Phil Kelly. He had relocated to Bristol and I travelled down there to help him with some work in his new house. He was employed as a mentor to the inmates at Ashfield prison and asked me if I would consider sharing my story. I was simultaneously excited and scared. Phil broached the idea with the prison chaplain, who gave it the green light. I didn't need to be asked twice and was soon in front of a group of inmates. Once I'd been where they were, a prisoner stuck in jail and now here I was, a preacher sharing the Gospel of Jesus and speaking of the glorious salvation found only in the Son of God. I was back in prison, but as a visitor, which felt strange. Knowing personally how hopeless I had felt during the years I had served inside, I wanted to show these men how God had turned my life around and could do the same for them.

My testimony didn't get off to a good start however, with some of the cons shouting out and taking the Mickey out of my accent. The chaplain stood up and told them all that I'd come a long way to speak to them and the least they could do, was listen to what I had to say. I knew that most of them would be there just to get out of their cell and wouldn't be really bothered about listening to me. I began to tell them about my childhood and how I descended into a life of crime that saw me shunted from prison to prison. A silence descended and you could hear a leaf rustle, or pin drop. When I concluded, I urged them to give their lives to Jesus, telling them that, yes, they would still be behind bars but they would be truly free indeed.

I asked for anyone that needed prayer to come to the front. I guess

I should have asked permission from the guards who were annoyed that about fifteen prisoners made a beeline for me. These men must have really been moved by God because they were willing to risk the ridicule of the other inmates. Prayer was more important than pride and I was overjoyed to pray for and with them. However, the guards weren't so enthusiastic because the inmates were supposed to be back in their cells. "Just let me pray for one more please boss, just one more boss", I pleaded with the guard in charge. I never got the time I would have liked, to pray with every one of them as they were led away back to their cold bare cells. I prayed that their hearts wouldn't remain cold and bare towards God and their lives would be transformed from prison to praise, jail to Jesus.

While I was thankful for these trips and holidays that were a time of rest and relaxation, they also served to make me yearn for a time when I would enter into that eternal rest, free from all stress, worry and heartaches, for a time when I will enter the next world, which knows no troubles.

Back in Sheffield, real life was about to prove to be anything but trouble-free as I was about to be evicted. I busied myself helping out with a newly planted church, which was in an old synagogue on Ecclesall Road. This road is unique in Sheffield. It's popular with students and is a cool place, with lots of cafes, bars and independent shops. It's a very sought after location and to get this building and be able to open a church, was wonderful. The building was beautiful from the outside but was definitely in need of some tender loving care to bring the inside up to scratch. A couple who attended Philly, as it was a church -plant were to be the leaders. They were supposed to be supported financially from Philly until the church became self-sustaining.

I don't know what went wrong because I wasn't party to all the details but I do know the funds weren't in place to be able to do so. Because of this, I was left alone most days as meetings took place to try and get things sorted. I remember being all alone up a high ladder leaning across, paintbrush in hand, while the ladders wobbled like jelly at a kids party. The thought flashed across my mind that if I toppled from my precarious perch, I'd be praising God in heaven today rather than this weekend in church. Thankfully, the Lord kept me safe and the decorating was finished. The church was named The Well, and opened a few days later. The new church doors may well have swung open but the doors to my flat at Crookes were to slam shut.

The owners wanted their keys back and me out. A disagreement had ensued over service charges that I couldn't afford. I asked for more time to pay these off but was refused point- blank when my support worker began to question the validity of the charges. I'd been friends with these people a long time and I felt upset and betrayed to be asked to leave. I've no doubt they saw the situation differently and I've no desire to fall out with them. I hold nothing in my heart against them; after all, it was their flat to do with whatever they wanted. I'm sure we could have both handled the situation better, but the fact remained; I was left looking for somewhere else to live.

Chapter 50

Handsworth

I was given six weeks to vacate the Crookes property. The only place available was in the South East area of the city, right across town. It was only a mile away from St Ann's Hostel that had been my temporary home all those years ago. The flat was on a council estate in Handsworth, a decent area. It was the best I could have hoped for under the circumstances, as I didn't think I would be given my own wing at Buckingham Palace any time soon. It was like every other council estate, it had its diamonds and its duck eggs. Many of the residents were good people, with whom you could happily pass the time of day. Others kept themselves to themselves.

When I first moved on to the estate, it was in the middle of a spate of burglaries. There had been five in just a week. I know it may seem like I would be getting a taste of my own medicine if I suffered this fate and it did nothing to help my paranoia. Because of this, I found it hard to settle in and was soon to regret moving here altogether, when I managed to alienate my neighbours. I dropped a leaflet through the letterboxes of my fellow residents. It introduced who I was and offered my services free of charge to anyone who needed help with shopping and odd jobs. However, it was my follow up flyer that caused the trouble.

I was attending church three times every Sunday, as had been my habit for many years. Some Saturday nights, when I was feeling ill, downcast or tired, the thought would always shoot through my mind that I shouldn't bother with church the next day. I ignored these negative notions because I knew they didn't come from God. He commands His people not to give up meeting together. Jesus promised that wherever two or three are gathered in His name He would be there, in the midst of us. (Matthew 18:20) I would always be glad I'd been to church. I would feel uplifted and nourished.

To many people church sounds boring and you may wonder why I go to church three times in one day? The answer is that they don't have four services. People like to spend time immersing themselves in things they enjoy. If a football fan is really passionate about his team, he will go and watch them through thick and thin. I know it's a bad analogy to equate watching twenty-two grown men chasing a bag of air to worshipping the creator of the universe. The fact remains, my passion is God, so I desire to worship and learn about Him. The place to do that is church. My testimony wouldn't mean much if I couldn't be bothered to get out of bed and go to church.

Anyway, a couple of months later after returning home from the first of a trio of Sunday services, I felt encouraged. I decided to show my gratitude to God by posting a flyer containing my testimony and a DVD through the letterbox of my neighbours. I hoped it would lead to conversations about my faith and give me a chance to share the gospel. Returning home that night about half past nine, I let myself in and stuck the kettle on to have a cuppa before I went to bed. I'd only been in for about half an hour when there was banging at the door. It was the lady from downstairs. She worked for the police in witness protection I believe. She was very angry and very loud asking me what right I thought I had posting material through people's letterboxes. She told me I had really upset my next-door neighbour. I apologised politely, telling her that it wasn't my intention to offend anyone; I just wanted to bless and help people. My words didn't have a positive effect and she made her way back downstairs, but not before leaving me in no doubt what she thought of me.

I knew it wasn't really me she was angry with, but God. The Gospel does offend people because it tells them they're sinners and that they need forgiveness. I realise this is unpleasant and unpalatable to hear. Most of us are proud and like to think we're good people, like this policewoman. When people realise and accept this bad news, the Gospel becomes a message of hope to the hopeless, of love, joy and peace that can be found and experienced through faith in Jesus.

Back on the estate, I was the talk of the town. The jungle drums of local gossip beat out the tale of an ex-con religious nutcase who was amongst them. I was about as popular as a leper at a handshaking convention. My next-door neighbour was well known in the area and talked to all and sundry. To say my name was mud would give mud a bad name. My desire to bless and help people had backfired drastically. I felt isolated and vulnerable. From my physical appearance people would judge me as being far from vulnerable, it just isn't an adjective anyone who doesn't know me would use to describe me. The truth is I struggle to cope with paranoia at the best of times, and now the open hostility and rumours flying around the local community were pouring petrol on the fire of my fragile mental health. It has taken me a long time and concerted effort to win people round.

The policewoman moved out and that helped. My next-door neighbour was ill and I was able to help her, I think she finally realised that I didn't have any ulterior motives. She sadly passed away recently. I'm so glad we were reconciled and she came to realise that I only had her best interests at heart before she died. I suppose it must have been quite a shock for my neighbours to discover someone who has been convicted of the things that I had, living in their midst. People assume that a leopard never changes its spots.

I remember a time I spoke in church, of how I was once a thief and had even stolen from churches. I went on to say how God had changed me and as I was doing so I saw a woman reach down to retrieve and cradle her handbag. She needn't have worried. I can honestly say that you could trust me with your life savings and I wouldn't touch a penny.

Perhaps parading my past misdemeanours to my new neighbours too soon caused them alarm. To them, my offers of help and friendship could have been a ruse but I was eager to give God the glory for what He had done in my life. Hopefully, many have come to know me now and can discern that I'm genuine.

I tried to help a local lad who was on drugs. I invited him to my men's group, which I'd hosted for years. One of my friends, Tony, played the guitar and we would sing a couple of worship songs, followed by a short Bible study. We'd then enjoy some food and finish by watching a film. I always invited a couple of others from the estate who weren't Christians as well as my regular friends. Of course, my prayer was that one day they will know for themselves the things we sang and talked about from the Bible. My men's group was called The Eagle Has Landed after one of my favourite films, a war film starring Sir Michael Caine. I love films and always have. I have a cinema pass and often go by myself to get out of the house. Even if I'm unwell, it's a place I can go where I'm alone but not stuck in the four walls of my flat feeling like the world is closing in on me.

Chapter 51

Sharing the Good News

My greatest desire was not for people to come to know me but to know God. I wanted to tell the world about how wonderful Jesus was and that salvation was only to be found in Him. I've always sought to share the Gospel with everyone I meet and have recently gone back on the streets once a week. A group of us stand on The Moor, a pedestrianised area near the city centre. It's a part of the city I've avoided for a long time because I had a bad experience when I first came to Sheffield.

I was walking down The Moor, past a large group of youths that directed their verbal venom at me. They told me to go away rather impolitely and questioned my parentage while reminding me of my generous waistline. I'm sure you can decipher from what I've told you, what the content of their vitriolic outburst was. You may think this abuse should be water off a ducks back to a man that has seen and heard the things I have in prison. But, my paranoia and anxiety can make abuse difficult to deal with. I'm glad I can bless people now in the very place I was slandered. Now, each week, I can't wait for the day when I talk of Jesus and share the Gospel.

If you're ever around on a Thursday afternoon from 1pm until 3pm, come and say hello. I'm the big, wide, bald-headed bloke giving out flyers, talking and praying with people. I'm there on the streets rain or shine, seeking to share the good news. When I stop someone, I always start by asking if I can pray for them or if anyone in their family needs prayer. I've come to see that this is certainly not enough and it's vital that I share the Gospel with them too. After all, what good would it be to focus on the things of this life, which are only fleeting and neglect the life to come that lasts for all eternity. I sometimes ask people if they know where they will go when they die. I would ask you, dear reader, the same question.

The Bible teaches that heaven and hell are real places and my dearest wish is for you to be sure that you're able to enjoy a glorious paradise for all eternity. The alternative is not only awful but final. Forever is a long, long time. Jesus is the way to heaven, the door to paradise and only in Him is salvation, forgiveness and eternal life found. This is the message I want to share with you. It's my message as I talk to people on the streets of Sheffield about a far better place. A place where there are gates of pearl and streets of gold. These city streets are only temporal but I'm telling them of a lasting, enduring heavenly city. I always finish sharing my faith by handing out tracts, little booklets that explain the Gospel. I even have a short version of my story printed, explaining how God has transformed and saved me and how that same salvation can be experienced by anyone, through faith in Jesus Christ. I've been giving out my flyers since 1999 to anyone who will take them. Down through the years, I have passed out more than fifty thousand of these testimonies.

A lot of people ignore me, which is fine. Some can be hostile and that's not so fine. If people react badly or negatively, I try my best to be courteous. I thank them for their time and move on. If any conversation I'm having with people on the streets shows the first signs of developing into an argument, I've found it best politely to move on. On rare occasions, people can be abusive. I never try to respond in kind to their insults but offer a silent prayer for them, asking the Lord not only to open their eyes to the truth of the Gospel but to help me forgive them. In these difficult moments, the words of Jesus are of great comfort, Blessed are you when people revile you and say all manner of evil things about you. Great will be your reward in heaven. (Matthew 5:11-12)

Thankfully, bad reactions are rare and I've never encountered physical violence, only verbal abuse. There have been times when things have looked like turning ugly. Perhaps the worst experience I had is with another Christian man. It's a man I knew from my time at Philly. I was talking to a lady who had stopped and taken a flyer from me when this guy came up to us and started to preach. His preaching style was loud and confrontational.

The people who had been happy to stop and chat with us, now gave us a wide berth, keeping well away from the shouty Christian man. The lady too, soon moved on. Any hope of a fruitful conversation evolving had been destroyed by the decibel level of the man who stood behind me. I quietly approached the preacher and told him that we met every week in the same place. I politely asked if he would consider moving somewhere else so we could continue talking to people. The guy reacted very badly and started shouting, "I rebuke you, I rebuke you." I walked away as people were starting to stare.

The very next day, I was in a city centre bank when the same guy walked in. I thought this would be a good time to apologise and explain myself so we could shake hands and be friends. After walking over to him, I simply said I was sorry. I explained the reason I'd asked him to move was that I couldn't hear the lady to with whom I was speaking and it was preventing any conversation. He grew very angry and said I had no right to stop him from preaching the Gospel. He started shouting again in the middle of the bank, "I rebuke you." I was being rebuked right in the middle of a busy bank in front of people.

Here were two people who profess to represent Jesus. I felt ashamed and began to feel very angry as the man kept shouting out his rebuke. I thought he was going to punch me he was so angry. He was a big bloke but I wasn't scared of him. In fact, I knew I could make mincemeat of him and I'm ashamed to say that I wasn't far away from doing something that would actually have warranted a rebuke. He just wouldn't listen to me and kept shouting that phrase. Whatever people thought, I can only imagine.

Two Christians, who stand on the streets telling people about God's love, stood in a bank eyeball to eyeball. Again, I had to walk away but I was raging inside. Truth be told, I felt like squeezing his windpipe and silencing him for good. I went straight for the bus home, upset and very angry. I knew that my anger wasn't good and I was shocked at the ferocity of my feeling. If I hadn't walked away, I think I would have punched his face in. On the bus, my phone buzzed with a text. It was my rebuker and he said he would like to apologise. I blocked his number and sat silently fuming. I got off the bus and rang a friend, explaining what had happened. He listened patiently as I vented my spleen and gave me some relevant Bible passages to look at.

When I got home, I put some Christian music on and sat down and looked at the Scriptures I'd been given. They spoke clearly, of how I needed to forgive this man. I dropped to my knees and prayed to ask God for His forgiveness over my anger and harbouring bitterness in my heart. God took away my anger and gave me a feeling of peace. I reached for the phone and texted this man back accepting his apology and offering him my renewed friendship.

Another time, I was passing the cinema and there was a group of women talking together and also a large group of teenagers. I approached the women and handed out some of my tracts. I then walked over to one of the youths and handed out another. Straight away, he was suspicious and aggressive. The rest of the youths crowded around to read what I'd given him. Sensing hostility, I carried on walking to the tram stop, which was about twenty feet away. I could hear their voices becoming increasingly angry as I took a seat at the empty stop. I prayed, asking God to defuse the situation.

These were only teenagers but there were about twelve of them and who knows if they carried knives. I didn't want to hurt anyone but I knew that I'd have to defend myself if they came after me. Please Father, don't let it come to that, was my silent petition. Immediately following this, I heard the guy to whom I had given the tract shout out the order to get him to the rest of the group. At the same moment, a group of people appeared from nowhere and a Muslim woman came and sat next to me.

The youths gathered close by, snarling and staring at me. I glanced up at the CCTV cameras above me. At least, if they did attack, the police would know I hadn't started any trouble. One of them crossed over the tram tracks towards me and I readied myself. Instead of attacking me, he asked me which way the tram travelled on this side of the tracks. I answered him politely and he turned on his heels and retreated. Once on the other side, the wolf pack dispersed without the cold glint of sharp steel being brandished, throwing only dark looks of disdain my way, instead of stones or fists. This kind of reaction is extreme and thankfully rare, as I'm much more likely to be ignored.

Many people do take the tracts and stop to talk. It's my prayer that God would use any conversation, witness and tracts to bring others from darkness to light. I leave these tracts in bars, buses and libraries. I always offer to help people practically as well as spiritually. The Bible says to tell people about the love of God, but then to leave them cold, hungry and in need is not good. Faith has arms, legs, and not just a tongue. Real love blesses the stomach as well as the soul and helps those who are desperate and in need, starving men don't want the Bible, they want something to eat. Give them food and help in any way possible, then people will see you're genuine and you can share the Scriptures.

I remember one night, talking to a poor Polish man about the love of God. That man had nothing apart from a sleeping bag. He had no coat to keep out the cold. After finishing speaking with him, I left him my coat. John Wesley, the English preacher, along with George Whitfield, was responsible for turning our country upside down in the seventeen hundreds by preaching the Gospel and seeing the Holy Spirit moving powerfully in people's hearts. How I would love to see something similar these days. Whilst I can't preach like these two giants of the faith, I can at least seek to live out Wesley's famous quote;[2] Do all the good you can, by all the means you can, in all the ways you can, in all the places you can, at all times you can, to all the people you can, as long as you can.

This is the way I now try to live my life. Of course, I fail miserably but that won't stop me from trying. I can never take away all the grievous

---

2 Famous quote attributed to John Wesley.

wrongs I've committed but I can seek to live right, to live a God-honouring life. I spent so long living for myself and not caring who got hurt. I can't change the past but I can impact the future and do my best to make a difference.

It seems the least I can do is to offer my strength and time to help others. Whereas I once did my best to empty houses, I now help to fill them. I once stole belongings but now I help to deliver furniture to people who have very little. I volunteered with a church -based charity service called BESOM. They help to find houses and furniture for displaced people. Living the kind of nomadic life that I once had is a subject close to my heart. I enjoy meeting these people and they seem really grateful that we can provide good quality donated furniture. I often get to share my story with them.

I have also volunteered to work in soup kitchens and worked twice a week in a local food bank until recently. The food bank is run by a local church. Well, I say local, it's about three miles away. Twice a week, I'd walk there and back whatever the weather. I was able to spend the journey time praying. The food bank work was great because it gave me a chance to help people practically and care for their physical needs. At the same time, I'm sometimes able to help people spiritually by sharing the Gospel.

As you have read, I've had some less than savoury stand-offs with mental health workers. Down through the years, I've had some good ones and some not so good ones. I've often vented my spleen and let them know in no uncertain terms the frustration at them being unable, and in some cases unwilling, to help me. My behaviour towards them hasn't always been what it should, despite the mitigating factor of my illness. I regret some of the things I've said and the way I've behaved due to my suffering. Much to my surprise, God made an opening. For a short time I provided help to trainee mental health workers, this proved to be an open door for me to witness for Him. I never envisaged that such an opportunity was ever possible for me. God brings about the unexpected and gave me the challenge of standing in front of a room full of university students. It all started when my support worker, Steve, asked me a question.

"What do you want to do in life, Nigel?"

I didn't need time to think about my reply, I blurted out what was on my heart. "I want to help people. I want to share my story and tell people about my mental health issues and share my faith with them. I want to reach out to people"

Steve smiled, as it must have been the reply he hoped to hear. He told me that he knew a woman at Sheffield Hallam University that would be interested in speaking with me. A few days later, I found myself in the Robert Winston building in Sheffield, about to speak to final year health students for an entire hour. My stomach was doing somersaults and my heart pounded as I stood surveying the packed room. These students were about to qualify and be sent out onto the front line. They would be in at the deep end dealing with people just like me. With a dry mouth and stammering lips, I began to share my story with them. As I talked, I began to relax and was able to share my story and of course, I didn't leave out what God had done for me. Three years later, I'd progressed to twelve talks a year.

I got paid £22 each time I spoke, for doing the thing I love, sharing my story and the Gospel. I liked to use the money to buy the students sweets and chocolate. I've got used to public speaking and I'm not so nervous nowadays. I really enjoyed it but sadly, it came to an end. A new boss started at the university who didn't like me speaking about God and sharing my faith during my talks. It's my hope that God opens that door again one day.

Chapter 52

Face to Face with Death

I like to keep busy and find that if I have nothing to do and nowhere to go then along with loneliness and boredom, depression will try to gatecrash the party. So, along with walking the five-mile round trip to the food bank twice a week, I go to a chess club, a bible study, a prayer meeting, an English class as well as hosting my own men's group. On Sundays, I attend three churches and, on top of this, I try to spend time with friends. I don't like life when it gets dull. Occasionally, I like to get away from it all and attend conferences or just take myself off into the countryside.

Whilst I was away on one such trip, I found myself walking down a country lane. As I was sauntering along enjoying the fresh air and being in the great outdoors, I noticed a police car driving towards me. Motioning the car to stop, it slowed to a halt at the side of me and the policeman let down the window. I told him that I just wanted to thank him for his service and the good job the police do under very difficult circumstances. He looked at me quizzically, probably trying to decide if I was winding him up. I wasn't, I know the police have a hard time and get plenty of flack and abuse. I knew only too well how I had treated them down the years and wanted to make amends for my behaviour. I shook his hand and left the bemused bobby with one of my flyers.

Another time, I ran into two armed policemen in a fast-food restaurant. My mind went back to the last time I was in such close quarters with two police officers carrying guns in Amsterdam. This time my hand wasn't curled into a fist but open to shake their hands, thank them and pass them my story.

I also offer security advice to anyone that needs or wants it. I'm usually able to suggest ways of making people's property more secure. As a result of my long years of robbing houses, I'm able to look at someone's house and immediately know at which point a burglar would try to gain entry. I've fitted extra locks for people and given tips to make their houses safer.

Every year, I make sure I give generously to the British Legion poppy fund and have long since paid off my debt of shame. I no longer drink, smoke or take drugs. I made a vow to God never to do any of these things, as I know that for far too long these vices held me captive and brought shame on my proclamation of faith. I have deliberated long and hard whether to include one area of the recent breakthrough in my life that God has brought about. I've decided to include it even though, once again, I'm bearing my soul for all to see.

Since my early teens, I've had a problem with lust and have masturbated every day. I found myself not able to sleep until I had done so. Although the days of me paying for sex have long since gone, the fact remained that I had an addiction to pornography. As a Christian man, I knew this was wrong and tried for a long time to break this addiction. Afterwards, I would feel ashamed and would ask for God's forgiveness and help. God has answered my prayers. I've thrown away and deleted all pornographic images. I no longer need to perform my former nightly ritual.

I try my hardest to live a good life even though I know that I feel I let God down every day and that it is only His kindness, grace and love that brings forgiveness and friendship with the almighty God. I still struggle with my mental health and try to get away every few months for a couple of days to ward off the onset of illness. I found just a couple of nights in the countryside will refresh and reinvigorate me. Of course, I take my flyers with me. I take them everywhere I go, even on my retreats.

It was on one such trip that the flyers got me into trouble and the whole thing turned into a nightmare. I was supposed to be on a break to recharge my batteries and try to relax but I would end up leaving in a much darker state of mind than when I arrived. I should have known it wasn't going to be a great couple of days when things started badly. The place I had booked was supposedly a Christian retreat that was a sanctuary geared towards those suffering from illness.

The guy who ran the place, Roy, arranged to meet me off the train. After our initial greeting, we began to make our way out of the station to his car. As we were doing so, there was a lady with a buggy and child that was struggling to negotiate the steps that led to the exit. After helping lift the buggy, I left her with one of my tracts. Roy wanted to know what I'd given the lady. I told him that they were Christian tracts that contained my story and explained the Gospel. He immediately demanded that I gave him all my tracts. I explained that I wouldn't be giving them out in the hostel but had brought them along for when I was out and about, and for anyone I may meet. He was insistent that I hand him all my tracts even though they belonged to me. Not wanting to cause trouble, I gave him my tracts.

Travelling back in the car, I tried to make small talk but it was hard work. Although he had previously told me he was a Christian, when I asked him about the church he attended, he mumbled something in reply I didn't catch. He then refused to give a reply when I asked him again. I hoped this wasn't going to set the tone for the trip. Unfortunately, what was to follow would haunt me for months to come and would be something I don't think I'll ever forget as long as I live.

That first day, I settled in and took a walk to explore the grounds. The next day, I went into Richmond and sauntered around the town. I was able to give out a few of my DVD's that Commandant Roy didn't know anything about. When I returned to the hostel, I felt ready to leave the next day. Things hadn't felt right from the beginning and I was looking forward to retrieving my tracts and setting off for home. My room was on the third floor and staying next door to me was a man who I'd only greeted a couple of times. He'd appeared to be nice enough but was reluctant to chat to me, although I had seen him talking to a lady who he seemed to be friends with. I'd seen them around and complimented the lady on the music she had been playing on a CD player. We'd made small talk and she chatted away but I had only said a quick hello to the chap. After breakfast, I returned to my room to pack my few belongings ready to set off for home.

As I was completing this mundane task, I heard a female voice that was anything but ordinary. She was screaming for help and it seemed to be coming from the room next door.

I shot outside to see what was causing such shrieks of horror. She was outside the man's room with the door slightly ajar and she was hysterical, screaming that he had hung himself. She squeezed back through the small gap into the room. I was unable to get through the door as something was blocking it from opening wide enough for my considerable bulk to gain entry. Looking down, I saw a foot slightly protruding. A man was lying behind the door and I had to shove it hard to move his prone frame. His body had fallen from the hook on the back of the door from which she'd struggled to prise him off. I managed to slide through the half-open door and surveyed the scene. What I saw filled me with horror.

The man was on his back, his lifeless face grey and his lips blue, his eyes open but seemingly unseeing. The next ten minutes all seemed to blur. I tried to calm her down, asking if she'd phoned an ambulance but the truth was I didn't feel very calm myself. I was all fingers and thumbs trying to unlock my phone to call the emergency services. Under extreme pressure, panic set in and I couldn't remember my passcode. Eventually, I managed to phone the emergency services but then had a blank when they asked me the address. Thankfully, the noise had alerted another resident and we were able to let them know our location. They told me that the ambulance was on its way and in the meantime, I was to give mouth to mouth and start chest compressions.

I don't know how long the ambulance took but it felt an age. It was horrendous, blowing into that poor man's mouth. The taste was unpleasant and there was an eerie sound of gurgling in his throat. Sweat was bucketing from me as I tried to keep pace with the chest pumping and the blowing into his mouth, making sure his head was tilted back so his airway was open. All the time, I was accompanied by the sound of the distraught, grief- stricken woman. Every passing minute I longed for the ambulance to arrive to relieve me of my responsibility and efforts to keep the man from entering into eternity. The noises he made gave us hope that he may survive and yet I feared that if he did, it would leave him in a vegetative state. After what seemed like an hour, the ambulance arrived. There wasn't enough space in the room for them to work on him properly, so I lifted him onto the landing and the paramedics began to work on him. They used a defibrillator to shock him. I thought that it must be faulty because his body didn't jump from the power of the shock, like in all the films I'd seen.

They told me afterwards that in real life, it wasn't like that. Unfortunately, there wasn't to be a Hollywood happy ending as the machine failed to shock his heart back into beating. Despite all our efforts, the man had succeeded in taking his own life. Had it been a spur of the moment decision after an argument? Had he really wanted to die? Or was it a tragic cry for help whilst his friend was outside smoking. Knowing she would be back shortly, to come sauntering in and find him swinging from a coat hook? Had he really been so desperate that he'd had enough? I will never know. One thing for sure is I can never ask him. When they finally pronounced him dead, his friend collapsed. It left me shocked and with a feeling that somehow I should have been able to save him. The ambulance crew tried to reassure me. They even called me a hero, but I knew the truth ; I was no hero. I had just watched a man die and the taste of death was still on my lips.

It would be a long time before I could start to put this tragic incident behind me. Coming face to face with death forces you to consider your own mortality, I was full of dread that even though his glazed, empty eyes would never see anything again on this earth, he would be standing in judgement before God in all His glory and that his soul would be lost forever. I was an emotional wreck because of what I'd witnessed and just wanted to go home but I had to wait three hours until the police had finished investigating.

Travelling home, my mind was in turmoil. Knowing personally how it felt to be suicidal, having had these thoughts plaguing me down the years, I knew it could so easily have been me. If only I could have had five minutes to talk and pray with him. I know that I didn't have a magic wand to make his problems disappear but I could have told him about a God who cared and in whom he could find love, forgiveness, grace and mercy. I hadn't given him a flyer or told him about Jesus. I resolved to share the Gospel with as many people as I could, to offer hope instead of despair.

One day soon, my eyes will close and they will put my body in a box. If I'm able to, I'll give the ambulance driver a flyer as he takes me on my last ever earthly journey. If I could slide a flyer through the lid of my coffin, I would. I know I shouldn't joke about death, this episode brought home to me how serious death is and what eternal consequences it will usher in.

Chapter 53

My Life in Black and White

It was whilst living in Handsworth that the idea of writing a book really started to take shape. For years, friends have said I should write a book telling my story, of how God has transformed my life. I dismissed their ideas straight away and was flatly against writing a book. I knew that if I was ever to pen my life story, I would have to reveal all the awful things I've done. All my skeletons would have to be released from their cupboards. I would be airing my dirty laundry for the entire world to see, no thank you. I'm deeply ashamed of my past life and the thought of baring my soul was horrifying.

However, my friends kept telling me to do it. A feeling grew within me that God may well be behind their suggestions. I began to give it serious consideration, was it was right to make public the life I've led? The more I thought about it, the conviction grew that I should. My story shames me but it glorifies God and gives testimony of His goodness and grace. I hoped it would give people hope because God saving someone like me clearly shows that whilst redemption is needed for all, it is possible for anyone.

I soon became certain that I should commit my story to the pages of a book, but who would write it for me? I'm no writer and needed someone to take on the task for me. I started to ask around. I was attending a church on Sunday mornings and also volunteered at their food bank. It was there that I met a woman who said her daughter would help me if I paid her. So, I started to meet up with her and tell her my story, which she would put into words. Unfortunately, it wasn't working and despite her best efforts, nothing came of it that I could use. We stopped meeting and I was left frustrated and bemused. I had felt sure that God wanted me to tell my tale but didn't know how to go about it. I concluded that it would never happen. Of course, the very fact that you're reading these words is a testament that God had other ideas. He was to bring about the commencement of this project in an unusual way.

I guess it all started one Sunday night at The Well. I was talking to my good friend, Daniel Smith, who, after asking how I was and listening to me list my problems and woes, thought for a moment. He suggested I come with him on Sunday morning as he had found a church that had great teaching and was really strong on the Word of God. He said that it would really help me to grow in my understanding of God. When using binoculars, you put the small side up to your eyes to enhance the image you're looking at so that it appears closer and bigger than it really is. If you turn the binoculars around and look through the bigger end then things look much smaller.

I think Daniel thought that if I could comprehend the majesty of God then my problems, although real, would somehow seem smaller when surveyed through the lens of God's sovereignty. Because we're human, troubles can often seem overwhelming. Facing my trials in my own weakness without realising God's awesome power only magnified the challengers facing me. Anyway, I agreed to go with him. The preaching was brilliant, totally God-centred, bringing out Biblical truths that put fire into your bones. Not a fire born out of hype but a desire to serve and love God.

The Pastor, Kevin Bidwell, is an excellent Bible teacher and the best preacher I've ever heard. However, the worship was very different to what I was used to and I didn't think it was my cup of tea. They sang without a band or even a solitary guitar. At The Well and back in my days at Philly, I could be found down at the front dancing and worshipping God. Daniel introduced me to a few people that day. One of them, I later found out, was my local postman. Not long after I bumped into him on my street and he invited me down to the Wednesday night Bible study. It was when he was driving me home one Wednesday that I asked him if he knew of anyone who could help me with my book. He said he would be happy to help, and that's how the whole project began to take shape.

We've become firm friends and we meet up twice a week to talk about the book, often over a meal and a game of chess. I would trap his king and then he'd trap me by asking me for dates for the stories that I regaled him with, from my past. Whilst there's nothing wrong with my chess skills, I can't say the same for my memory. I can remember perfectly what happened but I have struggled to get the account of my life into chronological order. Eric Morecambe, in one of his sketches, once famously defended his piano playing to composer, Andre Previn, who had accused him of playing the wrong notes. Eric retorted;[3] "I'm playing all the right notes, not necessarily in the right order." I can testify that everything written on these pages has happened to me but you will have to excuse me if the order is questionable.

We were on the verge of finishing the book when all hell broke loose. I thought my story was ready to be told. It turned out there's another chapter, a twist in the tale, a scorpion sting at the end. I was about to experience a breakdown. A meltdown of monumental proportions was about to tear my world apart.

---

3 Eric Morecambe 1971 Morecambe & Wise Christmas Show

Chapter 54

Meltdown

It was late February 2020 when I asked my mental health team about changing my anti - psychotic medication. I'd been on the same tablets for twenty-three years and I hated the affect they had on me. I'd feel like a zombie some days, listless and lethargic and didn't have the energy to do the things I needed to do. I'd manage my tablets so that if I was going evangelising the next day, I wouldn't take them, so I was able to function properly when I needed to. I knew it wasn't a great idea to mess about with my medication too much but I wanted to be able to talk to people, to feel at least a degree of normality. It was agreed that I could try new medication. The ones I'd been on for so long worked fine but it was living with the way they made me feel that I struggled with. I really wanted to find a new medication just as good but without the stupefying side effects. I was about to make a grave mistake and unleash a breakdown of epic proportions. A dark abyss of mental torture was about to open up and I would fall head first into it.

At first, all seemed well. Taking these new tablets gave me much more energy. I experienced a newfound vitality and felt normal for the first time in many years. I was even surprising myself how well I was doing because by this stage, the government had enforced the first lockdown due to the Corona virus. We weren't allowed to leave our houses, only to get essential supplies. Instead of sending, me spiralling out of control and making me anxious, it didn't bother me at all. I stayed indoors and spent a lot of time chatting to friends on the phone, playing chess over the airwaves and generally keeping myself busy. But, things were about to change. The storm was coming.

As my old medication left my system, fear and paranoia moved in. It started one night when I heard voices on my balcony and thought people were climbing over from next door to get me. Earlier that day, I'd seen a local woman going into my next-door neighbours flat. In the past, this woman had been abusive towards me and this did nothing for my new, fragile state of mind. In fact, it proved to be the removal of the pin in the grenade of my sanity. Things were about to explode badly.

I began to imagine that people were conspiring to get me. My state of mind darkened with terrifying conspiracies swirling around my brain. I started to believe that the neighbours were plotting to kill me. And it wasn't only them that I thought were out to get me. I also suspected that a local lad who I was trying to help had grassed me up to his dealer. I had refused to give him money and insisted on buying him shopping instead so he wouldn't use it for the drugs that were messing up his life. I'd seen the lad talking to another youth driving a Mercedes. I concluded he must be the dealer and thought they had both given me the dead eye.

That night, my fears grew legs and gained voices. I called the police twice during the evening and they came out to investigate my report of youths climbing over my balcony. They reassured me that no one was trying to get into my flat. They doused a towel with cold water and put it on my head in an attempt to calm me. In my terror, I'd kept all my doors and windows shut, the conditions in my flat were stifling and suffocating. The police said they could see steam coming from my fevered brow. The temperature on the outside of my temple was matched equally by the fevered fears on the inside. In my mind, I was convinced that the neighbour had enlisted some local youths to get me. The police's reassurance failed to stem the horror in my head. I'd had no sleep all that night and I didn't sleep the next day. I paced about, my mind a whirl of worries and fears.

As darkness fell again, so the shadows that lay on my mind blackened. I was terrified and began again to hear voices on the balcony. I heard my door handle being tried and imagined I could hear the sound of a gun being cocked. What made it worse was that I couldn't use my mobile phone to make or receive calls for some reason. I could only send texts. In my mind, I believed the police had disabled my calls so that the neighbours could get me. I was terrified and sent text messages to all my friends to call the police and ambulance services. It was the middle of the night and all my friends were asleep. I'd texted Andy constantly, he is a friend of mine who lived locally, to come round and help me.

Dave, another friend of mine, called an ambulance and the police when he saw my messages. The ambulance arrived first but wouldn't come in because I had a hammer in one hand and a knife in the other. They decided to wait for the police as I was very agitated and anxious, understandably they didn't feel safe. Whilst they were waiting, Andy arrived. After talking to them, he came in and got me to put down my weapons and I began to feel much calmer. My mind had been awash with terror and fear.

The best way I can describe it is to ask if you have ever been woken up in the night by a sound and thought intruders were in the house. If you have, then you will know the fear, it makes you think that your heart is going to jump out of your chest and squeezes your gut until you feel like vomiting. That feeling drains away the moment you realise that there's really no one there and you're able to breathe a sigh of relief and drift off back to your peaceful slumbers. Well, this same feeling plagued me constantly without subsiding. In the daytime when other people were around, it was bearable, but each night was pure torture.

I realise now that I was gravely ill and I was seeing and hearing things that just weren't there. At the time, the fear that gripped me was chilling and all consuming. I'd even been sitting with the frying pan in my hand to block any bullets fired from next door. It may seem laughable now but it was anything but in my confused and desperately ill state of mind.

The police arrived shortly after. My friend asked the paramedics to admit me to hospital. They said that the incident would be logged but I needed to speak to the mental health team who dealt with my care. The paramedic couldn't do it there and then because they didn't open until nine. The police asked Andy to stay and talk to the mental health team for me, as I wasn't making much sense. The paramedic was confident that they would find me a bed where I could come under the care of people who could help me. His confidence was misplaced. The woman who Andy eventually spoke to was more interested in the fact that he had broken the Corona virus rules than my health. He tried to explain that he was only in my flat because it was an emergency situation and was doing his best to maintain social distancing. He spoke of his concerns for me and the possible consequences of my actions due to the serious mental paranoia I was suffering. The woman bluntly told him that nothing could be done due to the global pandemic and that I needed to stay put and continue with my new medication.

There was no way I could stay at the flat so I threw a few things in a rucksack and went uptown. I sat on a bench and phoned around hotels. My mobile had been fixed by the policeman that came to my flat. They had been unable to catch imaginary intruders but they were able to help me make phone calls again. Unfortunately, I found out that no hotel was open, except for NHS workers. What was I to do? I phoned a friend called Simon who I knew lived on his own. He agreed to put me up for one night. At least it would give me twenty-four hours breathing space.

Whilst at Simon's, a friend found a Christian hostel in Mansfield that was willing to accommodate me. There were two stipulations for me getting into the hostel. One was that I would be quarantined on the top floor along with two other new inmates that were moving in. This would be for fourteen days in case we were infected with Covid. The other was that I would have to give up my flat so that my housing benefit would pay for my keep at the hostel. It was a big decision but one that I didn't have to think long about. I would essentially be homeless once again. Even so, I jumped at the chance to move to Mansfield, as I didn't ever want to return to the flat where I thought people were trying to kill me.

I thought I'd be leaving my troubles behind but the fear and threat didn't emanate from my neighbours on the Richmond Park estate. These came from my mind. I wasn't leaving any trouble behind because it was travelling with me, in the dark recesses of my tormented imagination. I didn't realise this as I caught a train from Sheffield to

Worksop and was chauffeured from there to the hostel. I had just a rucksack with a few personal items in it. I only had one T-shirt and one clean pair of underwear with me, as I couldn't face going back to my flat. My biggest regret was that I didn't have the one photo I had of my mum. What if they set my flat alight, trying to burn me alive tonight? I would lose the most treasured possession in the world, the image of the woman who brought me up not far from where I was now staying. In reality, the only thing that I was in danger of losing was my mind.

On the second night in the hostel, I called the police again. I'd been up all night hearing voices outside my door. The voices were chilling. They spoke to one another, he's in there, let's kill him. When the police arrived, they listened to my story and checked the hostel's CCTV. Of course, they found no murderous intruders, because they weren't real. They were a product of my paranoia. They showed me the CCTV to try to calm my fears. I was warned by the hostel that if I called the police again, I would have to leave. I didn't want to be thrown out; I would have nowhere to go apart from back to my flat. Besides, I was getting on well with the two other guys who were also quarantined on the top floor. I especially enjoyed Matt's company. He was a recovering heroin addict. He had moved into the hostel to try to give up the drug before it gave him up to the grave.

As we were not able to go out, there wasn't much else to do but chat to one another. I told him my story and he told me his. I tried to encourage him in his fight with such a deadly addiction. I told him all about God and how He was real and had delivered me from addictions like those with which he was wrestling. I urged Matt to look to God for strength and help. The truth was I needed God's help myself, as each night, the voices and images terrorised me. I knew I couldn't call the cops so I sat holding my door handle shut, once again expecting a bullet to be fired through the door.

The night after that I was again, convinced people were outside my room trying to kill me. I held a chair in front of me for protection. The minutes crawled into hours with me still holding the heavy chair as a shield. My arms and back were on fire with the physical effort of holding the chair. I didn't dare lower my defences, expecting my assassins to strike any moment. Sweat was pouring down my face and my head was as hot and fevered as my warped imagination. The pale light of dawn crept through the window but did little to ease my terror, as I stood rooted to the spot. My ordeal finally ended when one of the staff knocked on my door to ask me if I wanted a cup of tea, only then could I relax, knowing the night was over. I was finally able to put the chair down after a seven-hour vigil. I was exhausted both mentally and physically.

During my time in Mansfield, I was surviving on a couple of hours of sleep a night at best. In the daytime, I was phoning round talking to the housing people trying to arrange a flat somewhere that I thought would be safe. These things take weeks to organise at the best of times and these certainly weren't the best of times with our nation gripped in the middle of a global pandemic. I was supported by a group of loyal friends that I spoke to on the phone every day. Paul Moore kindly drove down from Sheffield, bringing me much needed clean clothes and supplies. I also tried to contact my mental health team to let them know where I was and what was happening. I asked to be put through to my caseworker, Claire, who I'd always got on well with. She was always gentle and caring with me and I felt I could trust her.

Unfortunately, the person I was put through to was the woman who had berated Andy for being at my flat. I'd never got on with her, as she was always harsh and uncaring. She told me flatly that I would have to deal with her. I replied that I wasn't willing to talk to someone who didn't like me and hung up. Ten minutes later the manager of the hostel appeared and asked me to follow him downstairs into his office. Once there, he told me that he was going to have to ask me to leave because he'd found out that I'd had weapons on me at my flat. I told him they were purely for self -defence and that if they made me leave, I had nowhere to go except back to my flat, where people were trying to kill me. I also asked him who had told him about the weapons. Of course, he wouldn't tell me. He was sympathetic towards my situation but told me he had no choice but to ask me to leave. He felt so sorry for me that he gave me a lift back to Sheffield.

Chapter 55

Terrors and Troubles

So, my rucksack and I made the journey north, knowing I had nowhere to go. The only option was going back to my flat. I tried to sneak in unnoticed but heard my neighbours shout that Nigel was back. I sat there in my flat feeling under siege and terrified at what would happen that night. I hadn't been there long when I heard my door being kicked and the door handle rattled. I rang the police again and this time I fled the flat. It was a sunny day and people were out and about. I asked them to help me, explaining to them that people were trying to kill me. The reaction I received was understandable, they thought I was off my head on drink and drugs and told me in no uncertain terms that I was mad. In my confused state, I just thought that they were in on the plot to kill me. I was standing with people around me, pleading with them to help me when the police turned up. My neighbours weren't shy in letting the boys in blue know they were wasting their time and they were responding to the imaginings of a deranged delusional.

They told the police to leave, assuring them that nothing bad was happening; it was all in my mind. Whilst this was true, how they acted only further fuelled my paranoia. My heart sank as I watched the panda car drive away, taking with it any hope of deliverance from my imaginary foes. I made my way back to the flat and locked myself in, fearing the worst.

Sure enough, all hell broke loose that night. I heard and saw people trying to get into my flat. I called the police again. I was very ill. Time crawled by and I had no chance of sleep coming to relieve my tormented state of mind. At about 2am, I saw two youths trying to get into my flat. I shouted at the top of my voice at them, trying to scare them away. They didn't leave because they weren't really there. In my mind, they were now pushing at the door about to get in.

I took my hammer, ran into the bathroom, and whacked the window. The glass exploded out and the sound of breaking glass woke many of the neighbours. One of whom rang the police. I also smashed up the flat for good measure because the sound seemed to have scared off my imaginary intruders. I wasn't arrested but I did receive a caution from the police. I called my friend, Paul Moore, and he came round and sat with me. He tided my flat and spoke with the mental health crisis team who had been alerted by the police. Paul was told by them that, although they couldn't find me a bed in a hospital for that night, they would try their best to get me in the next day.

Andy came round with some fish and chips as I was starving. He took me out for a walk around a local beauty spot. It was a gorgeous summer day and it seemed strange to be out looking at the tranquil lake after the terror of the previous night. Andy dropped me off at my friend Peter's. He had arranged for me to sleep overnight in the church he attends. I hoped it would only be for the one night as I was expecting to be admitted to hospital. These events should have been the catalyst for me to be admitted for expert care. I was told the next day that there was still nowhere for me to go. Ten weeks of lockdown had seen an avalanche of people who needed help with mental illness. The NHS just didn't have the resources to help everyone.

That night, in the church, the shadows once again moved, morphed and tormented me with the familiar images and noises of the previous nights. I imagined that the neighbours had somehow followed me and were out to get me. Of course, the only thing following me was my illness. I was convinced I heard cars and thought the youths from Richmond Park were once again about to mount an attack. I suddenly saw figures trying to break into the church. I barricaded myself into the back room. Looking around for weapons to defend myself I picked up the only thing available to me, a pitchfork. You may well be tempted to laugh as you picture the situation in your mind's eye. For me, it was terrifying. I was frantic; again, I was unable to make phone calls.

I texted Peter asking him to come down telling him that youths were in the church and about to get me. It must have taken Peter no longer than ten minutes to respond to my SOS text. Those minutes seemed like an age, as I stood ready with my pitchfork to skewer the scumbags that I expected any second to burst through the door and find me. When Peter arrived; there was no sign of the intruders. The next day, Peter offered to put me up downstairs in his house, as I was terrified of being alone. This was the same Peter who the church had sent to visit me all those years ago when I lived on The Manor. I'm so grateful for his kindness and for the fact that he was willing to let me share his house with him and his family. It wasn't easy for him because, even though other people were in the house with me, I still suffered from fear and paranoia. I was constantly asking him if the doors and windows were locked. I was hearing cars all day and imagining people coming for me.

One day, I went for a walk and thought I saw Louise, my neighbour, hidden behind a bush. In my head, passing cars were driven by my old neighbours, tailing me. Peter tried to look after me and assure me I was safe, at the same time as caring for his family. His kind words and those of my other friends failed to reassure me because paranoia and fear are deaf to reason and logic. I was constantly on edge living in a perpetual state of anxiety, expecting at any minute to be attacked and killed.

I was still trying to read my Bible, pray and listen to sermons when I could. It was hard to set my mind on heavenly matters when constantly watching the door, windows, and experiencing stark terror. This proved to be the case when I had joined the online midweek church meeting. As Kevin, the Pastor, was leading us in a Bible study, I suddenly shouted out for them to call the police as intruders were in the house. The embarrassment I feel when I think about this is palpable. It demonstrates how real the danger felt to me that I would interrupt the exegesis of our esteemed minister. These delusions hoodwinked my senses and caused paranoia-fuelled panic attacks. These would continue for another ten days or so before finally a suitable place was found for me. Poor Pete and his family patiently endured my frantic fears and waking nightmares. I woke him in the dead of night, on more than one occasion, telling him intruders were trying to break in and I phoned the police as well. He had to get up, cancel the police and try to calm me down. He called the mental health crisis team and, once again, explained the circumstances and the severity of my illness.

Finally, a temporary bed was found for me on a secure unit at the Northern General Hospital. Later that day, Peter drove me there and I was admitted. That night, I prowled the corridors, shouting for the staff to help me and call the police. I'd seen hooded characters at the doors with guns. I imagined that the youths from Richmond Park had once again found me and even thought Peter's son had told some local gangsters of my whereabouts. There was no logical reason to suspect Peter's son as he didn't frequent with any shady characters and was a good lad. It's just that one day I imagined I saw youths outside Peter's kitchen window trying to get in to kill me. Shortly before, I'd noticed Peter's son on the phone and putting two and two together, I came up with a million and one. I feel deeply embarrassed at suspecting the son of my mate who had done so much for me. He and his family had shown me great love, taking me in when I had nowhere to go and putting up with all the madness and mayhem I caused them. I'd like to take this chance to express my gratitude and offer my apologies.

Now the figures that had stalked me these last few weeks had followed me from my mate's house and were banging on the hospital door, ready to shoot and kill me. Although to you, these things will seem bizarre; in my troubled mind, these things seemed very real. I kept shouting that they were going to kill me but no one came. My shouting carried on for hours as the terror and torment once again took hold. No one on the ward was getting any sleep with me around and one exasperated woman comically shouted that they should hurry up and shoot me. I can see the funny side now but back then, I was in the stranglehold of psychosis and its crippling fear.

The next day, a team of burly men came to escort me across town to Nether Edge Hospital. They assured me that it was safe to go with them and they would look after me. The date was Friday 12th June 2020. I was given a Section Two, which meant I would be admitted to the Michael Carlisle Centre at Nether Edge Hospital for twenty -eight days, for assessment and treatment under the Mental Health Act. I was placed in the Stanage Ward, which is an acute mental health inpatient ward. To my friends, this was a great relief and an answer to prayer. I was now back at the same hospital in the very same ward I'd been in eighteen long years ago. The place I had met Sharon in 1992. But, this time I was in a much worse state.

Chapter 56

Stanage

Thankfully, after weeks of serious mental illness, I was finally in a place where I could be cared for. Believe me I needed it. My illness didn't magically dissipate the moment I was admitted. The paranoia was still there. I still heard the cars and imagined that people were trying to break in. I was convinced someone had a gun and was going to shoot me. I imagined a gunman was in the unit and dived behind a settee. In doing so, I knocked a woman out of the way. It shook her up. Getting in the way of sixteen stone of petrified, paranoia-driven craziness, moving as quickly as he could wasn't pleasant. After they had calmed me down, I tried to apologise. I couldn't get the idea out of my head that a gunman was about to get inside the unit. I was terrified. I tried to rip the metal bars off from underneath a table tennis table so I could twist and bend them around the door handles to stop the assassin from gaining entry. The staff came running to stop me before I dismantled the poor ping-pong table.

Another time I was in the toilets and thought people were trying to get in through the roof. I stood on the toilet rim to check the ceiling was secure. I pushed the roof tiles hard to see if they would hold and they came down on top of me. I fell and hit my shoulder and hip on the toilet, hurting myself. Staff came running and found me covered in dust and plaster. I must have looked funny but my condition was no laughing matter. I became convinced killers had come onto the wing to kill me. In a blind panic, I ripped a set of drawers apart with my bare hands, ready to use them as a weapon. I legged it into my room' slamming the door behind to escape. My door began to swing open. It was one of the staff who had followed me to check on my welfare and to see why I was demolishing hospital furniture. But to me, the turning of my door handle signalled not help but horror. In my confused mind, it was assassins coming to shoot me. I threw the heavy wooden drawer with all my might. Thankfully, the door hadn't opened wide enough and my mahogany missile crashed into the back of the door. A couple of seconds later and it would have done some serious damage to the nurse looking in on me.

Unfortunately, in another incident, I did hurt a nurse unintentionally. I was in the bathroom and heard the sound of assailants coming for me. I kicked the door with all my might sending it crashing into one of the staff. the poor lass was only tiny and my kung fu exploits left her with a bruised and painful shoulder. I was mortified I'd hurt her and very upset. I apologised profusely and continued to do so every time I saw her. She had every right to be angry and upset but she was so gracious and understanding. She realised that I would never hurt her on purpose and saw how badly I felt at having caused her pain. She was kind and caring and I would call her my angel, which would make her smile. I wasn't making many people smile in Stanage. Another time, one of the patients was talking to a member of staff. This woman had a pen in her hand and I became convinced she was about to stab the nurse in the eye with it. I wrestled the pen out of the poor woman's hand.

I was so bad that it was decided that I had to be put on one-to-one care. Someone had to be with me at all times, wherever I went. Even though I now had a constant companion, it couldn't stop my mind from imagining that people were about to break into the unit to kill me. My psychologists, Pete and Claire, did their best to help me, teaching me coping strategies and breathing skills to deal with my paranoia-induced panic. The truth was that I was very ill, my nerves frazzled and fried with constant fear and paranoia. I placed glass bottles on the window ledge of my room and on the floor so that intruders would knock them over and the sound would alert me to their murderous intentions. Whenever I returned to my room, I would check under the bed and behind the shower curtain for any hiding, hooded assassins.

One time, convinced they were inside the unit, I took off my shirt and covered myself in toothpaste. My lopsided logic being that in a fight with attackers, I would slip from their grasp. In reality, the only thing I was in danger of fighting was plaque and the only person that had lost their grip was yours truly. The nurse found me hiding in the bathroom, and gently but firmly reassured me that I was safe and I should clean myself up.

Living in the environment of a mental unit where people would often shout out and alarms and buzzers would sound, only heightened my nerves. I was still strung out crazy and expecting violence and attack. Things were so bad one night that I lay on my bedroom floor with my head inside my bedside cabinet. Staff would check in on me, tell me everything was okay, and try to get me to lie on the bed. I only felt safe with my head stuck inside the drawer, hoping it would shield me from the bullets that I expected to be fired at me. I continued to try to sleep this way night after night for weeks, my head encased by wood. I must have looked a strange and surreal sight, a man suffering from extreme delusions and enduring mental torment and torture. At the lowest point, when I felt all alone, God sent me people to help me and to reassure me that He still loves and cares for me.

One of the staff was a Christian; his name was Roland. We would sit together, share Bible verses, and pray. The way this man prayed moved me and caused me to glorify God. I knew God was real and that despite the severity of my illness He was still my God, my Salvation. I also knew one of the nurses, Lee, who worked on the ward, from the Presbyterian Church. He spent time encouraging me and playing chess and table tennis with me. Two other nurses were Christians and one of them prayed for me. I even did a Bible study about the storm-tossed boat on the Sea of Galilee with Peter, one of the psychiatrists. Once again, God was surrounding me with His people.

One scripture a friend sent me from the book of Isaiah, declares that even though we go through waters, we wouldn't be drowned and even though we walked through fires, we wouldn't be scorched and burnt. (Isaiah 43:2) I was certainly in the deep water of mental illness and the raging fire of paranoia and torment but God hadn't forgotten me.

Even though the tempest was raging, God was my rock and refuge. His promise never to leave or forsake me held firm. There is a Bible passage in Daniel, telling of how three men of God were thrown into the fiery furnace and Jesus was with them. Well, my Saviour was still with me through the fires of mental illness.

He has promised never to lose one of His sheep. I'm living testimony that God's promises to His people are yes and amen, in Jesus Christ. His promises are as valid for someone all alone in a mental hospital as they are for a church full of believers singing His praises. In the pitch black of night, when despair and discouragements come crashing like furious waves pounding us and we can't discern God's presence, He still has us safely in His love and care. He will see us through to the breaking dawn through troubles and trials. Although to many people, I may have seemed like a lost cause, I was safe and secure in my Father's hand, despite the madness that swirled in my mind. One particular blessing was that my friends were also allowed to visit me as the Government slowly lifted the lockdown restrictions. It was nice to see friendly faces again. I was especially grateful to Joy who visited me two or three times a week, bringing me clothes and supplies. I remember the first time she came. In my mind, youths had surrounded the hospital and were trying to get into the ward to kill me, and in walked Joy.

"How have you got in here?" I asked my friend, "We're surrounded."

"Nigel, there's no one out there trying to get you; it's all in your imagination."

Joy's words reduced me to tears because I knew she wouldn't lie to me and the terrible things I was seeing and hearing were all down to my serve paranoia. I started sobbing as the reality of my illness hit home. Peter also came, bringing me a new phone as I'd lost the one I had. Others came too, in fact, I had so many visitors, the staff was amazed and wanted to know why all these people came to see me. It's simply that God's people are faithful friends who never give up on you. In this aspect, they reflect God's character who loves His people despite all their sin. God's love and grace are truly amazing.

My visitors all tried to reassure me I was safe but of course, I was very ill and couldn't be cured by the common sense of my friends. Still, it was good to see familiar faces. After meeting with the psychiatrist, it was decided that I should be put back on my old medication, which was now to be given to me by injection. After a few weeks of this treatment, there was a significant improvement. The paranoia that I'd experienced for the last two months slowly and gradually began to subside and I was taken off one-to-one care.

I no longer had a nurse to shadow and follow my every step. I still felt anxious and didn't immediately stop seeing and hearing the imaginary threats to my life.

Chapter 57

Calm after the Storm

It would take a long time before I was able to look back, and realise the delusions were a product of my mental illness. I was battling the worst mental breakdown I'd experienced since my prison days. Thankfully, things began to improve; the hurricane was passing. Whilst I still needed to recover, the worst was over. The fierce storm was abating but it had left a wake of destruction strewn behind it.

I'd smashed up my flat and that wasn't the only thing that I'd wrecked. I'd worked hard to have a good relationship with my neighbours on Richmond Park. I'd often order cakes from my friend Nicky, who ran a catering business. I would have Bible messages iced on the cakes and give them as gifts to my neighbours. I liked to bless people and now I felt those relationships were broken beyond repair. I'd blessed them by constantly calling the police and trashing my flat.

My caseworker suggested that when released, I should return to Richmond Park and live in my flat, as it had yet to be allocated to a new tenant. This filled me with fear because although I was much better, I still hadn't fully recovered. I also wasn't too keen on seeing what kind of reception I'd get, walking back into my neighbourhood. I was guessing the ticker tape and balloons would be in very short supply. Thankfully, it was agreed that a new place was to be found for me, and I would be placed on the priority-housing list. I was told I would be allocated a flat and I either had to accept it or face the daunting prospect of being homeless.

I wanted to go back and live in the Upperthorpe or Crookes areas I knew well, but I would have to take the first property to become available. I made it a matter of prayer, knowing that God works out His purposes in the lives of His children and has known from before the foundation of the world the things that would befall me. I don't believe in blind fate but rather in an all-seeing, all-knowing God who directs the steps of His people. He has known for all eternity that I would need a new place to live and I was happy to trust in Him.

It seemed that I wouldn't be going anywhere soon though. My psychiatrist informed me that they were issuing me with a Section Three order. This meant that they could keep me for up to six months. The thought of being stuck in Stanage until Christmas dismayed me. In an effort to stay positive, I helped others; this also had the added bonus of keeping me busy. I enjoyed games of table tennis; luckily, the table was still standing despite my best efforts to dismantle it. I began to use the gym and really enjoyed working out and getting a sweat on.

I was also allowed to go to the local shops as long a member of staff was with me. These were all welcome distractions and signs that I was slowly beginning to recover. That is exactly how it felt, slow. These privileges could only take place when there were enough staff members around. On days when this wasn't possible, I'd feel trapped. Being cooped up twenty-four hours in the claustrophobic cauldron of a mental health unit, would sometimes bring my frustrations to the boil. I kept calling my room, my cell and the patients, inmates. The fact that I didn't do this purposely wasn't solely the product of the long years I'd served in prison but what I felt about being confined there.

As I got better, I tried to be a blessing and help to both staff and patients. As I inched my way to recovery, I was allowed to go to the shops on my own. I would go and buy sweets and treats for the staff and patients. To cheer everyone up, I arranged music and film nights. I would also order a takeaway and pay for those who couldn't afford it. I tried to be a positive influence with other patients. I also stepped in a couple of times when it seemed that violence was about to break out.

A particularly ill patient was threatening one of the staff. I told him that if he laid a hand on the staff member, I would knock him out. He took no notice and I ended up having to push him hard, backwards. After getting to his feet, he backed off when he saw I was serious. I had no appetite for violence but I wasn't going to stand around and watch a member of staff be assaulted.

Part of my recovery was to be allowed a two-hour leave as long as accompanied by a friend. Anna came and took me for a picnic in the park. I went to a local cafe with Andy and played chess. I could tell I wasn't back to my normal self yet, as he beat me. Luke took me to the pub for a meal. Most people take walking in the fresh air for granted, but for me, these couple of hours out were precious times, beacons of hope and a reminder that the sun was still shining beyond the clouds. Then finally, after two and a half months in a secure mental hospital, I was well enough to be moved to a halfway house. This was a place where I'd still receive care and supervision but where I would have my own room, a place where I could have more freedom to come and go as I liked.

And so, I was transferred to Wainwright, the halfway house support care facility. I spent sixteen weeks in there. My mental health continued to improve. Because I felt better, I was eager to move into my own place. Although I was well enough after a few weeks, it took what seemed an age for a flat to be found for me. This wasn't without its frustrations and life at Wainwright wasn't always idyllic. I had a couple of run -ins with the staff after suspecting people were stealing from my room.

Life felt too repressive and claustrophobic. I longed for my own place and the freedom it would bring. As I got better, I aimed to be a blessing once more. I painted a large fence and shed, organised movie and music nights and of course, more importantly, shared my faith with anyone I could. After a storm, everything seems calm with a freshness in the air. After the storm of my mental illness, I finally made a fresh start. A new flat was found for me on the outskirts of the city. It's on the edge of Derbyshire and I have the beautiful countryside right on my doorstep.

Amazingly, I moved in on the 11th of December, the day of my fiftieth birthday. It seemed God was giving me a wonderful present: my sanity back and a lovely flat for my birthday. I can say without hesitation that God is good. I look forward to loving, serving, and getting to know Him more and more. I thank God for bringing me safely through this awful time of sharp trial. I don't know what awaits me in my future but I do know that God will be with me, as He's been with me through thick and thin, storm and sunshine.

Chapter 58

Future Hopes and Present Struggles

You have read of my past but what of my future. God has redeemed and rescued me to give me hope and a future. One heartfelt hope is to fall in love with a godly woman with whom I can share my life. Not just for the physical aspect of the relationship but for someone I can love and cherish. Ideally, she would have a passion to share Jesus with people. That would be the absolute cherry on top of the cake. I long to fall in love and be loved in return, if the truth be told, I'm lonely. It would be wonderful to have someone to share my life.

I tried a Christian dating agency but without much success. I think I've tended to scare off women by giving a full account of my past in the opening greeting. I did this because I didn't want to be dishonest. I pray that God has a woman for me, one who won't be put off by the life I've lived and all the terrible things I've done, someone who shares my love for God. I know it wouldn't be easy for anyone to live with my mental health issues, but still, I have hope in my heart that there is a special someone out there for me who I can shower me with love and affection.

God has done so much for me through the years. I still have a long way to go on my journey with the Lord and still face many challenges. I'm still hoping and praying that God will heal me from all mental health issues. My paranoia still plagues me daily. I often think people are talking about me and watching me. I imagine that people are poisoning my food, following me and seeking to do me harm. I sometimes think that the events that befell me during my breakdown, were real and not due to my illness. At times, I'm extremely worried that people will try to break into my flat and attack me. I imagine the neighbours

293

are trying to listen to me when I'm alone. When I'm having a bad day, all these thoughts torment me and I can't seem to get any peace of mind. I can constantly feel troubled and worried. I'm on strong antipsychotic drugs to combat these symptoms and to help me cope with life. The medication itself has a disabling effect on me and makes me feel drowsy and lacking energy and motivation. I also take Diazepam and other pills to help me sleep. I have to be honest and tell you that when I'm having a really bad day, the desire to end my life is still there. I know this is wrong and fight against these feelings and desires. I know it must be hard for people to understand who haven't suffered from mental health problems.

On bad days, I long to be finally free from these torments. My heart yearns for heaven and to be with my heavenly Father in the land of milk and honey. Things can seem so bleak I still greatly desire to leave this life and be with the Lord. And yet, I know that God calls me to endure and press on and has promised to help, support and give me the grace to endure.

God was with me in the dark recesses of a prison cell and a mental hospital. I know He'll be with me in better times and circumstances because I know my heavenly Father loves me and will cause all things to work together for my good. Whilst I know I've still got so far to go, I can look back in amazement at what God has done for me. I'm just so thankful for His grace and goodness towards me, once a robber, reviler and an addict seemingly destined to be left languishing in a prison cell. In all probability, my body would have been rotting away in the ground by now. I was heading towards an early grave, until God's kindness and love stepped in. God had mercy on me.

Me, who didn't deserve forgiveness and salvation, I am forever grateful to God for sending Jesus Christ to live a perfect life, die on a cross and be raised from the dead so that I have eternal life. I've made seven crown court appearances, been in eighteen different prisons, two probation hostels, four bail hostels, three secure mental units and countless other outpatient centres. In my mind's eye, I can look back and see myself, blood gushing from my stomach, as I tried to kill myself. I remember being naked in a cell drinking my own urine and covered in my own faeces. I was addicted to drink, drugs and nicotine. It seemed I was a lost cause but as Charles Wesley says,[4] the blood of Christ can make the foulest clean. His blood availed for me. Hallelujah. And His blood will avail for you if you make Jesus Christ your Saviour.

I look forward to my future with renewed thanks in my heart towards God. God seems closer to me every single passing day. My relationship with him seems to get more passionate, intense and joyful. It was twenty-four years ago, that God saved me, and I love Him more now than ever. I love spending time praying to my heavenly Father. I read the Scriptures, the Bible, God's book of love, and I'm fed and nourished daily from the living oracles that speak deeply to my spirit and heart. Don't feel sorry for me, in all my struggles. I've found Jesus Christ, the pearl of great price, full of wisdom, truth, grace and knowledge. He is altogether lovely. Oh, what love God has poured out on me, bringing me to know the Lord Jesus Christ as my Saviour.

I know that whatever happens to me for the rest of my life that God will be with me. When my time comes to leave this short life, He will bring me safely home to heaven where I will be finally free from the torments of mental illness; where God, Himself, will wipe away every tear; where heartache, pain, disease and death will be replaced by everlasting joy. Yes, I still have a long way to go, but I praise and thank God every day for his goodness and grace towards me.

This is my story, thank you for reading it. The story of how God has taken me from darkness to light. But, what about you dear reader? You have read of the love the Lord has lavished on me. Don't you desire to experience this same love, to be forgiven, to know the joy of the Lord, to have hope and a future, not just for a few short years but for all eternity? I hope this book has been a real blessing to you as you have read about my life. It wasn't for entertainment that caused me to write this book. It was care and concern for your soul and a desire that you, too, could have the same sure hope of heaven. As you finish reading my story, my prayer is that your own spiritual story begins. I strongly urge

---

4   O for a Thousand Tongues to Sing-Charles Wesley 1739

you to read the following message.

God bless.

Nigel Owen James Williams-May 2022

EPILOGUE

A Note from Nigel and Friends.

John tells us that the reason he wrote his Gospel was so that the people who read it may have eternal life. I hope you have enjoyed reading about my life but your entertainment is not the main reason for me writing my life story.

Above all, it's my hope and prayer that you will come to believe in Jesus Christ and so experience the same marvellous salvation that I did.

You may well be thinking that you have not lived the life that I have nor have you done all the terrible things you have read about in this book. I have no doubt that this is true in the case of 99.9% of people. Compared to me, you are a good person. Again, you won't find me arguing with you on this point.

You may well believe that you don't need forgiveness and salvation because you're a good person. So the question that needs to be asked then is: Do good people go to heaven?

The Bible answers this question in quite a startling way.

It tells us that, Yes, good people go to heaven but that there are no good people so none get to heaven on their own goodness or by the things they do.

There is none righteous, no not one. (Romans 3:10)

We are told that it is appointed for man to die once and afterwards to face judgement. (Hebrews 9:27)

We must all appear before the judgement seat of Christ to give an account for everything we have done. (2 Corinthians 5:10)

All the secrets of our hearts will be revealed and we will have to answer for everything, even down to the thoughts we have had and every careless word we have spoken.

We will have to stand before a Holy and Awesome God.

There are only two outcomes of our appearing before the judgement seat; Either we will be condemned and sent to hell for all eternity or we will be justified in Gods sight and sent to heaven to enjoy an endless paradise.

Given the gravity of this news, and that our eternal future is at stake I'm sure you'd agree that this is not something we should leave to chance.

The sad fact is most leave it to chance. Many today are atheists and die having to stand before an almighty God they thought didn't exist. Others cling to the hope that God is a God of love and hope that he will overlook their wrongdoings. They find comfort in that, in their own estimation, they are good people, they're better than others in society and certainty better than I was.

But as we have already seen, God clearly says that there is none good enough to earn salvation. I know only too well that it's not what the person on trial thinks about themselves. Whether they consider themselves innocent or guilty makes no difference at all.

No, it is what the judge says that counts. So we need to measure ourselves by God's standards. He alone is our judge. Let us honestly seek to measure ourselves by His commandments.

1. You shall have no other gods before me

2. You shall make no image.

3. You shall not take the name of the Lord in vain.

4. Keep the Sabbath

5. Honour your Father and Mother

6. You shall not murder

7. You shall not commit adultery

8. You shall not steal

9. You shall not lie

10. You shall not covert

If we are honest, we all have to admit to breaking these commandments. We have all wilfully broken them. You may well be tempted to ask how many of God's commandments do you need to break before you have blown it and are sent to hell.

The answer is that if we have broken one only once then a holy God will and must punish us and cast us away from His presence for all eternity. But the truth is we have all broken all ten of God's commandments.

Because the breaking of God's commandments starts in the heart and Jesus taught us that if we look lustfully after someone then we've committed adultery in our heart (Matthew

5:28) and if we've hated anyone without cause then we're guilty of murder. (1 John 3:15)

Which of us hasn't told a lie?

Which of us hasn't used God's name flippantly?

Which of us hasn't coveted (desired) what belongs to others? Which of us hasn't stolen?

Which of us hasn't lusted after someone in our heart and committed adultery?

And so we see before we even look at the Sabbath or putting any other gods before our creator we have all failed miserably.

We have all fallen short of God's standards and are corrupt in His sight. (Romans 3:23)

A Just and Holy God will rightly find us guilty when we stand before Him and it will be a terrible thing to fall into the hands of the Living God who will condemn us to hell for all eternity.

That's the bad news, but there is hope. There is the Gospel; the good news. God still loves us despite our sins and rebellion.

He sent Jesus Christ His Son to earth.

He came and kept the Law perfectly never breaking any of the commandments.

He willingly gave up His life to die an agonising death on a cross. And because He was without sin, death could not hold Him and three days later, He gloriously rose from the dead, never to die again.

Indeed one day soon, He is coming again and it will be too late for everyone who hasn't found salvation in Him. But there is forgiveness, reconciliation and eternal life for anyone who repents of their sins and believes and trusts in Jesus Christ. If you're honestly willing to follow, trust and obey Him then ask God to forgive you and commit your life to Him by trusting in Jesus.

Jesus said these words in John 8:12: I am the light of the world. He who follows Me shall not walk in darkness but have the light of life.

His promise still holds good for anyone who will believe in Him. Ask Him to have mercy on you and to lead you from darkness to light. Following Jesus is not the easiest life but it's the best.

Jesus has been my shade in the burning desert;

He's been my rock, refuge and shield.

He is my hiding place in the day of trouble and distress.

He is altogether lovely, the friend who sticks closer than a brother and will never leave or forsake me. He is my Saviour.

My greatest hope and prayer is that He'll become yours.

God bless, Nigel.

I heard the voice of Jesus say,

I am this dark world's light;

Look unto Me, thy morn shall rise, and all thy day be bright.

I looked to Jesus, and I found in Him my star, my sun; and in that light of life, I'll walk till travelling days are done.

I Heard the Voice of Jesus Say-Horatius Bonar, 1808-89

BIBLIOGRAPHY

Chapter 45

Forever with the Lord- James Montgomery 1835

Chapter 51

Quote attributed to John Wesley

Chapter 53

Eric Morecambe-1971 Morecambe & Wise Christmas Show

Chapter 58

O for a Thousand Tongues to Sing-Charles Wesley 1739

Epilogue

I Heard the Voice of Jesus Say-Horatius Bonar 1846

To tell us what you thought to the book or to contact Nigel for speaking engagements please get in touch With Nigel

Nigel-fromdarknesstolight@outlook.com

With Andy

Kaliberkid@hotmail.co.uk